Sacrifice as Terror

Global Issues

General Editors: Bruce Kapferer, Professor of Anthropology, James Cook University and John Gledhill, Professor of Anthropology, Manchester University.

This series addresses vital social, political and cultural issues confronting human populations throughout the world. The ultimate aim is to enhance understanding – and, it is hoped, thereby dismantle – hegemonic structures that perpetuate prejudice, violence, racism, religious persecution, sexual discrimination and domination, poverty and many other social ills.

ISSN: 1354-3644

Previously published books in the series:

Michael Herzfeld
The Social Production of Indifference: Exploring the Symbolic Roots of Western Bureaucracy

Peter Rigby
African Images: Racism and the End of Anthropology

Judith Kapferer
Being All Equal: Difference and Australian Cultural Practice

Eduardo P. Archetti
Guinea-pigs: Food, Symbol and Conflict of Knowledge in Ecuador

Denis Duclos
The Werewolf Complex: America's Fascination with Violence

Thomas Hylland Eriksen
Common Denominators: Ethnicity, Nation-Building and Compromise in Mauritius

Thomas Hylland Eriksen
Common Denominators: Ethnicity, Nation-Building and Compromise in Mauritius

Sacrifice as Terror

The Rwandan Genocide of 1994

Christopher C. Taylor

Oxford • New York

First published in 1999 by
Berg
Editorial offices:
150 Cowley Road, Oxford OX4 1JJ, UK
838 Broadway, Third Floor, New York, NY 10003-4812, USA

Paperback edition reprinted in 2001

Berg is the imprint of Oxford International Publishers Ltd.

A French version of this book is to appear at Editions Octarés Toulouse
"Applications de l'anthropologie".

Library of Congress Cataloging-in-Publication Data

A catalogue record for this book is available from the Library of
Congress.

British Library Cataloguing-in-Publication Data

A catalogue record for this book is available from the British Library.

ISBN   1 85973 273 9 (Cloth)
       1 85973 278 X (Paper)

Typeset by JS Typesetting, Wellingborough, Northants.
Printed in the United Kingdom by Hackman Print, Tonypandy

Contents

Acknowledgements

Writing is an eminently solitary exercise where one is alone with one's thoughts, one's feelings, and the anguish of the empty page, but the discipline of anthropology can never and should never be a solitary pursuit. This work has proven to me the truth of both these propositions. I would never have written it without the gentle encouragement, and sometimes prodding, of friends and colleagues. I feel that I may have tried the patience of some in taking so long, and if so, I apologize.

It may be that the events of which I speak in these pages are more to be forgotten than remembered but, since my wife and I were evacuated from Rwanda, it has been impossible not to relive every day some tiny bit of the pain and anger that both of us felt during the first weeks of refugee existence in Nairobi, Kenya. Many times while writing I have found myself obliged to stop and to do something intensely physical in order to dissipate the rekindled negative affect. Luckily I have usually been close enough to a bicycle or to a swimming pool to transform spiritual pain into muscular exhaustion. But if I have suffered, what I have suffered pales in comparison to what I know many Rwandan survivors continue to suffer. Many former friends and acquaintances, having survived the massacres, have subsequently died simply of a broken heart. Some have taken their own lives. Others have drunk themselves to death. Others live on as permanent emotional cripples, unable as yet to find joy in life again. What I have written can hardly do justice to them.

It is impossible to sufficiently thank all those Rwandans that I met in Kenya and who shared their thoughts and emotions with me. I hope that my presence among them was as therapeutic for them as it was for me. Among these refugees was Jean-Marie Vianney Higiro, former director of Office Rwandaise de l'Information

(ORINFOR), one of the few Rwandan journalists who, during the events leading up to the genocide, continued to exercise his profession with the highest standards of integrity and who educated me about the political situation in Rwanda before the genocide. I also remember one young boy about eight years old who told me about several encounters he had had with *Interahamwe* and how each time he had managed either by wit or by sheer luck to elude his pursuers and therefore death. Yet he continued to be haunted by the fact that he had been forced to leave his dog behind him in Rwanda and that he was unsure as to whether the dog had survived. He was aware that in all probability the rest of his family was now dead, but it was this one being who had depended solely upon him for sustenance and love that worried him most. I could not help but be awe-struck by this little boy.

But if this boy managed to show me something affirmative about humanity in what were probably the darkest days of my existence, I can hardly say the same about the world at that moment. For while in Nairobi I was profoundly aware, as an American, that it had been implicit from the outset of hostilities that saving my life and that of other Europeans and Americans was a higher order of priority than that of saving African lives. Where bodies are concerned, the social mechanisms of triage are always at work. This continues to be the case in Africa's numerous conflicts to this day.

Many friends and colleagues expressed their concern for me during those bleak days in Nairobi and I remain grateful to them. Richard Gringeri, Andrew Apter, Kurt Tolksdorf, John Napora, Roger Nance, and Fred Damon stand out particularly in this regard. I must also thank Fred Damon for keeping up an almost daily exchange of faxes with me while I was in Nairobi. These faxes were among the first of the gentle encouragement mentioned above and they helped me to step back a little from the events and to see them as would an anthropologist.

I must also thank my former AIDS Control and Prevention Project (AIDSCAP) colleagues, who were extremely supportive and helpful to my wife and to me while we were living in Nairobi. I particularly thank Rose de Buysscher for helping me rescue and repatriate much of my library and field notes. I would also like to thank Constant Kabwasa in this regard. Several other AIDSCAP staff members also helped me in Kenya. I thank Rukarangira and his wife for being the witnesses at my wedding at the magistrate's office in Nairobi, and I also thank 'Ruka' for lending me a ring for a few minutes so I could place it on Esperance's finger. Jean Moulin of the Belgian Embassy and his wife also helped Esperance and me live through a particularly difficult time.

As for the writing of this work, I have profited from the perspicacious critical remarks of many colleagues. I would like to thank John Gledhill for his reading, extensive comments, and kind encouragement concerning an earlier version of this work. Vincent Crapanzano was also very helpful with his remarks pointing to the desirability of better framing the context and the argument of the middle chapters with a thorough initial discussion of Rwanda. My former Chicago colleague and friend, Ray Fogelson, has also offered valuable comments and advice on parts of this work.

I have presented earlier versions of chapters at various professional meetings. I presented a paper at the 1997 Satterthwaite Colloquium where I benefited from the comments of Dick Werbner and other participants, including: Birgit, Stefan, Kit, Simon, and Alex. I would also like to thank Roy Wagner for his comments on an earlier version of the same paper. Rene Lemarchand also provided kind encouragement concerning one of the chapters, as did Alex Hinton. Others whose critical remarks and suggestions have proven invaluable include my University of Alabama, Birmingham (UAB) colleagues, Tom McKenna and Brian Hesse, and three of my former colleagues and friends at the University of Chicago, Richard Gringeri, John Macaloon, and Andrew Apter. More recently I have benefited from remarks made on the penultimate version of this text by a French colleague, Jean-Francois Bare, who, along with his wife, Annie, is helping me to prepare a French version of this work. I would also like to thank another French colleague, Claude Raynaut of the University of Bordeaux-2, for the many conversations that we have had together not only concerning the present work but about anthropology in general. Other people at Bordeaux-2 have also been quite helpful including Mmes. Laurence, Marie-France, Marie-Helene, and Sheherazade, as well as Charles Cheung who has put his cartographic skills to work on the two maps in this book.

I have also been fortunate to receive financial support during some of the time that it took to write this book. I heartily thank the Virginia Foundation for the Humanities (VFH) for one semester of support at the University of Virginia. While at Virginia I also benefited from interaction with my colleagues at VFH, with Roberta Culbertson, and with several University of Virginia (UVA) faculty

members who read and commented on my work, including: Joe
Miller, George Mentore, and Chris Crocker. I also thank the African
Studies programme at the University of Illinois at Champaign-
Urbana for providing me with a small summer stipend that afforded
me the possibility to use their impressive library.

Finally, I would like to express my appreciation to my wife,
Esperance, who lost parents, relatives, close friends, and her entire
life's savings as a result of the genocide, but who has managed to
continue to live a life free of hate and bitterness.

Introduction

How does one make sense of events that defy reason – events like those that occurred in Rwanda during 1994, costing the lives of one million people, one seventh of the country's population? How many ways are there to understand mass violence and murder? What constitutes sense under such circumstances? Is it singular? Is it plural? Or is it neither, nothing but a useless conceit driven more by the scholar's need to explain than a world's desire to understand? How do we harness the tools of anthropology to make such an event comprehensible? What kinds of understanding can prevent future violence in Rwanda? Are there 'magic bullet' insights out there whose revelation might break the cycle of crime and counter-crime that have plagued the region for the past forty years? Will Rwanda's people ever be able to bridge the chasm that ethno-nationalism and genocide has left among them?

And where to begin? With the historical antecedents? The political divisions? The social tensions? External pressures? Class disparities? Gender disparities? Or, as some have suggested, internal cultural proclivities to violence? How does one speak dispassionately of the unspeakable, the horror of genocide – a genocide that took the lives of close friends and colleagues? These are questions that have tortured me ever since I was evacuated from Rwanda on 9 April 1994, just two-and-a-half days after hostilities resumed between Rwandan Government Forces (RGF) and the Rwandan Patriotic Front (RPF) when President Juvenal Habyarimana was killed in a missile attack on his personal plane on 6 April 1994.

With some notable exceptions, most media depictions of armed conflict in sub-Saharan Africa have tended to reinforce negative Western stereotypes about Africans. The genocide in Rwanda did nothing to dispel these impressions and, if anything, rekindled them with added intensity. Yet how quickly many of us in the West forget

Rwanda

the crimes against humanity that our predecessors committed in Europe and in the Americas: the horror of two world wars, the Nazi holocaust, and the wars of extermination that native American populations suffered at the hands of people of European origin. Was the violence perpetrated against native Americans not genocide? Has genocide been uncommon in this century? Armenians, Jews, Gypsies, and Bosnians would certainly beg to differ. Yet Africa retains a privileged place in the minds of many Westerners who need to think of themselves as 'civilized' and of others as less so. Where Africa is concerned, 'heart of darkness' images continue to lie close to the surface of consciousness. The spectre that persists juxtaposes contradictory images of verdant freshness and putrefying decay, of noble beings still intimate with nature yet propelled by archaic and primal urges of savage bloodlust. How quickly we forget that three of the greatest mass murders in this century – the genocide of the Armenians by the Turks which took up to two million lives, the Stalinist campaign against the kulaks which killed six million, and the Nazi holocaust which claimed between five and six million souls – were perpetrated by white people against other white people. Nor have Asians shown a much better record when it comes to annihilating their fellow man. The enormous loss of civilian life that characterized the Japanese conquest of Manchuria is one example, the violence that accompanied the partitioning of India and Pakistan another, the 1970 purge of 'communists' in Indonesia a third, and the Khmer Rouge 'killing fields' where almost two million died yet a fourth.

On virtually all continents, although under different circumstances, mass murder and genocide have seemed to some political leaders and their followers like rational courses of action, yet the cumulative effect of their presumed rational choices has been irrational. And rarely has the 'world community' in the form of the League of Nations, the UN or some other supra-national entity stepped in to put an end to the killing. Even in Bosnia today it is difficult to argue that NATO involvement in the peace-making process was primarily motivated by the desire to put an end to rape, genocide, and 'ethnic cleansing'. As for Rwanda of 1994, there can be no ambiguity. Humanitarian motivations were simply too weak to affect policy. As ordinary people in the world looked on in horror, the leaders and institutions of its strongest nations chose to play Nero. During the months of April and May at the UN Security Council, 'general fatigue on the part of the international community regarding participation in peace-keeping operations' (Boutros-Ghali, 1996: 50) led to a reluctance to commit manpower and money to what was fast becoming yet another twentieth-century killing field.

When Ghana offered to send several hundred troops, difficulties were encountered in equipping them (Boutros-Ghali, 1996: 50), and other nations offered only to send non-combatant support units. In the United States, fear of being held to the 1948 Geneva accords on genocide, which required intervention, led spokespersons for the Clinton administration to scrupulously avoid using the term 'genocide' to describe what was occurring during those fateful months of 1994. Although one can partly understand the US administration's hesitancy to act in Africa in the wake of the Somalia intervention, which cost the lives of eighteen American soldiers, US inaction, and that of the other developed nations in the world, resulted in the probable deaths of one million Rwandans.[1] But there was something deeper and less savoury behind the inaction. In the minds of many, the Rwandan holocaust was simply African tribalism rearing yet again its atavistic head. There was nothing to be done. The UN had tried and failed to bring peace to Somalia and closer to home there were more serious preoccupations. The quagmire of Bosnia continued to boil like Hecate's cauldron with every Security Council action serving only to show the world that the UN was a paper tiger. Was the world community prepared to take on another basket case? For the one million Tutsi and Hutu moderates who lost their lives in the Rwandan holocaust, it was this thinking that prevented anyone from doing anything to help them. As for the French action, 'Operation Turquoise', which came at a time when most of the genocide's victims had already been killed, it served more as a means of rescuing the shards of a former client government than of saving innocent lives (Prunier, 1995).[2]

How poorly the world powers read the situation. But for that matter, did a sincere desire really exist at the time to understand it? The US was going through a phase when it was weary of intervention; and only France and Belgium had much interest in Rwanda. Belgium, the former colonial ruler of Rwanda and its principal Western sponsor after independence, had ceased its military assistance when it became clear after 1990 that the Rwandan Government was systematically abusing the human rights of many citizens (Chretien, 1997). France had leaped almost without thinking into the breach left by the Belgians, and the son of then President

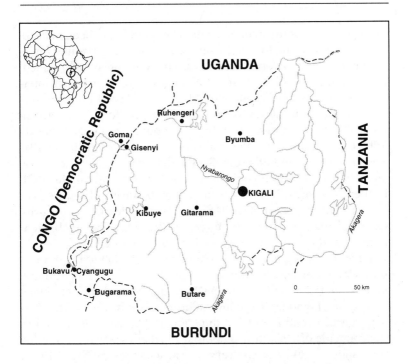

Francois Mitterrand, Jean Christophe, was given the task of bailing out 'old man Habyarimana' and saving the French language in central Africa (Prunier, 1995). There was little of value to the world economy in tiny Rwanda – no oil, no strategic minerals, no precious stones. Although there were a few cassiterite (tin ore) mines, these had been shut down in the mid-1980s due to low world market prices for tin. Rwanda's principal exports, coffee and tea, were commodities that brokers could easily obtain elsewhere. In the absence of strategic or economic interests, only humanitarianism could have brought the world community to action in Rwanda.

Had the world community acted and acted decisively, the horror of genocide could have been arrested in its tracks. Rwanda of 1994 was not Somalia, it was not Cambodia, and it was certainly not Nazi Germany. The Hutu extremist militias in Rwanda did not possess 'technicals' nor did most of them have firearms of any sort. Most were unemployed or underemployed adolescent males armed with clubs and machetes and imbued with the assurance that they were acting out the will of their country's leaders with the support

of the majority of their compatriots. They could have been neutral-
ized with little or no loss of life on the part of an intervening force.
As for Rwandan Government Forces, who were indeed well armed,
that is another story. These latter might have resisted an intervention, but their resistance would not have lasted long. In four
years of war with the Rwandan Patriotic Front, Rwandan Government Forces had shown that they were poorly organized, poorly
led, relatively unmotivated, and only effective when backed by
French artillery and advisors. Rapid and unambiguous action by
an intervention force could have bottled up most of the RGF
in their garrisons. Instead, shortly after the death of ten Belgian
soldiers who were part of the UN peacekeeping forces, the Security
Council chose to reduce its forces in Rwanda to an ineffectual
number and to observe the genocide from the sidelines.

When I journeyed to Rwanda in October of 1993 to begin work
on a USAID project intended to slow the spread of HIV (human
immune deficiency virus) and AIDS (acquired immune deficiency
syndrome), it had not been my intention to study the war that had
begun with the RPF invasion in October 1990 and culminated in
the genocide of 1994. It was not that I had any special distaste for
such subjects. On the contrary, in earlier stints of fieldwork in
Rwanda during 1983 to 1985 and in the summer of 1987, when I
studied popular medicine, I had encountered human malevolence,
albeit of an individual nature, that had sometimes resulted in illness,
misfortune, or death. I had studied the underside of the Rwandan
character, as well as its creative and life-affirming side. On rare
occasions I had also witnessed the lingering racism that some
Rwandans held for members of other ethnic groups. But I had
always felt that the moral intelligence of most Rwandans would
predominate over the ignorance and malevolence of the few. My
experience with Rwandans of all groups, after all, had usually been
positive. More often than not, they had shown kindness to me. I
could never have predicted, in 1985 or 1987, that events would take
the turn that they did in 1994. I had seen too many instances, with
my own eyes, of Hutu and Tutsi living close to one another, co-
operating with one another, fraternizing with one another, and
sometimes intermarrying. Moreover, in October 1993 and during
the months that followed, I had too many other things to think
about and to do than study the war and the political situation in
Rwanda. Nonetheless, I could not evade the reality of the war, whose
events continued to intrude, growing more ominous with each

passing month. I found myself drawn into the maelstrom, at a distance at first, then more closely and irrevocably.

Once, in December 1993, while I was descending Kigali's Avenue de Kiyovu in my Jeep Cheorkee, I noticed a Mercedes with most of its windows shattered parked in a driveway off to the side. Around it stood four men with pensive expressions on their faces and a motorcycle police officer busily writing on a notepad. Later I would learn that a grenade attack had been made on a prominent Hutu member of the democratic opposition. As he was alighting from his car, two men passing by on a motorcycle had thrown a grenade. The man escaped with minor injuries, but his assailants were never caught. It is not likely that the incident was ever seriously investigated, although obviously the victim of the attack had alerted the police. I was quite shocked, as I must have passed the vehicle only minutes after its driver was attacked, but even more shocking was the blasé attitude of most of my Rwandan acquaintances who considered it business as usual.

A couple weeks later, in January 1994, I was driving my closest Rwandan friend, Victor, and his wife, home from work. They lived on the side of Mount Kigali in the Nyamirambo section of Kigali. Although their house was not a palace, it was pleasant, surrounded by a beautiful garden, and was high enough on the mountainside to enjoy a magnificent view of Kigali below and of the hillsides in the distance. On some of these distant hills one could make out white specks dotting the landscape. With Victor's high-powered binoculars, one could readily discern that the white specks were tents – tents that had been placed there to accommodate the large number of internally displaced people from northern Rwanda who had fled the RPF's 1993 February offensive. One could even make out numerous human shapes moving among the tents. That Rwanda was a country in the throes of a war was hard to ignore when one could see its consequences from a vantage point within Kigali's city limits, even if binoculars were required. But that cool, rainy January evening as we began the steep climb up the dirt road that led to Victor's house, no one was thinking about the war. Despite the rain, we were all in a good mood. We passed a little bar, where Victor suggested we stop and order brochettes. We entered, found a table, ordered, and when our beers arrived began to patiently sip away knowing that the *brochette-frites* could take anywhere from twenty minutes to an hour. But I felt uncomfortable there. The atmosphere in the place was strange, too silent for the number of clients, although not overtly hostile. Everyone seemed to be attentively listening to the radio. It was Radio Television Libre de Mille Collines (RTLM) – Rwanda's infamous 'hate radio', principal disseminator throughout the country of virulent anti-RPF and anti-Tutsi propaganda. Naturally Victor was nonplussed; he was a Tutsi. Although his wife was Hutu, I could read the tension on her face. She had good reason to be frightened: to be Hutu and married to a Tutsi was, to some Hutu extremists, more reprehensible than simply being Tutsi. We had come to the bar at an awkward moment, at a time when its patrons were listening to a station that we all loathed and feared. I grew nervous.

'Let's get out of here,' I said to Victor.
'That will only draw attention to us,' he replied.

We tried to be invisible, tried to disappear into the green plywood walls, tried to blend in with the sound of falling rain on the corrugated iron roof, but we had grown too frightened to open our mouths, mute and fidgety patrons waiting for their brochettes. Soon the radio orator reached a climax in his speech, he wasn't speaking anymore, he was screaming: 'Hutu powa, Hutu powa, Hutu powa'. Several voices in the bar took up the chant like a Greek chorus: 'Hutu powa, Hutu powa, Hutu powa'. Some even raised clenched right fists, punctuating each shout in a gesture reminiscent of the Black Power salute. But these were not an oppressed minority here. They were the majority and they still controlled the government. A shiver traversed me; the same chill that I remember feeling when once I saw newsclips of the Attica prison uprising in New York State during the 1970s when at the end, the police and prison guards had retaken control. There had been enormous loss of life – forty or so inmates had died and several guards. As the police left the prison, they and onlookers shouted 'White power! White power!' Bigotry is an equal opportunity employer.

On another occasion bricks were thrown at the car in which I was a passenger. The driver, a close Rwandan friend, managed to throw off the aim of our attackers by driving straight at them. The bricks hit the hood of the car, just beneath the windshield. In yet another incident, my friend, Victor, sustained a knife wound to his face as I pleaded with his attackers and three police officers observing from a safe distance to let him go. I did not see the knife and did not know he was injured until the incident was over. Had I seen it, I probably would have chosen flight rather than back alley negotiation.

On some days during the last months before the genocide there were glimmers of hope that the political problems were close to a solution. 'The President's people are trying to negotiate a general amnesty. It must mean they're getting serious about peace,' I heard one day in the corridors of USAID. On other days the optimism that continued to be expressed among Western diplomats, even as late as February and March of 1994, sharply contrasted with the pessimism and despair that Rwandan acquaintances expressed in my presence. Several of my male Rwandan friends asked me to help them procure any kind of firearm. Female friends expressed anxiety about sexual attack and told me of precautions that they took to avoid it (see Chapter 4).

After January 1994, the situation in Rwanda never improved. There were several serious incidents, several assassinations, mini-rehearsals for the coming pogrom. Once, in late March, the gardener I employed at my house came to work carrying a pair of blood-stained jeans. As he proceeded to wash them, he mumbled away about someone nicknamed 'CDR,' after the extremist Hutu political party, Comité pour la Défense de la République. Apparently 'CDR', who was a notorious assassin of Tutsi, had himself been assassinated in a Nyamirambo bar the previous evening. Albert had been seated right next to him. CDR's blood had spattered all over Albert's clothing. Someone had taken revenge – maybe the RPF, maybe an RPF supporter. All Albert said about the incident and what was happening in general was 'Abahutu bica abatutsi' ('the Hutu are killing the Tutsi'), although clearly it was sometimes the other way around. I began to wonder about Albert. Is he an *Interahamwe*?[3] What was he doing with such a person? What if he tells some other *Interahamwe* that I am living here with a Tutsi woman?

I had always liked Albert. He was hard working and efficient, and always seemed eager to learn more. Occasionally I had even seen him in one of the Nyamirambo nightspots that my closest Rwandan friends and I sometimes frequented. One night in early March, at the Cafe Rio, I invited him over to our table. At the table was a Rwandan Army officer, Lieutenant Joseph, Hutu but the farthest thing from an anti-Tutsi racist. There were two others: someone I didn't know very well but who was Hutu. and another friend of Lieutenant Joseph's and mine, who was Tutsi and a known RPF supporter. Despite the mix of ethnicities and political tendencies, we were all relaxed and having a good time. There was no animosity between Phillip, the Tutsi, and Joseph, the RGF soldier. In fact they appeared to be very good friends. They had known each other since childhood as both had grown up in Nyamirambo. Yet here they found themselves at opposite poles of Rwanda's political crisis. Neither seemed to care that evening; their friendship transcended that. Then Michel came in the bar, saw us, and came over to the table. Michel was another Tutsi, and fairly well known for his pro-RPF sentiments. His father had been arrested in October 1990 along with hundreds of others and put in Nyamirambo stadium. All the prisoners had endured harsh treatment at the hands of their captors. Michel's father had even been shot through the leg during an apparent riot in the stadium, although he managed to survive. As a joke I called out to Michel as he came over to our table, 'Inyenzi! Inyenzi!' the pejorative term that RPF soldiers and supporters were known by. Everyone at the table howled with laughter, almost falling from their chairs. Even at this tense moment (just a week or so earlier, there had been two assassinations of high level political leaders) the political situation could be viewed with a degree of irony. Most of us there at the table clung to the belief, despite all the evidence to the contrary around us, that cooler heads among the leaders of both sides would prevail and that the crisis would be resolved without further bloodshed.

That, of course, turned out to be a vain hope. Several attempts to install the 'transitional broad-based government' failed during the months of January, February and March. Finally, in April, President Habyarimana was summoned back to Arusha, Tanzania where he met with several of the region's top political leaders including President Museveni of Uganda and Burundian President Ntaryamira. The message to Habyarimana at these meetings was a stern one, as he was widely perceived to be behind the repeated failures to fully implement the August 1993 Arusha accords that he and his government had signed with the RPF. He was told that he had better do something to see that the accords were fully implemented or else risk dragging the whole region down in flames. It was en route back to Kigali in the early evening of 6 April 1994 that his private plane carrying him, Burundian President Ntaryamira, several highly placed Rwandans, and two Burundian cabinet ministers, was shot down by two shoulder-launched surface-to-air missiles. That day remains indelibly etched in my memory.

A couple of hours after I returned home from work that evening.

I received a call from the American community's neighbourhood warden. Virtually every American in Kigali who worked for the US embassy, USAID, or for an NGO during the troubled times after October 1990, kept in touch with others via telephone and two-way short-wave radio. There had been one or two emergency evacuations since the beginning of the war in 1990 and people needed to be informed of rapid deterioration in the security situation. Every neighborhood with a sizeable American community had a 'warden' who would contact others in the neighbourhood by phone when there was trouble. In addition, every Friday morning at 07.00 we would receive a transmission over the radios issued to each one of us to verify that each person's equipment was in working order. Everyone had a code name and would respond in turn to a call from the American who captained the network: 'This is White Angel calling High Five. Do you read me High Five?' The usual response was: 'This is High Five, White Angel. I read you loud and clear.' Then 'White Angel' would contact the next person on the list until all members of the American community who had been issued two-way radios had responded or in some way been accounted for. On 6 April my phone was working but not the two-way radio; it had broken down just a week before and a replacement was on order. Over the phone, the warden advised me to stay at home that evening as there were rumours to the effect that the President's plane had been shot at. He did not know whether anyone had been hurt.

At the time I thought the threat to order was not serious – just a pretext on the part of the President's more extremist supporters to set up roadblocks and rob anyone they happened to catch in their traps. That was their usual *modus operandi* and I had come close to getting caught in such binds more than once. Twice stones had been thrown at my car. On the evening of 6 April the neighbourhood warden lacked precise details, but I assumed he was correct in warning us to stay at home. My fiancée, who was a Rwandan Tutsi, and I retired at around midnight as usual. Neither of us thought that anything momentous was in the works. Then, at about 03.00, our house watchman came to the bedroom window and woke us up. He said, 'they've just announced on the radio that the President's plane has been shot down near the airport and that he is dead. Everyone is supposed to remain at home.' I asked him if he preferred to stay inside the house, but he declined. We drifted back to sleep. About one hour later we were awakened by loud shooting, small arms mostly, but more horrendous booms as well: grenades, artillery, and mortar fire. The degeneration of the situation that I had witnessed for months, but tried to deny so tenaciously that night, had come to a head.

Nine months of shaky truce between the Rwandan Government Forces and the Rwandan Patriotic Front were over. The RGF started the attack, blaming the RPF and all Tutsis in general for the death of President Habyarimana. As part of the Arusha accords the RPF had been allowed to bivouack one battalion of 600 men at the Conseil National du Developpement, a large building and fenced-in compound in a Kigali suburb called Remera. Not far from the RPF encampment, the UN troop contingent had its headquarters. Shortly after Habyarimana's assassination, the RPF announced over their radio station, 'Radio Muhabura', that they had had nothing to do with it. They had not fired the missiles or authorized anyone else to do so. They issued a general appeal for calm, saying that they would not take hostile action unless attacked. Their appeal fell on deaf ears. By early Thursday morning they were under heavy fire. Later that morning they asked the UN for permission to leave their compound to defend themselves. That permission was granted. Nevertheless, much of the ordinance that we heard exploding during the early hours of 7 April was not directed at military targets such as the RPF headquarters. Political opposition leaders and important Tutsi were being surrounded at their homes by RGF soldiers or Hutu militia members and slaughtered, along with everyone in their households.

My fiancée and I remained at home for the next two days as fighting raged all around us. I moved a mattress into the house's central corridor. There were bedrooms on both sides of this corridor whose windows and doors I closed. I placed other mattresses on their sides and propped them up against both sides of the corridor to act as a buffer in the event that bullets or shrapnel might penetrate the walls. I closed all the other windows and doors in the house opening a few of them only when noise of the fighting appeared to subside. Into the protected space of the corridor I brought a radio that received two bands of commercial short wave and listened to it until its batteries went dead, then I hooked it up to a 12 volt car battery until it died about a day later. It was from listening to the BBC World Service that we obtained the most accurate information about what was happening in Rwanda. All we heard on Rwandan radio was the occasional announcement that the President had been killed and that the population was to remain at home. These announcements, always the same, came about once every hour. The rest of the time they played classical music, often lugubrious classical music like Mozart's Requiem, a hauntingly beautiful piece but scandalously ironic given the context. Were the people at the National Radio of Rwanda (not the same as 'RTLM') aware of what they were doing or were they merely throwing anything they could get their hands on onto the turntable? Was this their way of mourning Habyarimana? I don't know, but the Requiem must have been played at least six times in forty-eight hours. It was surreal – the national radio playing Mozart's Requiem and advising people to stay put like sitting ducks until the army or militia could get there to rob and kill them.

By the late morning of 7 April, we were fairly well aware of what was happening around us. Our house watchman, for example, had learned from the watchman in the next house, who had learned from the watchman in the house next to his, that Liberal Party leader, Landouald Ndasingwa, who lived two doors away from us, had been murdered. He had been killed along with his Canadian wife, Hélène, their children and even, apparently, his wife's ageing mother. The news came to me as a shock; I had once considered both 'Lando' and his wife, Hélène, to be friends. Both had worked for the United States Information Service during my earliest stint of fieldwork in Rwanda and both had helped me during that time. I was deeply saddened by their deaths and shocked by the fact that it had all happened just two houses away from where I lived. From the front room of our house, I could just barely see above the front wall of our enclosure and discern the heads of people walking one way or the other. Many were carrying objects and bundles on their heads. They were looters carting off Lando's and Hélène's belongings. What is to stop them from coming in here, I thought? What will they do when they see that I am living with a Tutsi? They will rape her in front of me and then kill us both. This fear was reinforced when our watchman told us that twice soldiers had come to our gate and asked him if Belgians lived there. He had told them that we were Americans. We were not yet on the list.

Chaos had broken out all around us. Still our tap water continued to function and we had enough gas in the butane tank to cook food. The electricity had been out for some time, so it was not long before the food in the refrigerator would begin to rot. I decided it was best to cook up all that we had as cooked food can last longer without refrigeration than raw food. Whenever I thought it was safe, I was out in the kitchen cooking away.

Oddly enough our phone still worked. On Thursday 7 April, I called people I knew and received several phone calls from Rwandan, Belgian, and American friends. Everyone confirmed our worst fears that, as one Belgian friend put it, *le grand nettoyage a commencé* ('the big cleanup has begun.'). In another conversation, an American friend who had a vantage point from his house, which afforded him a view of much of our neighbourhood, told me that our section was a focus of particular activity. He told us of a house that had been surrounded by Rwandan soldiers who then proceeded to bombard it with rockets and rifle-propelled grenades. Soon all that was left of it was a pile of rubble. He did not see how any of the occupants in that house could have survived the onslaught, nor could he understand the degree of overkill that was clearly being directed at the regime's opponents.

Fighting subsided a little during the afternoon of Thursday 7 April. I went out into the yard and chatted with Belgian neighbours who lived on one side. I had never met them before but found them to be quite friendly and pleasant. The man had a two-way short-wave radio and from time to time talked with someone over it. He told whomever he was speaking to contact the American Embassy and let them know that I was all right. These neighbours bolstered my spirits. They had seen incidents like this before in Rwanda, like the night of the RPF invasion on 4 October 1990 when RGF soldiers patrolling in Kigali shot their guns at anything, either because they believed that the enemy had entered the city or they wanted to cow the population into believing it. My neighbours thought that the present situation would be resolved without too much delay. I didn't tell them what our watchman had told me earlier – that soldiers were knocking on gates and asking if Belgians lived there. Later I would learn that Belgians, as well as the RPF and all Tutsi in general, were being blamed for the downing of Habyarimana's airplane. Two white men wearing Belgian uniforms had apparently been seen in the vicinity of the place where the missiles had allegedly been fired. Later, on 7 April, ten Belgian soldiers who had been guarding an important Rwandan Hutu opposition politician, Madame Prime Minister Agathe Uwiringiyimana, had been taken prisoner by RGF forces and then brutally slaughtered. In the days that followed, the UN withdrew all but a couple of hundred members of their peacekeeping forces.

The lull on Thursday afternoon lasted for about an hour or so. Then, as the shells began falling again, I retreated back into the house. Later that evening I received a call from an officer in the Rwandan Army. I was completely surprised. He said, 'Hello, Chris, this is Lieutenant Darius of the Rwandan Army. I met you at Daniel's house. I am Daniel's cousin. Remember Felicia's naming ceremony? I met you there.'

'Ah yes, I remember now. How is Daniel and his wife and his children?'
'They are fine. Daniel just wanted me to call you and tell you that you are in no danger. The shots are being very well aimed. The targets are very specific.'
'What about the shots that go off course? One of my neighbours had a shell land in her yard. It blew all the windows out.'
'That was just an accident. Anyway, don't worry. Nobody's trying to get you.'

I was not completely reassured. How much had his cousin Daniel told him about me. Did he know that my fiancée was Tutsi? Did he know where we lived? On the other hand if someone was going to come and kill us, they would just come and do it, wouldn't they? My mind raced on, swinging between fear and relief. I tried to ignore these thoughts. It had been a kind gesture to call. I could not really believe that I was on anyone's hit list, but then what about those errant shells?
On Friday morning, shortly before 07.00, I received a few more phone calls – people wondering if I was all right and if I was holding up under the strain. One American friend asked me, with a touch of his typical humour, 'have you buried your stereo yet?' Clearly we were going to be evacuated at some point and if so, we would be unable to take much with us. The stereo was dead meat; all my possessions were dead meat. Everything that I had brought to Rwanda – car, computer, stereo, CD collection, books, clothes, papers, lecture notes, field notes, everything. I knew it then. Kiss it all goodbye and be thankful to get out of Rwanda alive. The last call I received that morning was from a Rwandan employee of our project. He was Hutu and therefore not in danger from *Interahamwe*, but wondered if anything could be done to get him and his wife out of their neighbourhood. I didn't really know, but I did my best to reassure him. As we were talking the phone suddenly went dead.

No more phone. We were completely cut off from the rest of the world.

That afternoon the fighting subsided just as it had the day before. Do these soldiers respect the siesta hour, I wondered? A Tutsi woman who was a friend of my fiancée's came over to our house from across the street. Her eyes were bloodshot. She had obviously been crying. Her brother, his wife, and all their children had just been killed where they lived in Nyamirambo. A neighbour of theirs had called and told her the news that morning before the phones went dead. She had also learned about several Tutsi who had been killed in another section of Kigali, Gikongoro. It seemed apparent that a genocide was under way. I wondered about Victor, his wife, and their children. After an hour or so, the pause ended and once more all you could hear was the sound of explosions, shots being fired, and the thump of mortars being dropped into their launch tubes. Outside in the yard, you could hear the passing bullets clearly. They would buzz and whistle over our heads. As the fighting grew more intense, our neighbour scurried back across the street to her house. We closed the tall metal gate and retreated inside to our mattress-lined corridor. I worried about my fiancée's parents. How would two frail people in their sixties escape this horror alive?

As of Friday 8 April, our house had not yet sustained any damage, although grenades and mortar shells had indeed fallen in our neighbourhood. Apart from the friend of my wife from across the street who had had a shell land in her yard, an American woman who lived next to us had also had a shell land in her yard and it had caused some damage to her house. These were the explosions that I had felt the previous night and I had thought at the time that they were direct hits on our house. 'So far we have been lucky', I thought to myself. Months later I would return to Rwanda and visit our former dwelling. Then I would see one or two broken windows where bullets had passed through. We could have survived that, I mused at the time. I also saw windows that had been completely smashed away in the front door, clearly the work of looters attempting to gain entrance into the house. We probably would not have survived them.

Friday night, 8 April, was the worst night. The battle for Kigali between RGF and RPF soldiers was now well under way. Mortars and artillery shells must have been flying right over our heads, for behind our house at a distance of about a quarter of a mile to half a mile there was an RGF camp. From the front porch of our house,

I could make out the hillsides of Remera where the RPF battalion had its encampment. We were directly on the line that joined these two points. This was not a comforting thought. Sleep that night came only in short bits. You would nod off under the sheer inertia of fatigue only to be reawakened by the boom and tremor of a nearby explosion. Sometimes, while asleep, an especially loud explosion would cause all the muscles in my body to contract involuntarily and I would leap from the mattress, expecting to see soldiers in front of me. I would dream of this before wakening, a ring of Rwandan government soldiers their bayonets pointed at my chest. They would rape Esperance, kill her, and then kill me. Years later, I would occasionally have the same dream.

At around midnight I heard what sounded like firecrackers slowly advancing in our direction. It was small arms fire, I guessed – rifles and pistols. Every now and then a more substantial explosion punctuated the cracks and pops. Those must be grenades, I thought. The noises inched closer and closer to us, growing louder as they advanced. Soon they sounded like they were right on top of us, with every grenade explosion shaking our house. Both of us listened, clinging to the bedsheet as if it were a shield, petrified with fear. That's it, I thought; a grenade or mortar shell is going to come down right on our house, right on our heads. But the noises moved on. They must be out in the street right in front of our house, a firefight between an RPF patrol and RGF soldiers. I followed the noise of the battle, imagining where it was going as it receded into the distance. First it moved to the left past our house and then further down the street. Then it began to move toward the rear. It seemed to be heading in the direction of the RGF camp behind us. It must be an RPF patrol trying to attack the camp. Soon the shots were being exchanged with such frequency that it was hard to distinguish one from another. 'They're attacking the Rwandan Army base behind us', I said to Esperance. 'I hope they kick the shit out of them.'

The battle became furious, but after only about ten minutes or so it began to move the other way. Why were they giving up so quickly, I wondered. I wanted them to overrun the RGF camp. Although I had met soldiers on both sides in the days leading up to this and considered one RGF soldier a friend, as a group I trusted the RPF more. They were much more professional than the RGF. I was also well aware of what the RGF soldiers were up to. They were murdering innocent people in their homes and then looting their possessions. They were committing genocide. But the RPF attackers were not going to take the camp that evening. They were withdrawing. They were coming back the same way that they had arrived. Slowly the cracks and booms grew louder once again. Then they were on top of us a second time. This was worse. They had rattled a hornet's nest and the hornets were in hot pursuit. One explosion shook the house so badly that I thought for sure that it had been hit. The battle moved down the street. Gradually it dissolved into the general din of that night's shots and explosions.

Weeks later I would learn that an RPF patrol had indeed attacked the RGF camp that night. Some people had even seen RPF soldiers in the streets of our neighbourhood, Kimihurura, that very evening. I would also learn about the tactics employed by the RPF. During the day they kept their distance from RGF strongpoints, preferring to bombard them from afar with light artillery when they had it, mortars and small arms when they didn't. At night, small RPF patrols would attack at the edges of RGF bases – quick hit-and-run missions. They could not beat a numerically superior force with a sustained assault,[4] so they harassed it, wearing away its morale. Their aim was to rattle their enemy's nerves until it spooked and ran.

On Saturday morning, 9 April, the battle continued but with less intensity. One would hear short bursts of automatic rifle fire and occasional booms from mortar and artillery. I felt confident enough to venture out of the corridor and inspect the inside of the rest of the house, thinking that I would certainly find a portion of it that had been blown away. But it was still intact. Not even a sign of shrapnel damage. I was utterly amazed. I opened the front door of the house, walked out into the yard and around the perimeter of the house. I saw nothing in my yard that looked like a crater from a mortar shell or a grenade. We had come through another night unscathed. I chatted with the neighbours. By now the car battery that had sustained the radio for at least twenty-four hours, was dead. My neighbours were the only source of news and they knew about as much as I did at that moment. Occasionally a car or pickup truck would zoom down the street in front of the house. Hoping it might be the UN, I walked over to the metal gate and opened it slightly to get a better look. The cars were not those of the UN. They were those of ordinary Rwandan citizens carting off loads of cargo, motorized looters squirreling away their booty in wholesale quantities. When will it be our turn to be looted? When will they come here?

Then I heard the noise of a helicopter. As it drew closer I could read 'UN' on its underside. Two Rwandan soldiers on the other side of the street also saw the helicopter and began firing their automatic rifles gleefully in its direction. The helicopter banked upward and retreated back in the same direction from which it had come. It was not going to take any risks. The two soldiers laughed uproariously, tiny Davids staving off a monstrous, mechanical Goliath.

Sometime after noon that day, I heard a loud banging on the gate. 'Chris! Chris! Get your stuff together. We're being evacuated. You've got five minutes to get your stuff together.' It was Chris Grundman of USAID. He was going around the neighbourhood, rounding up Americans. I opened the gate and he ran into our house. 'Get a white cloth or a towel and put it on the antenna of your car.' Then he saw a sheet on a bed and began tearing it apart. 'Here take this and tie it to the antenna. Drive over to the American school. You'll meet Rwandan soldiers along the way. Don't speak any Kinyarwanda to them. Hurry up, you've got five minutes. We've gotta get out of here.' Then he ran out, jumped into the car that a Rwandan appeared to be driving and took off.

Esperance, my fiancée, took a few minutes to put some of her clothing in a suitcase. I went outside and yelled to the American woman who lived next door. I told her to get ready and that we were being evacuated. 'I know,' she said. 'Wait for me, it'll only take me a few minutes.' Am I the only one who's in a hurry, I wondered? Do I need to be early for my own funeral? I tried to take it more slowly. I waited for Esperance, then loaded up our car, drove out into the street, and waited for our neighbour. She took her time. I turned off the ignition. When our neighbour was ready, she came out, started up her car, and proceeded to follow me to the American school, which was about a mile or so from where we lived.

I was the first to encounter a group of Rwandan soldiers. There were four of them standing beside a green Peugot that must have been their means of transportation. They had probably looted it from someone in the neighbourhood. One of them carried a translucent plastic jerry can, two thirds full of what appeared to be gasoline. I knew it wasn't for their car; it was for setting houses on fire. Another one of them had a rifle with a grenade on the end of it that he enjoyed sticking in my face. 'Where are the arms?' he asked in broken French. 'Where is the money? Where you going? Where you come from? Where is your house?'

I tried to summon my composure, though I could feel the trembling in my legs. 'We're being evacuated. We don't have any arms. We're supposed to go to the American school.'

'Give us the weapons!'
'We don't have any weapons,' I replied to the one with the grenade on his rifle. He walked around the car and stuck the rifle in Esperance's face.

He asked her questions in Kinyarwanda. Luckily for her, she remembered Chris Grundunan's advice. She feigned ignorance of Kinyarwanda and would only respond to the soldiers when they asked her questions in French. Had she responded in Kinyarwanda, that would have affirmed what they already suspected from Esperance's physiognomy – that she was Tutsi. They would have killed her right then and there.

'Who are you? Where is your house?'
'I am that man's wife', she said pointing to me. 'We live back there,' pointing in the direction from which we had come.'

Another soldier who seemed more reflective than his eager comrade, began to pose other questions. 'What nationality are you?' he asked.

'I am an American,' she responded in French. Luckily he didn't speak any English, for if he had tried that on her, it would have surely given her away.
'A black American?'
'Yes, a black American.'
'Show me some identification.'
'He has it,' she said pointing to me.
'Show it,' he told me.

Luckily I still had a picture ID with me that said, 'Ambassade des Etats-Unis' (United States Embassy). It didn't mean that I was a diplomat or that I was an important person, nor did it say anything about Esperance. All the card meant was that as an American and indirect USAID employee, I could enter the US Embassy in Kigali without a great deal of screening from the guard at the entryway.

But the Rwandan soldier did not know that. To him it must have seemed that I was someone that he shouldn't hassle too much.

'OK. You may go,' he said as he moved to the side of our car.

His colleague with the rifle grenade looked disappointed; he had wanted to do more.

Feeling that wave of relief that comes only after a stay of execution, I crossed a wide intersection and waited for our neighbour on the other side. I could see the soldiers and our neighbour's car but I couldn't see exactly what was going on. I had wanted to put some distance between the soldiers and us, but I was concerned about her. They were clearly taking more time with her than they had with us. Finally they let her proceed. When we had both arrived at the American school and parked our cars, I asked her what had happened. She began to cry, 'Why didn't you wait for me?' she pleaded.

'I did. I just didn't want to be that close to them. Esperance is Tutsi and I think they knew that.'
'They stole my jewellery,' she sobbed. 'One of them said I was his wife and that I was going to have to stay with him. He touched my breasts. I gave them all the money I had with me.'
'I'm so sorry, Barbara. What could I have done?'
'I know you couldn't have done anything. I'm sorry. It was just so awful.'

When we arrived at the American school we saw at least sixty people and about twenty or thirty cars. Someone told us to sign our names in a notebook that was being passed around and to indicate how much gas we had in our car. My gas gauge was almost on 'E'. Someone said that we should leave the car there and double up with someone who had more gas. We found someone – Jackie, an employee of Project San Francisco. She had come by herself in a little white Suzuki. She was happy to let us ride with her. The plan was to drive in a long convoy of cars each bearing a paper American flag scotch-taped to the rear window and a white towel or sheet tied to the antenna. We would drive southward from Kigali to Butare. There was no hostile action between the opposing sides along this route as virtually all RPF soldiers were concentrated in areas to the north of Kigali. Then we would continue on southward to Bujumbura, Burundi. We waited for others to show up at the American school for another hour or so. Soon, though, the noise of grenades and mortar shells began to intensify. Directly to the side of the American school, I could see a small group of Rwandan soldiers who were launching mortars in what seemed to be the vague direction of the CND. One could hear the booming thump of each shell as it was launched. I had a sinking feeling; it will not take long for the RPF to determine where those mortars are coming from and they will respond with ordinance of their own. This will place us right next to an important target. Others must have been thinking the same thing for, shortly thereafter, it was decided that we should leave. The front gates of the compound swung open and a long line of cars began filing out.

In order to gain access to the Butare road we had to pass through parts of the Kiyovu section of Kigali and through Kigali's large traffic circle known as the Round Point. As our cars filed through, groups of Rwandans lined the streets and watched us. Some waved and smiled. Others looked at us in a blank and slightly puzzled way. I felt what it must feel like to be a rat deserting a sinking ship. Over and over as I looked at those faces the words repeated in my head: *après nous, le déluge.* But who among us, I also thought, would choose to stay in Rwanda at this time.

Some of the Rwandan onlookers had clearly been looting and were laden down with booty. Others were there apparently just as spectators. We could see that many shops had been broken into. As we proceeded, we could not help but notice that the beer distributorship just a few hundred yards downhill from the Round Point had been particularly hard hit. A large mound of broken brown glass lay strewn in front of the building. Nevertheless, none of the Rwandans that I saw in the vicinity were drinking, nor were they carting off cases of beer. This type of loot was clearly not destined for ordinary citizens.

Soldiers from the RGF stopped us at our first roadblock, hardly half a mile downhill from the Round Point. These soldiers seemed to be in a terrible mood. Many had bloodshot eyes either from lack of sleep or from drinking alcohol and smoking marijuana, which were both in evidence. Cases of unopened Primus beer could be seen here and there and some soldiers were sitting upon the plastic crates. They paced ominously up and down the long line of cars, some carrying weapons that I had never seen in my life even at military parades. Catching sight of Esperance, one of them came over to our car and said 'muraho', the standard greeting in Kinyar-wanda. She didn't respond. He came over to our window and asked us some questions in Kinyarwanda. It made me extremely nervous, but she didn't flinch. Then he asked us some questions in French. We answered his questions and he walked away. There were several more roadblocks. Each one seemed to take an infinity. At just about every barrier, a soldier or two would come over to the car and say something to us in Kinyarwanda in the attempt to flush out Esperance as a fleeing Tutsi. Our convoy was the first one that they had had to deal with. I learned two weeks later in Nairobi that subsequent convoys had fared very badly at the hands of these soldiers. Suspected Tutsi or Hutu opposition politicians were pulled from cars and summarily executed, either in front of everyone or later. One Rwandan whom I met about week later at the Nairobi airport told me that the car he had been travelling in had been fired upon, one of its occupants killed, and two others wounded, but they had managed to traverse the barrier and outdistance their pursuers.

Several miles south of Kigali we arrived at the Nyabarongo River and, of course, there was a barrier before the bridge. I could see two soldiers sitting in a car drinking Johnny Walker Red Label straight from the bottle. Others sat along the side of the road, drinking Primus from large bottles that contained three-quarters of a litre. This group seemed to be the most undisciplined of all those we had met thus far. But I thought to myself that if we got through this roadblock all right, the rest would be easy. 'This is the boundary of the sacred Rwandan kingdom,' I said to Jackie and Esperance. 'Once we cross over this river, we will be OK. We will be in southern Rwanda and out of the territory that every Rwandan regime considers to be its most sacred turf.' Neither of them had any idea of what I was talking about – the pedantic murmuring of a stressed-out professor. They both looked at me indulgently, as if the degradation in my mental state were more worthy of pity than of scorn.

Of course my previous symbolic studies of Rwandan sacred kingship combined with the lack of sleep over the last three nights was what was generating this fantasy. In the present context, it couldn't possibly have been appropriate. This was, after all, a modern nation state with legalistic and not sacred boundaries. But oddly enough, my prediction proved to be true. Every subsequent roadblock on the way to Butare, and there were only four more, was a cake walk. The RGF soldiers that we encountered at these barriers could have easily belonged to another army. They were polite, relaxed, and more disciplined than the ones that we had encountered up until then. They would smile and even engage in small talk with us. Esperance even struck up a conversation with one in Kinyarwanda, much to my horror – but the soldier was very pleasant and wished her and all the rest of us well. I advised him not to go to Kigali at all costs. He seemed genuinely surprised at my grim description of the situation there. This was very odd, I remember thinking. Are their communications so poor that they don't know what is happening in Kigali?

We encountered the last blockade right before entering Rwanda's southern city of Butare, but it was an easy one and only cost us a few minutes delay. Upon entering Butare we decided to stop at the Hotel Ibis for a short pause and a bit of refreshment. I had always loved this hotel with its large arcaded patio, cold soft drinks and beer, and its various simple but tasty dishes: *frites, boulettes, saucisses,* and *brochettes.* I ordered a Coke, gulped it down and ordered another. I also ordered a few *boulettes* (spicy meatballs). French-speaking journalists came up to us and asked questions. I told them what scum I thought the Rwandan government and army were and gave them my name. Minutes later Esperance said to me, 'What if we have to come back to Rwanda and the same people are still in power?' This was a depressing, but realistic appraisal of the situation. What if the bad guys win? I went running out in the street to find the journalist, and when I found him, asked him to delete my name, which he proceeded to cross off his notepad. Then I returned to my table in the hotel only to be barked at by one of the leaders of our convoy who told me that I had better hurry up and finish my Coke and *boulettes* as we were going to leave in exactly two minutes. I told him that we were in no danger in Butare, but he was insistent and angrily so. 'What a pain these people are', I thought, 'and what poor judges of where there is danger. This is not sacred territory.' Butare, as it turned out, did not experience violence until weeks later.

At the end of what must have been a ten- or twelve-hour journey, we arrived in Bujumbura and went to an upscale, modern hotel. There all the American refugees assembled in a large conference room and listened to a representative from the US Embassy. We filled out forms and then were told by a hotel employee how and where to register to get a room. All anyone could think about was sleep. The next day virtually everyone who had come with us was air-evacuated by US forces to Nairobi. Esperance and I stayed behind as an Embassy official had expressed doubts about whether, as a Rwandan, Esperance should be allowed on the flight.

We ended up staying a few days at the hotel. With each passing day we would meet the occasional Rwandan escapee – usually, but not always Tutsi – who had slipped through the dragnet and the inferno. One person we met was Karimu, a close friend of Victor and me. Karimu recounted an extraordinary story of his escape. He and two friends had hidden within a pile of adobe bricks that they had arranged in such a way as to make it look like a simple storage pile. They were friends of a sympathetic Hutu woman who owned a bar, and the bricks were on her property. She had allowed them to conceal themselves there. They would remain hidden in the brick pile all day. In the early evening they would listen to the bragging of *Interahamwe* who had come to the bar to drink. Under-employed and destitute during ordinary times, the killers could now afford to eat and drink at will on the proceeds of whatever they had been able to steal from their victims. Karimu and his friends remained ensconced in their brick pile for several days, although in the dead of night and when she was sure no one else could see them, the bar owner would tell them that the coast was clear and they would venture out of their hideaway for short periods.

Karimu told me that the *Interahamwe* he had overheard while hiding among the bricks spoke of what they were doing as 'our work' (*akazi kacu*). They would begin hunting Tutsis down in the early morning and continue until sunset. At night they collected in the bars to drink and to talk over the day's events, whom they had killed and whom they would look for the next day. They would usually leave the bar well before midnight, sometimes expressing concern that if they stayed out too long and drank too much they would be no good for 'work' the next day.

I asked Karimu, 'Did you hear anything about Victor?' Karimu looked at the floor momentarily and then looked back toward me, 'Victor is dead.' I half expected this news, but felt the blood leave my face. After a period of incarceration in 1990, Victor, far from becoming more circumspect, had never kept his pro-RPF sentiments secret. Still the news hit me hard. Karimu went on to explain that Victor and Phillipe had been somewhere in Nyamirambo on the night of 6 April. At around 23.00 they learned that the President's

plane had been shot down. Victor decided to go home, fetch his
three children, and consider what to do from there. He and Phillipe
drove to Victor's house. When they arrived, Presidential Guard
soldiers were lying in wait for them. Both were shot dead and,
although Victor's three children witnessed the whole incident, they
were not harmed. Monique, Victor's wife, had not been at home.
She was at her sister Rose's house in Kicyukiro. Rose was married
to a very senior member of President Habyarimana's political
party, the Mouvement Revolutionnaire pour le Développement et
la Démocratie (MRND) and Rose herself was active in the women's
Interahamwe.

I said to Karimu that this had to mean that Rose or her husband
had sent the soldiers to Victor's house to wait for him and to kill
him when he arrived. Victor, married to Rose's sister, had been a
close friend of the Rose's family in the years before the RPF invasion. In the summer of 1987 when I resided for a time with Victor
and Monique, members of that family were frequent visitors. I knew
both Rose and her husband quite well. Then in 1990, Victor was
thrown in prison as a supporter of the RPF even though, at the
time and like most others so imprisoned, he did not support the
RPF cause.

Victor told me that during his confinement he had been beaten
nearly every day. They would knock his head to the cement floor,
yet take care not to drive him to unconsciousness. His captors gave
him a choice: become an *Interahamwe* and recruit others or stay in
jail. Victor did not give in. After a few weeks, Rose's husband
interceded to secure Victor's release. He was able to obtain this
because of his high position in the MRND. Victor might have shown
some appreciation to his brother-in-law. Instead, he became an
ardent and vocal supporter of the RPF. Because of this he sometimes
quarrelled bitterly with Rose's husband. On one such occasion he
prohibited Rose and her husband from ever again setting foot in
his house to visit Monique. Victor's personality changed as well.
He began to drink heavily and at times, and to be abusive to his
wife. It was because of an incident of abuse three days earlier that
Monique was staying with her sister Rose on the night of Victor's
murder.

There was strong reason to suspect the involvement of Rose and
her husband in Victor's death. During the first day of the massacres,
the interim Rwandan government sought to liquidate its most
articulate and visible critics and prominent opposition politicians,

whether Hutu or Tutsi. As Lieutenant Darius had told me on 7
April, 'the shots are being very well aimed'. Victor, although an
RPF supporter, had not been a politician. Secondly, his children
had been spared and this departed from the usual pattern. In
virtually all cases where someone was earmarked for execution by
the *Interahamwe* or the RGF, everyone in the family would be killed.
The only logical explanation I could find for why Victor's children
were spared, was because the soldiers had been specifically instructed
to bring them to Monique unharmed. Such special arrangements
to kill some, but not all the members of a household, bore the
imprint of an influential person. Who else could it have been if
not one of Rose's family? Karimu agreed that that was probably
how it had happened. This realization depressed me. I had once
been friends with those people. One evening, in May of 1993, I
had had dinner at their house in Kicyukiro (a suburb of Kigali).
Later that month when I returned to the US, Rose gave me a
package to send to her daughter who was studying at a college in
California.[5]

Esperance and I stayed a few days longer at the hotel in Bujumbura, then took a commercial flight to Nairobi. We spent the next
four months in Nairobi, our ears still ringing from the events that
we had just lived through in Rwanda. We would meet with former
friends and acquaintances and learn of the death of others. Because
of the horror of the genocide and the subsequent discrediting of
those associated with it, most Rwandans, whether Tutsi or Hutu,
claimed to support the RPF. Only a few did not. One among my
former friends who was not an RPF supporter and who thought
that elements of the MRND should eventually be allowed to participate in a new Rwandan government, pointed out to me that, unless
this was done, 'ethnocracy' was likely to remain the dominant mode
of governance for years to come. Once the RPF took over Rwanda,
which appeared more and more likely as the war progressed, the
Tutsi extremist contingent within it would seize control and there
would be an abusive 'Tutsi-cracy' in Rwanda where once there had
been an abusive 'Hutu-cracy'. Things should return to the state
that they were in during the 1980s, he claimed: limited Tutsi participation in politics, but fill rights for Tutsi in the economic arena.
At the time I dismissed my friend's ideas, although in subsequent
years, much of what he predicted has indeed come to pass. In
hindsight I am forced to confess the naiveté of my own beliefs at
that moment.

In April and May only a trickle of Tutsi refugees made it to
Nairobi. A few had probably gone elsewhere, to Burundi, Tanzania,
or Zaire. Estimates claim that probably 80 per cent of Rwanda's
Tutsi did not survive the genocide (Chretien, 1997). Once in Kenya,
Rwandan Tutsi were met with hostility from the Kenyan government. Kenyan President Daniel Arap Moi had been a close friend
and ally of Habyarimana and an opponent of the RPF. As weeks
and then months went by, more and more of the Rwandan refugees
entering Kenya were Hutu, fleeing the RPF advance. These refugees
were treated much better by the Kenyan government and were even
permitted to engage in the international arms trade to re-equip
the RGF. By mid-July 1994, most of the RGF had been forced to
flee to eastern Zaire.

In Nairobi it was common for Esperance to encounter people
whom she had known to be *Interahamwe* in Rwanda. Once, while
we were on a public bus and about to get off, she caught glimpse
of just such a character. He was a relative of Rwanda's first Hutu
Prime Minister during the 1960s, Mbonyamutwa. The two exchanged
angry words before we descended. Completely flustered by the
encounter, Esperance fell to the pavement as she stepped from
the bus. But the worst moment of our stay in Kenya came when
Esperance learned of the death of her mother and father, residents
of Kigali's Muhima quarter. Up until that time, Esperance had
maintained the hope that somehow her parents would manage to
survive. Never in the days leading up to this event, when I knew in
the bottom of my heart that she would one day learn the worst, did
I try to dissuade her. Clearly this war was not something from which
one could easily take refuge.

Virtually every Rwandan we met in Kenya had lost relatives,
friends, and property. Some were anxious parents worried about
children who were still somewhere in Rwanda. Most were destined
to be sent to other countries as refugees, unsure of what they would
encounter or of how they would make a living. Most assumed that
they would never return to Rwanda, whether or not the RPF won
the war. I talked to as many as I could. Many recounted stories of
having avoided death two, three, or more times. Several were Hutu
who had not sided with the genocidal regime and had been obliged
to flee for their lives because of it. Some had given help to fleeing
Tutsi only to be targeted as *ibyitso* (traitors) in turn.

Of course there is no single way to talk about the Rwandan
genocide and I do not attempt, in the pages that follow, either a

monocausal explanation of it or even any 'explanation' in the proper sense of the term. Instead, what I attempt to do is to partly unravel a tangled skein of order and disorder. In what appears to be an example of total systemic collapse, there was order in the disorder, elements of pattern in the midst of apparently total chaos. For one thing, there is the fact that the genocide was well-planned and organized in advance by Rwandan politicians and their intellectual allies. Beneath this level of rational decision making lurks the eerie irrationality that one million people could be eliminated in only a little over three months, not by gas chambers and the bureau-cratized machinery of an industrial society, but by the hands of youthful militia members and ordinary citizens wielding knives, machetes, and clubs. Yet even amidst this irrationality there lurked a certain kind of order in that many of the techniques of cruelty were mythically and symbolically conditioned – they followed mean-ingful forms, a 'mythic logic'.

Understanding the Rwandan genocide requires that we under-stand something about the historical and political preconditions, but an analysis of the social and cultural factors that imparted a specific form to this tragedy is also necessary. These concerns build upon what has already been written about the genocide, for since I returned to the US from Africa in September of 1994, at least six books have appeared. These concentrate on the historical and political factors. A recent book by Gerard Prunier (1995), for example, is an excellent work in this vein.

In the pages that follow I will attempt to elucidate factors that were manifest in the genocide at more or less apparent levels. At the most apparent level, I will briefly summarize Rwanda's political history. Then I will discuss the intellectual substrate of extremist ideologies in Rwanda and Burundi, most notably the notions and ideas that are associated with the 'Hamitic hypothesis'. Of European origin, Hamitism has continued to provide ethnic extremists, whether Hutu or Tutsi, with a set of prefabricated notions that have served as a basis for claiming rights to the land and as a template for ethnic stereotypes. Unfortunately, these stereotypes and their associated versions of history have been internalized by many Rwandans and Burundians. Taught new ways to hate by Europeans, central Africans have learned the lesson only too well, becoming the authors of their own repetitive tragedy. To this day, these stereotypes and versions of history serve as raw material for extremist ideologues who exploit them according to the perceived

needs of the moment. In the discourse of Hutu extremism, Hutu
autochthony is opposed to the supposed foreignness of the Tutsi. In
the discourse of Tutsi extremism, Tutsi intellectual superiority is
opposed to Hutu intellectual inferiority.

Yet it would be premature to attribute all causality to discourse.
Discourse is never produced in a vacuum, nor can it resist for ever
the facts about human existence, although in certain historical
circumstances these may be poorly understood or apprehended.
After Copernicus and Galileo, for example, it is impossible for any
but the uninformed or the extremely recalcitrant to conceive of
the human place in the universe in the same geocentric and
anthropocentric way. Nor do human beings, as some would have
it, reinvent culture and therefore 'truth' from one day to the next.
Every invention or cultural construction is contingent upon every
previous construction and constructions that defy all empirical
evidence to the contrary tend not to survive in the long run. Sooner
or later, most are abandoned. Human beings may do irrational
things, even with an apparently tragic persistence, but they are never
completely blind, never completely stupid. False conceptions of the
world and of the human place in it are subject to refutation and
are often completely discarded, as was the Ptolemaic model of the
universe.

For these reasons we cannot criticize the Hamitic hypothesis
solely on the basis that, as discourse, it was colonialist, Eurocentric,
racist, and immoral. Although all these criticisms may be true, the
dragon of 'Bell curve' type hypotheses (in which I would include
certain aspects of the Hamitic hypothesis) is more adequately and
permanently slain by empirical evidence to the contrary than by
the charge that it occupies the moral low ground. Although we
certainly need to understand the Hamitic hypothesis as discourse,
we also need to confront it as fact and this may mean that we cannot
refute it in its entirety.

Moving from the ideological to an ontological level and from a
conscious domain of experience to a less-than-conscious domain, I
will then argue that the genocidal violence followed culturally
specific forms and that these require symbolic analysis in order to
be understood. In particular we need to understand more about
Rwandan notions of the body, notions of being and personhood,
notions of good and evil, and notions about orderly and disorderly
social life. These are factors referred to by Bruce Kapferer in his
work on ethno-nationalism and violence as ontology (1988). Build-

ing upon Kapferer's work as well as that of Pierre Clastres, Pierre Bourdieu, and John Gledhill, I maintain that specific ideas and representations involving the body have to be included in our understanding of ethno-nationalist violence. The ultimate origin of political violence is the human body. The expression, "to take up arms," seems proof enough of this assertion. However, and more importantly for our purposes, the ultimate destination of political violence, the tableau upon which the dictates of oppression are inscribed is also the human body and not all polities write their signatures in the same way. But what is a starting point cannot be our terminus. The mere assertion that the violence was enracinated in specific cultural dispositions, that it was symbolically conditioned begs the question. We need to understand what these cultural dispositions were and are, what Rwandan habitus was and is from the vantagepoint of a Rwandan social actor. We must, therefore, make some effort to decipher the cultural hieroglyphics of torture and violation.

While the preceding might be included under the rubric of 'structure', it also seems clear that, in employing Bourdieu's notion of habitus (1977), we attribute equal importance to human agency and to history. Rwandan ways of thought and action, though they manifest continuity with the past as I show in a discussion about nineteenth century sacred kingship, have not been sheltered from external influences, nor have they been mindlessly and mechanically replicated from one generation to the next. Rwandans have improvised, innovated, and transformed their ways of thinking and acting, even while tending to reproduce earlier structures. This is most apparent in the iconography of Hutu extremist literature, the images of which I discuss in some detail.

Pursuant to the issues of structure, agency, and the body, my final topic of discussion in this book concerns sex and violence or, in other terms, the question of gender and the genocide. The Rwandan events were not simply a conflict between groups of men – they were also about reconfiguring gender. In the years preceding the genocide, many Rwandan women achieved prominence in economic and professional life. In order to do this, they had to confront the patriarchal structures of post-colonial Rwandan society. Their success threatened some Rwandans including many who were members of President Habyarimana's party, the MRND, or those in the most reactionary Hutu party, the CDR. One of the earliest victims in the violence that followed President Habyarimana's death was the female prime minister, Agathe Uwiringiyimana, a southern Hutu member of the party known as the Mouvement Démocratique Républicain (MDR). Her death owed as much to the fact that she was a woman, and a particularly articulate and outspoken one, as it did to the fact that she was a prominent member of the democratic opposition.

In addition, in the months leading up to the genocide, Hutu extremists focused particular attention on Tutsi women. A great deal of conflict and ambivalence characterized Hutu extremist attitudes towards Tutsi women. On one hand relationships between Hutu men and Tutsi women were strongly condemned in extremist literature. Yet on the other hand, many high level Hutu extremists either had Tutsi wives or Tutsi mistresses. This placed them in an ideologically questionable position. Furthermore, these men often sired children who were legally Hutu but biologically mixed. People of mixed ethnicity, often pejoratively called 'Hutsi', were a thorn in the side of Hutu extremism. Potentially such persons could completely undermine the categories 'Hutu' and 'Tutsi', and render ethnicity irrelevant.

Notes

1. Estimates of the total number killed during the Rwandan genocide range from a low of about 500,000 to a high of well over a million. A recent attempt by local authorities in Rwanda to tally the number commune by commune yielded a figure of 1,300,000. Some Rwandans so counted may still be alive and living in other countries. On the other hand violence against Rwandan Tutsi and other survivors of the genocide continues to this day, especially in north-western Rwanda where forces hostile to the present government have been conducting guerrilla warfare. An estimate of one million killed is not unrealistic.

2. Other commentators disagree, pointing out that 'Operation Turquoise' did indeed save a few thousand Tutsi who would most probably have been killed. Recently a French parliamentary commission under the direction of Paul Quiles considered this question and others. While the 'Quiles Report' (1998) underlines many serious errors in French policy toward Rwanda before and during the genocide, it stops well short of directly implicating France. For a critical assessment of this report see S. Smith, *Libération,* 16 December, 1998.

3. *Interahamwe* means 'those who attack together.' Most Rwandan political parties had youth wings and for the MRND party, theirs was the

Interahamwe. Recruited largely from among young males who had drifted into Rwandan cities, the *Interahamwe* received political and arms training from MRND party officials, Rwandan Government soldiers, and possibly also from French military advisors. Practically every urban neighbourhood possessed at least one *Interahamwe* member and, in the rural areas, every hillside. They aided the pre-genocidal apparatus in keeping regularly updated lists of all Rwandan opposition party members and all Tutsis. Before the outbreak of wholesale massacres, the *Interahamwe* intimidated people on their lists with actual or threatened violence and extorted 'protection' money from them. Even before the genocide *Interahamwe* were occasionally given the authorization to set up roadblocks and to rob, beat, and sometimes kill the people they had trapped, or to steal or damage their vehicles. On two occasions I narrowly avoided being trapped in such roadblocks. During the genocide *Interahamwe* weapons of choice were the machete, the nail-studded wooden club, and the grenade.

4.   In early April 1994 the Rwandan Government Forces numbered somewhere between 40,000 and 50,000 men; Rwandan Patriotic Front troops counted between 15,000 and 20,000.

5.   On April of 1999 Ngirumpatse's sister-in-law, Monique, visited me in the Ivory Coast. She explained to me that it was not Ngirumpatse who was responsible for her husband Victor's death. Instead, neighbourhood *Interahamwe* from Nyamirambo had committed the crime. Intending to kill the children later, the *Interahamwe* had left the scene affording the children a chance to escape to a neighbour's house. Monique was then able to rescue her children because Ngirumpatse provided her with a car and a chauffeur.

CHAPTER ONE

Rwanda

Rwanda is the smallest African country south of the Sahara and possesses a superficial area roughly equal to that of the state of Maryland. Much of the surface is covered with lakes, swamps, or mountains that are too steep to farm. Rwanda is close to the equator ($2°$ S), but high altitude keeps it temperate. Most of its population, which is 95 per cent rural, lives at altitudes between 1,500 and 2,500 m. With a population that was close to 7.5 million people before the genocide and about 6.5 million after it, including approximately 1.5 million Hutu refugees, most of whom were repatriated from Zaire (now Democratic Republic of Congo), Tanzania, and Burundi, it remains sub-Saharan Africa's most densely populated country (over 250 inhabitants per square kilometre). Moreover, its population growth rate of over 3.5 per cent per year is one of the highest in the world. Population density in Rwanda compares to some of Japan's most populous islands, yet its average per capita GDP is one of the smallest in the world. To many observers, lack of available land contributed to the political tensions that led to the genocide (Chretien, 1997). Although far from being the whole story, there is some truth to this.

Rwandan farms are quite small, just a little over two acres on the average, whereas the typical Rwandan household consists of about nine people. Virtually all the arable land in Rwanda is under intensive cultivation. From much of the land, two crop harvests can and must be extracted per year in order for the people to survive. Subsistence crops include: plantains, sorghum, beans, maize, potatoes, sweet potatoes, manioc, wheat in some places, and rice in others. Many Rwandans also raise livestock including goats, sheep, and cattle. Cattle are the most prestigious form of livestock. Both Tutsi and Hutu own cattle where possible and the animals are exchanged in the most socially significant transactions such as

marriage and patron–client ties. Cash crops are also grown in
Rwanda including coffee, tea, and pyrethrum flowers (used in
pyrethrin insecticides). Tea tends to be grown on large state-owned
plantations, and numerous independent small farmers plant coffee.
These latter are among the most poorly compensated for their
product in the world (Chretien, 1997).

Not every Rwandan farm consists of only two acres; in the last
several decades a rapid process of class formation and socio-econ-
omic differentiation has produced something of a rural aristocracy
and a small urban bourgeoisie. Close to 17 per cent of the total
number of Rwandan farms are larger than two acres and these take
up about 43 per cent of Rwanda's total area of arable land, 60 per
cent of the total in Kigali prefecture (Chretien, 1997: 77). Before
the genocide, many of the owners of these larger farms were military
officers and/or MRND party notables with commercial interests,
prompting many to speak of Rwanda's élite as a 'military-merchant'
class. Although some Rwandan entrepreneurs have earned their
position in this élite by providing needed products and services to
the Rwandan economy, most gained their status due to their proximity to the organs of state power.

> More than competence, connections to the regime have given rise to a
> new form of pseudo-technocratic bourgeoisie and conferred prosperity
> upon it. Following the ups and downs of political favor, we see a rapid
> turnover in these *bourgeois gentlemen*. In three years one such high
> personality exercised four different functions: administrator of the
> pyrethrin factory in Ruhengeri, general director of the Social Fund of
> Rwanda, Prefect of Kibungo, and finally, Minister of Education. What
> pleasant diversity, what guaranty of effectiveness!
>
> Without over-generalizing, the claim is justified that a portion of
> the Rwandan bourgeoisie is simply parasitic and prebendal. One must
> also admit that a fraction of it does re-invest some of its earnings. Many
> industrial ventures started out as commercial operations.
>
> (Bezy, 1990: 51, cited from Chretien, 1997: 78, my translation)

Famines have occurred with some frequency in Rwandan history.
One particularly severe famine in 1927–30 undoubtedly hastened
the overthrow in 1931 of one Rwandan *mwami*, Yuhi Musinga, the
last non-Christian Rwandan king (Cornet, 1995). More recently
drought in the late 1980s coupled with a decrease in world coffee
prices, combined to produce famine conditions in some areas

during 1989–90. Thousands of people in south-western Rwanda fled as 'economic refugees' into neighbouring Zaire and Burundi. None of this was helped by a 'structural adjustment programme' that resulted in a sharp devaluation (40 per cent) of the Rwandan Franc (Chretien, 1997: 76). Without the massive input of food assistance during the 1990s, surely many Rwandans would have died of starvation.

During the 1970s and 1980s there were many assistance projects that aimed at increasing agricultural output and decreasing the birth rate. Some successes in achieving these goals had been realized; family planning projects, for example, had managed to bring the average number of births per woman down from close to nine to a little under six. Many other projects were operative in Rwanda in the 1970s and 1980s – so many, in fact, that Rwanda was sometimes referred to as the country with the most number of aid projects per square kilometre (Willame, 1990). These projects often did well in Rwanda because of the country's hard-working population, relatively high number of educated people, and until the mid-1980s, relatively little corruption by local standards. Other development analysts have pointed to the country's psychological and economic dependence on these projects and to the possibility that they may have been doing more long-term harm to Rwanda than good (Willame, 1990).

Early Colonial History

Until the late nineteenth century Rwanda had managed to avoid much contact with others beyond its borders. Arab slave traders for example, were unable to conduct raids on Rwandan soil because most of central and eastern Rwanda was well-organized under a centralized state ruled by a king (*mwami*). The fighting forces of this state, basically peasant militias with hierarchical ties to the *mwami* and his central court, could be rapidly mobilized to counter any external threat. For this reason, Islam, so important in neighbouring Tanzania and nearby Kenya, never gained much of a foothold in Rwanda. Only about 10 to 12 per cent of the pre-genocide population was Muslim.

As for European contact with Rwanda, it was not until the 1880s that Rwanda began to be seriously coveted by rivalrous powers in the 'scramble for Africa'. The first European colonialists to set foot in Rwanda were the Germans, who established a certain priority of claim to Rwanda and Burundi due to the fact that a German, Count von Götzen, had been the first to extensively explore the area and to sign a treaty with the Rwandan king at the time, Kigeri V Rwabugiri. But German claims to the region were contested by the British, already present in neighbouring Uganda to the north, who wanted the area as a link in their planned rail line from the Cape of Good Hope to Cairo. King Leopold of Belgium also had designs on Ruanda-Urundi due to its proximity to the Congo Free State and the possibility to extend a corridor eastward from the territory to the Indian Ocean (Louis, 1963).

These conflicting claims were settled at the Berlin Conference of 1884–85 when most of Ruanda-Urundi was awarded to Germany. England managed to retain much of the lands termed Mfumbira (adjacent to present day north-west Rwanda), although there were many people in the region who spoke Kinyarwanda. Kinyarwanda speakers also predominated on the Island of Ijwi in the middle of Lake Kivu, but the Congo Free State retained possession of it (Louis, 1963).

At the Berlin Conference the ground rules for colonialism were also established. The two main ones were 'effective occupation' and the 'civilizing mission'. A colonial power needed to demonstrate that its agents, soldiers, and missionaries, were effectively occupying the land and that they were 'civilizing' the indigenous inhabitants. At the time no one contested European anthropological assumptions, held by laymen and scholars alike, that societies could be unproblematically divided into those that were 'civilized' and those that were not. White Europeans placed themselves and all their cultural attributes at the pinnacle of civilization. Christianity constituted one of the most significant pieces in the European cultural mosaic and by sending the natives its proselytes, Europeans persuaded themselves that their interference in the lives of distant peoples was altruistic.

In the case of Rwanda, the first missionaries to accept the call were Catholic missionaries from Alsace who established their first mission in 1900. Unable to find willing candidates from Germany itself, at least at the time, the Germans decided to recruit missionaries from somewhere as close to home as possible and with some historical and cultural links to Germany. The only problem was that these priests were more often Francophone than German speaking (Linden, 1977).

Along with belief in Christ, the received wisdom of the eighteenth and nineteenth centuries associated 'civilization' with inherent biological and intellectual superiority. According to the 'Great Chain of Being' theory, northern Europeans were closer to God and the angels whereas Africans occupied a position closer to lower animals. The theory justified European domination of the planet as an inevitable corollary to the race's superior intellectual abilities. Added to the pseudo-science of the Great Chain of Being was another theologically inspired theory to explain the origin of seemingly anomalous advanced civilizational traits found south of the Sahara in central Africa. According to this theory, 'Hamite' Tutsi were responsible for bringing the rudiments of civilization to the region. Tutsi were presumed to be the remnants of a lost tribe of Israel, the descendants of Ham – Noah's son, banished to the south of the Promised Land. Following this hypothesis, descendants of Ham, being Caucasian, had an easy time conquering the less intelligent negroid peoples that they encountered in their inexorable move southward (see Chapter 2). As they moved southward the Hamites supposedly became darker skinned, though they did not lose all their Caucasian attributes.

Rwanda was destined to be the hapless focal point of these several convergent streams of thought emanating from nineteenth-century science and theology. If a state pre-existed the arrival of Europeans in Rwanda, it had to be the work of clever Hamite-Tutsi. Rwanda for the Europeans was composed of three distinct racial groups: the Hamitic Tutsi whose Caucasian affinities naturally predisposed them to rule, the Bantu Hutu whose stocky physiques naturally predisposed them to hard work, and the pygmoid Twa who, as an atavistic throwback to the ape, were a pariah race destined to disappear.

History of Ethnic Conflict

Much has been written about the two tiny central African countries of Rwanda and Burundi and, of course, one of the preferred subjects of discussion is the question of ethnicity and its effect upon political life in both countries. Before 1994, Rwanda and Burundi were characterized by a similar ethnic mix of approximately 80–85 per cent Hutu, 15–20 per cent Tutsi, and a little less than 1 per cent Twa. In sharp contrast to ethnic differentiation in other parts of Africa, where linguistic, religious, or regional differences figure prominently, Rwandan and Burundian ethnic groups share a single language and culture and are not, for the most part, regionally concentrated in specific areas. In pre- and early colonial times, a high degree of economic specialization characterized the groups. A larger proportion of Tutsi, for example, gained their livelihood from cattle herding than Hutu, who were cultivators. Nevertheless, many Hutu raised cattle as well as cultivating and many Tutsi raised crops as well as husbanded cattle. Only Twa neither cultivated nor herded cattle. A few were hunter-gatherers, but most were potters.

Since independence in 1962, many Twa have continued to make pots, but less difference in terms of economic activity can be observed between Tutsi and Hutu due to the diminution of pasture lands. Although there are still some Tutsi who live primarily from herding, most members of both groups cultivate the land and own cattle where this is economically feasible. Where religion is concerned, most Rwandans are Christian, and although there are more Roman Catholics than Protestants, religious preferences do not break down neatly along ethnic lines. Differences in physiognomy among the three groups exist, but these are statistical in nature rather than indelible markers of difference. Many Tutsi are taller and thinner than Hutu and have longer and thinner appendages, whereas members of the Twa minority tend to be the shortest in stature. Physiognomy, though often used by Rwandans and Burundians as a means of ethnic discernment, is not always reliable. Many people classified in a particular ethnic group do not have the group's typical features.

When the first German colonialists arrived in Ruanda-Urundi, they noted the local use of the terms, Tutsi, Hutu, and Twa. They also perceived that in the areas with which they had the most experience, many high-status individuals came from the Tutsi group. While this perception was more accurate in the case of Rwanda, where the most influential polity was a Tutsi-led kingdom, even in Rwanda the perception of absolute Tutsi dominance was an over-simplification (Newbury, 1988). In the central Rwandan Tutsi kingdom, there were Hutu who held high positions. In areas adjacent to the centre, Hutu also held positions of responsibility even though in most instances they recognized the authority of the Rwandan king. Finally, in the most peripheral regions that were nevertheless linguistically and culturally similar in many ways to central Rwanda, Hutu polities existed that maintained their autonomy *vis-à-vis* the central Rwandan state (Newbury, 1988). Many of these polities referred to their ruler by the same term that was used to designate the ruler in central Rwanda, *mwami* (Nahimana, 1993).

Operating under the assumptions of the Euro-centric Hamitic hypothesis and following British Colonel Lugard's idea of 'indirect rule,' Germans decided to administer Ruanda-Urundi indirectly through Tutsi. Although German tutelage over Ruanda-Urundi was destined to be short-lived, it established a pattern that would come to characterize relations between Europeans and Africans and between Rwanda's two most numerous groups, Tutsi and Hutu.

In addition to favouring Tutsi over Hutu and Twa, German colonialists helped the Rwandan king extend central Rwanda's control over peripheral regions, particularly in northern and south-western Rwanda. Although Rwandan kings had often waged military campaigns in these areas, the influence of the king and his court depended largely upon their presence. As soon as the king's soldiers headed back to central Rwanda, life would resume as before. After the arrival of the Germans, however, efforts began to definitively integrate northern Rwanda into the central state and to place Tutsi administrators there. During the early 1900s, the north was the scene of frequent violent confrontations between colonial troops allied to the central Rwandan state and local northern leaders. Many of the latter were inspired by the local traditional religion known as Nyabingi. These confrontations persisted until 1912, when the last Nyabingi leader, Ndungutse (who was a Tutsi), was killed (Lugan, 1997: 254). After his defeat, northern Rwanda became open to the in-migration of central Rwandan Tutsi associated with the Rwandan king.

Germany controlled Ruanda-Urundi for just a little over 20 years until the loss of its colonies at the end of the First World War. The League of Nations then awarded Belgium a mandate over Ruanda-Urundi. The change in colonial masters did not significantly affect relations among Rwanda's three ethnic groups, however. Tutsis continued to be favoured. Already, under the Germans, Catholic missionaries had established an administrative school at the royal capital of Nyanza. Students at this school were predominantly Tutsi. If anything, this tendency was accentuated under the Belgians – between 1932 and 1957 three-quarters of the students recruited were Tutsi (Chretien, 1997: 14).

When Belgium assumed control over Ruanda-Urundi, the policy of consolidating the central regime's hold over the north was continued. Northern Rwanda had managed over the centuries to retain a great deal of autonomy in relation to the central kingdom, thus extension of European, central Rwandan, and Tutsi control over the area during the 1920s was particularly resented. Jan Vansina refers to this period as a time when central Rwandan Tutsi 'colonized' northern Rwanda (Vansina, 1967).

After 1929, Belgian authorities further systematized indirect rule through Tutsi who had been educated at the missionary-run administrative school in Nyanza (Linden, 1977). The early Catholic missionaries educated this élite and transferred Hamitic ideology and prejudices to many of them.[1] For example, the first missionary ethnographers of Rwanda such as R Pages (1933) and A de Lacger (1959) popularized Hamitic themes that had first appeared in writings by John Henning Speke, Harry Johnston, and Charles G Seligman (Prunier, 1995). Many upper-class Tutsi understood that it was to their advantage to reinforce European perceptions of Hamitic superiority and they obliged with pseudo-historical fabrications that extolled their intellectual, cultural, and military supremacy. Although the Tutsi élite were only echoing what colonialists had told them, the story of Tutsi natural superiority and predisposition to govern took on the aspect of truth as the story was repeatedly told.

The substantialization of Tutsi superiority led increasingly to its institutionalization in the colonial state apparatus with predictable results where Hutu were concerned. Following Belgian administrative reforms of the late 1920s, social relations became less fluid and this was particularly apparent in patron–client relations. In pre- and early colonial Rwanda, the less powerful had always enjoyed a certain degree of latitude with regard to the powerful whose protection they sought in patron–client relationships. Historians have pointed out that during the nineteenth century there were numerous types of patron–client ties and that these were often mutually advantageous to patron and client (Newbury, 1988). Yet the most famous of these relationships, *ubuhake*, is portrayed by many social scientists as one-sidedly exploitative and generative of hierarchical differences between Tutsi and Hutu (Maquet, 1954; De Heusch, 1966). Although the *ubuhake* arrangement could be construed as exploitative, this aspect appears to have been relatively recent and more reflective of social inequality than generative of it (Vidal, 1969). In early Rwanda, some clients (or client lineages) could become prosperous, and there were limits on the degree to which a patron (or a patron lineage) could place demands on the labour and products of clients. A patron who overly exploited a client found that the latter would abandon the relationship and seek the protection of someone else. In any given local area there might be several different, redundant, and potentially competitive sources of patronage – land chiefs, army chiefs, cattle chiefs, and lineage heads. Under the Belgians during the late 1920s, the administrative system was 'rationalized'. Instead of a complex system of interlocking authorities who owed their allegiance to the Rwandan king but were locally in competition with one another, the Belgians instituted a system where the powers and responsibilities of local authorities were clearly delineated both vertically and horizontally. There was less redundancy and inefficiency in the reformed system, but less latitude for the weak. Clients, who were often though not always Hutu, no longer possessed the ability to choose a less oppressive patron. Domination in Rwanda became concentrated in the hands of a relatively small clique of Tutsi administrators and a handful of Belgian colonial administrators.

Hutu disaffection with the system grew as increasing demands for corvée labour were placed upon them, especially during the Second World War. Although this labour benefited the Belgian war effort, the official enforcing the exaction at the grass roots level was inevitably a Tutsi chief, the local representative of the central Rwandan government. Hutu protest grew more vocal in the years following the Second World War and continued into the 1950s. The Rwandan Catholic Church, which had achieved astonishing success in evangelizing large numbers of Rwandans, began to shift its orientation away from the Tutsi élite and toward the Hutu masses who comprised the majority of its converts. This shift was reinforced by the fact that the Church was recruiting more of its European missionaries from the blue-collar strata of Flemish speaking Belgian society and fewer from among the French-speaking élite (Linden, 1977). Flemish-speaking priests felt a certain affinity toward the Hutu, whom they helped to gain access to higher education. They even facilitated stays in Europe for some of them, such as Gregoire Kayibanda (independent Rwanda's first Hutu president), where they gained political experience in Christian Democratic trade unions (Linden, 1977).

General instability in the region and troubles in the neighbouring Belgian Congo accompanied the increasing politicization of Rwandan Hutu during the 1950s. Some of the more radical voices there, such as Patrice Lumumba, called not only for independence from Belgium but for a new strategic alignment in opposition to Western economic imperialism. In Rwanda, some Tutsi nationalists voiced many of the same themes: independence from Belgium, an end to the Rwandan monarchy, and alignment with the world's socialist nations. Fearing a 'leftist' drift on the part of the ethnic group that it had always supported, Belgian administrators rapidly shifted in favour of what had become the safer group, the Hutu (Prunier, 1995). Governor General Jean-Paul Harroy quickly set about the task of replacing Tutsi chiefs and sub-chiefs with Hutu, disingenuously claiming that he was acting in the interests of the oppressed masses and advancing democracy (Harroy, 1984). Nascent Hutu political parties received the blessing and support of the Belgian administration.

Members of the Tutsi élite also organized themselves during the late 1950s, with the Union Nationale Rwandaise (UNAR) as their principal party. Some attempt was even made to form a multi-ethnic political party, Rassemblement Democratique Rwandais (RADER), but by this time the situation between the ethnic groups was so polarized that the party attracted few supporters. Violence between Hutu and Tutsi political groups broke out in 1959, when UNAR supporters attacked a group of Hutu who belonged to the Association pour la Promotion Sociale de la Masse (APROSOMA) in Gitarama. This provoked reprisals on the part of Hutu against UNAR. Soon, generalized attacks against Tutsi civilians spread to other parts of the country, particularly to northern Rwanda, where Tutsi domination was relatively recent, brutal, and resented. Thousands of Tutsi were killed and tens of thousands fled to safety in neighbouring countries. Hutu mobs burned houses belonging to Tutsi and stole or killed their cattle. Then, in UN sponsored elections in 1961, the largest Hutu party, Parti du Mouvement de l'Emancipation Hutu (PARMEHUTU), won a large majority in the principal legislative body. Shortly thereafter, the Tutsi king fled the country and the first Hutu president of Rwanda, Gregoire Kayibanda, assumed power. Nevertheless, for several years following the fall of the monarchy, armed Tutsi refugee groups (called *Inyenzi* or 'cockroaches' by Hutu authorities) organized raids into Rwanda from just beyond the border in Burundi, Tanzania, or Zaire. Each raid provoked reprisal violence against Tutsi still resident in Rwanda, and thousands more were killed or driven into exile. By 1964, the refugee groups realized the futility of their strategy to retake Rwanda by force and grudgingly resigned themselves to diaspora existence (Lemarchand, 1970).

Despite the ebbing of the *Inyenzi* threat, Kayibanda found that he could exploit lingering fear of Tutsi for his own political ends. Occasionally agents of the regime incited localized popular resentment against Tutsi, targeting businessmen and others who enjoyed a modicum of social prominence. In the early 1970s when Kayibanda began to be troubled by increasing criticism of the regime and charges that he favoured southern over northern Hutu, despite the fact that the latter were well represented in the Rwandan army, he used the anti-Tutsi ploy again. In 1973, shortly after the massive 1972 killings of Hutu in Burundi, agents of the Kayibanda regime accused Tutsi of holding a disproportionate number of jobs in the schools, private sector, and Rwandan Catholic Church hierarchy. Many Tutsi school teachers, priests, and others were fired and harassed. Tutsi school pupils were identified in classes and then verbally or physically abused (Prunier, 1995).

At one level Kayibanda's strategy worked quite well; a general state of unrest quickly pervaded the country. Although fewer Tutsi died in comparison with the 1959-64 period, enough were killed to provoke generalized panic among them, and once again thousands streamed across the borders. However, Kayibanda had ignited a fire he could not control; soon the settling of accounts spread beyond Tutsi. Seizing the opportunity to establish himself as Rwanda's 'saviour' while re-establishing order, Kayibanda's Defence Minister, Juvenal Habyarimana, an army officer from northern Rwanda, took control of the country in a 'bloodless' coup d'état.[2] Promising to restore order and to assure fairness of opportunity, Habyarimana brought the persecution of Tutsi to an end and instituted a policy of 'regional and ethnic equilibrium'. According to this policy, state administrative jobs, secondary school, and university placements were to be apportioned on the basis of representation in the population. Southerners were not to be favoured over northerners, nor Hutu over Tutsi; each sector of the population was to receive a share of jobs, school placements, directorships, and so forth, according to its proportion of the population. In actuality northerners came to dominate the army, the government, and the economy. Tutsi were never given their full allotted portion (about 9 per cent) of state jobs or places in secondary schools and universities. Although many Tutsi lost their jobs or their chances for schooling under the principles of 'regional and ethnic equilibrium', Habyarimana's coup came to be supported among many of them, for they were no longer being killed or harassed (Prunier, 1995). The massive Tutsi exodus from the country ceased. Virtually no Twa ever received jobs or school placements, despite their allotted 1 per cent.

Until the late 1980s the Habyarimana regime enjoyed a favourable image among Western governments and donors. Christian Democratic parties in the Western world, particularly in Belgium, were taken in by Habyarimana's apparent devotion to Catholicism and the regime's insistence that it spoke for the masses. Specific opponents of the regime were dealt with harshly, but generalized ethnic persecution had come to an end. Tutsi did not enjoy the same educational and political opportunities as Hutu, but some managed to receive university training anyway. A few found jobs in the state bureaucracy, but many more worked in the private sector or for international organizations. Most Tutsi acquiesced to the unwritten *modus operandi* of the Habyarimana government; as long as they kept silent on political issues, they could go about their lives unmolested.

Economically, Rwanda was something of a showcase for development apologists during the early and mid-1980s. A hard-working peasantry and relatively fertile land kept the country self-sufficient in food. Coffee, the country's principal export, earned hard currency. Cassiterite (tin ore) mines operated in a few parts of the country. Rwandan tea, although exported in much smaller quantities than coffee, brought in additional earnings. Tourism continued to grow to the point that by 1987 it was the country's third most important source of foreign revenue. These factors kept the Rwandan economy growing and made the Rwandan Franc central Africa's most stable currency.

Despite its image of health, the Rwandan economy was more vulnerable than it seemed. Its central weakness was that it was essentially a monoculture dependent upon world coffee prices. Although cassiterite, the only commercially mined ore, added an alternative source of hard currency, by 1986 all Rwandan mines had been closed due to low world market prices for tin. Moreover, possibly because of Rwanda's strong currency, the country persistently ran trade deficits. Usually these were compensated by the high amounts of foreign assistance funds entering the country from Western donor sources. One of the highest population growth rates in the world, however, assured that any economic growth or increased agricultural productivity would be rapidly absorbed by additional mouths to feed. The agricultural sector was particularly vulnerable because close to 95 per cent of the population gained its livelihood from farming, and floods or drought struck frequently. In the late 1980s all these weaknesses combined with a sharp descent in world coffee prices to produce severe conditions in many areas.

The political situation in Rwanda also deteriorated in the late 1980s. Years of northern Hutu political and economic dominance had left people in the south and centre frustrated and angry with the Habyarimana regime and its associated political party, the MRND. When the latter were pressured by a French-supported democratization initiative to open the country to multi-party democracy, several opposition parties from southern and central Rwanda quickly came into existence. Yet the lingering problem of hundreds of thousands of Tutsi refugees living outside the country and seeking to return continued to be met with inaction on the part of the Rwandan government. Although negotiations with the refugee groups had been underway for several years, not much had been accomplished on the questions of Rwandan citizenship and eventual repatriation.

In the face of these threats to its monopoly over power, the Habyarimana regime responded in a way that was true to the pattern established by Kayibanda. It attempted in 1989 to reanimate popular resentment against Tutsi. In the years before this, the Rwandan refugee groups (majority, but not exclusively Tutsi) in Uganda and elsewhere began contemplating military action to achieve their ends. Their militarization was accelerated by events in Uganda, notably Ugandan dictator Milton Obote's campaign against Banyarwanda in the early 1980s in which as many as 80,000 people of Rwandan origin were killed. Many Rwandans living in Uganda joined forces with Yoweri Museveni in his fight to overthrow Obote, which met with success by 1986. Finally, in October 1990, after receiving advice from Rwandan politicians opposed to Habyarimana and the MRND that the Rwandan regime was close to collapse, the Rwandan Patriotic Front (RPF), composed largely of Rwandan deserters from the Ugandan Army, invaded Rwanda from Uganda. This may have been a miscalculation on their part. Habyarimana and the MRND could not have wished for a more felicitous turn of events. The so-called *Inyenzi* were back (even if 20 to 30 per cent of RPF soldiers were Hutu) and the whole issue of power sharing with southern Hutu and democratization could be side-stepped by claiming a higher order of priority – defeating the new Tutsi threat (Prunier, 1995).

As in the period from 1959 to 1964 and in 1973, Tutsi-baiting proved politically expedient. Intellectual supporters of the Habyarimana regime, mostly within the MRND party, and later the extremist CDR, resuscitated the story of Tutsi 'invaders from Ethiopia' and used it to great effect in propaganda. Rwanda's mass media were conscripted in this effort (Chretien, 1995). The most virulent and influential of these media was a Kigali-based radio station named 'Radio Television Libre de Mille Collines' (RTLM) whose electrical power was supplied by cables directly connected to the nearby Presidential Palace. Frequent denunciations of Tutsi could be heard over this station as well as scandalous innuendo, locally termed *'amakuru ashyushe'* (hot news), directed against opposition politicians whether Tutsi or Hutu. The station combined propagandistic diatribes with the latest Zairian or North American rock and pop music and was immensely popular among young Rwandans. Hutu extremists also made use of popular news reviews, such as *Kangura*. Sometimes these journals gave voice to elements that were more extreme in their anti-Tutsi virulence than Habyarimana himself. Occasionally, he was even attacked in the news reviews for being soft on Tutsi and on the Hutu opposition. One cartoon that I saw in January 1994 depicted then RPF General Paul Kagame (now Defence Minister and Vice President of Rwanda) perched on the back of Habyarimana's neck pulling his ears as if they were the reins of a horse. The caption beneath the cartoon announced ominously: 'Tutsi ingratitude: Habyarimana will die in March 1994' (cartoon from J-P. Chretien, 1995: p. 152). In other media, care was taken to refrain from airing anything suggestive of so-called 'Tutsi culture.' Traditional folk songs in honour of cattle, for example, were no longer broadcast, even though such songs had often been played on Rwandan radio during the mid-1980s.

Several local massacres of Rwandan Tutsi were organized and perpetrated by local MRND officials after the RPF invasion in 1990, but there was little evidence of widespread popular anger against Tutsi on the part of Hutu peasants (Chretien, 1997). On the battlefield, despite initial reverses during the first year of fighting, the RPF was more than holding its own. By 1992 it had managed to capture and administer portions of northern Rwanda. Only the massive material support and direct involvement of French troops

Figure 1.1 *Tutsi ingratitude: 'Habyarimana will die in March 1994'*
(Kangura, *December 1993, no. 53, p. 3)*
Kagame: On to Kigali.
Habyarimana: I've done everything I could to make you Tutsi happy.
Kagame: Who asked you?

prevented the Habyarimana regime and Rwandan Government Forces from suffering a humiliating military defeat.[3] Attempting to buy time the Rwandan government agreed to a ceasefire in 1992 and direct negotiations with the RPF in Arusha, Tanzania. A stalemate ensued punctuated by occasional violations on the part of the Rwandan government in the form of other localized massacres of Rwandan Tutsi. Growing increasingly impatient with the Rwandan government, the RPF took the offensive again in February 1993. Before being stopped by French artillery and field support of Rwandan Government Forces, the RPF offensive pushed to within 25 km of the capital city, Kigali. Hundreds of thousands of northern Rwandan peasants fled their homes in the wake of the offensive and eventually ended up in central Rwandan camps for the internally displaced. There the UNHCR and the International Red Cross ministered as best they could to their needs.

Finally, in August 1993, the Rwandan government signed a peace accord with the RPF that called for a multi-party government with

Figure 1.2 *Tutsi disdain for Hutu: 'It is said that Kagame refuses to shake the hand of any Hutu.' (Kangura, October 1993, no. 51, p. 14)*
Kagame to Habyarimana (in the buffer zone of Kinihira): 'You might as well know, I won't shake the hand of any Hutu.'

RPF participation. Although the President's political party was to be guaranteed a substantial number of seats in the legislature and several key ministerial portfolios, the powers of the presidency were considerably diminished under the Arusha accords. Habyarimana was destined to become a figurehead president rather than an absolute dictator. Furthermore, he risked being thrown out of office altogether, as presidential elections were scheduled for 1995 following a two-year transition period under a broad-based coalition government. Prior to the end of 1993, this government was to be put into place and to include representatives from the MRND, the major opposition parties, and the Rwandan Patriotic Front. Although President Habyarimana and members of the MRND signed the peace agreement, to many Rwandan politicians it was clear that the MRND was displeased. In the months that followed, Habyarimana and his coterie, including many who were more extreme than him, did everything possible to subvert the accords. During the early months of 1994, occasional violence had succeeded in creating an atmosphere of tension and near disorder. Hostilities between the two sides resumed on 7 April 1994 just a few hours after President Habyarimana was killed when his personal plane was shot down (probably by extremists within his own entourage) near Kigali airport.

In the next three months Rwandan Patriotic Front forces pursued a slow, methodical campaign against the Rwandan Government Forces. Outnumbered by the RGF, they used their forces sparingly and efficiently. Tending to concentrate their attack on one or a limited number of RGF strongholds at a time, the RPF always left their enemy an escape route to flee to other bases. This strategy, going after territory rather than trying to destroy the RGF outright, saved the RPF men and materiel, but it did little to stop the genocide. The RGF and their allied militias appeared to have a different strategy: destroy the RPF's presumed base of support among the population. As the weeks went by, both sides were winning in their own way. Chased from one stronghold to another, the RGF eventually found itself pushed into two small enclaves, one in the northwestern part of the country near Gisenyi and the other in the southwestern part near Cyangugu. As the RGF fled the RPF advance, it forced the local Hutu population to flee with it. Finally in early July, the RGF was pushed out of Rwandan territory, taking refuge in eastern Zaire along with their allied militias and nearly 1,500,000 Rwandan Hutu. The RPF had won the country, but 80 per cent of Rwanda's Tutsi population was now dead. Winning the peace, as events continue to show, would be much more difficult. The RPF had wrested control over a devastated, demoralized, and partly depopulated country whose bank coffers had been looted by the 'genocidaires'. Among the population remaining in Rwanda, the RPF enjoyed only limited popular support. Rwanda's infrastructure was in ruins, and most of its intelligentsia (Hutu and Tutsi) was either dead or no longer living in the country.

In the years since the RPF victory, the entire region has continued to experience instability. A massive aid effort on the part of the international community to feed and protect Rwandan Hutu refugees in eastern Zaire saved many from cholera and starvation. One unintended consequence of this action was that it allowed the former genocidal leaders of Rwanda to regroup and rearm, as the UN and other aid organizations refused to separate combatants from non-combatants in the camps. The same municipal authorities who had implemented genocidal actions in their localities back in

Rwanda emerged as leaders in the camps. When a revolt against Mobutu Sese Seko's government broke out in eastern Zaire in 1996, Rwanda sent in units from the Rwandan Patriotic Army (the renamed Rwandan army) to assist the rebels. Mobutu was toppled and replaced by Laurent Kabila, a leader who has not exhibited particular brilliance in leading the renamed Democratic Republic of Congo since his seizure of power. As a quid pro quo for their help, the RPA was able to use the intervention in Zaire to solve the problem of sorting out combatant from non-combatant Hutu refugees. They did this by attacking the camps. Fleeing the RPA assaults, hundreds of thousands of Rwandan Hutu streamed back to Rwanda, but thousands of other Hutu were probably massacred in the process. Efforts to investigate these massacres, sometimes mistakenly referred to as a Tutsi counter-genocide against Hutus, have proven futile.[4]

In the meantime, substantial numbers of Hutus who returned in the wake of the revolt against Mobutu have since been engaged in guerrilla warfare against the present Rwandan government, especially in north-western Rwanda. Often their actions strike very close to the capital of Kigali. As for the new government, dominated by leaders of the former RPF, it has had difficulties in remaining true to its previously avowed intention of creating a non-ethnic society. Many of the original Hutu members of the government, invited to participate shortly after the RPF victory, have since left the country and over 100,000 Hutus accused of crimes committed during the genocide continue to languish in overcrowded and unsanitary Rwandan jails. There have been encouraging signs as well, however: the economy is on the mend and many of the former planners and organizers of the genocide have been extradited to the International War Crimes Tribunal for Rwanda in Arusha, Tanzania. Whether some semblance of a 'rule of law' is taking form in Rwanda is debatable. Many Rwandans who were neither 'genocidaires' nor supporters of the RPF have had properties seized. Mysterious 'disappearances' have also occurred and not all of these can be blamed on Hutu ethnic extremists. If the present government remains true to its promise to transcend ethnicity in Rwanda, peace and stability have a chance, but if it proves to be as ethnocratic as every previous Rwandan government, it will be planting the seeds of the next genocide.

Notes

1. First and foremost, this class of Tutsi possessed a sense of superiority due to the fact that it was the élite and not because it believed itself to be a biologically superior race. Nevertheless, most Tutsi were not members of the élite and thus did not share its privileges and pretensions. As the élite gradually began to internalize Hamitic ideas, however, its 'superiority complex' took on the characteristics of racialist ideology.

2. Although President Kayibanda was placed under house arrest rather than killed outright, he did not survive much longer. Local rumour has it that Habyarimana's agents slowly poisoned him; others have it that he was effectively starved to death and denied medical attention. Virtually all the prominent members of Kayibanda's regime died in prison or under mysterious circumstances in the years following Habyarimana's coup.

3. Although the French government at the time claimed that its support of Rwandan Government Forces was limited to advisors and artillery officers, I met several RPF soldiers before the April 1994 events who claimed to have been in engagements against French ground troops.

4. Precise documentation of the events in eastern Zaire during 1996 has not been established because local authorities have made investigation difficult. From reports of witnesses to some of the events, however, it is likely that some units associated with the RPA participated in large-scale killings of Hutu refugees. Whether this qualifies as genocide is moot. The overwhelming majority of Hutu who had taken refuge in eastern Zaire managed to return to Rwanda safely and there is no indication of an organized plan on the part of either the Rwandan government or the RPA to eliminate all Hutu.

CHAPTER TWO

The Hamitic Hypothesis in Rwanda and Burundi

Introduction

In Frantz Fanon's words 'decolonization is always a violent phenomenon' (Fanon, 1968: 5). It is violent, he explains, because, 'decolonization is purely and simply the replacement of one type of human by another' (Fanon, 1968: 5).[1] Fanon's words have a prophetic ring to them when we consider the past thirty-five years in Rwanda and Burundi, for in these countries the process of decolonization has not been completed. As tragedies continue to unfold, it remains to be seen whether the colonialist species of human will eventually be replaced by a new person in Rwanda and Burundi. In central Africa, perhaps more so than in any other part of the continent, we witness the lingering effects of colonialism in the form of the Hamitic hypothesis. Since Rwanda's and Burundi's independence in 1962, the main proponents of Hamitism have not been Europeans – they have been Rwandans and Burundians. The people victimized have been other Rwandans and Burundians.

The Hamitic hypothesis as a model for understanding the history of East Africa emerged in Europe during the nineteenth century. It drew upon half truths and outright fictions of a religious and pseudo-scientific nature. Today its use and influence have persisted, although more in central Africa than in Europe. The people who should be challenging this history, intellectuals and policymakers in Rwanda and Burundi, are often the ones who employ it the most disingenuously. The terms 'Hamite' and 'Bantu', used as synonyms for Tutsi and Hutu, delineate the groups as 'races' with varying intellectual capacities. By casting Hutu as 'slow-witted' Bantus, and Tutsi as 'quicker witted' Hamite invaders, Hamitism has contributed

to the recurrent violence in central Africa and has impeded attempts
to reconcile the two groups. The categories 'Hamite' and 'Bantu'
are so commonly employed among central Africans that few question their meaning despite at least thirty years of historiography
that impugns the Hamitic hypothesis as Eurocentric and racist. As
Fanon warns in a chapter entitled 'The Misadventures of National
Consciousness', when an unprepared and egotistical bourgeoisie
takes power in the wake of departing Europeans, this élite only
reproduces the social relations that characterized colonialism in
the first place (Fanon, 1968: 95–140). This can lead in his words to
'ultra-nationalism, chauvinism, and racism', but on the part of
Africans against other Africans (Fanon, 1968: 101). Where Rwanda
and Burundi are concerned, I am again struck by Fanon's prescience,
for this is exactly what has occurred in the years since independence.

This tragic central African reality poses a number of problems
for the discipline of anthropology that have not been sufficiently
well addressed. Anthropologists today have no difficulty denounc-
ing colonialism or criticizing the axioms, methods, and conclusions
of colonial science and policy. Where our African interlocutors are
concerned the story is often different. Where their constructs are
at issue, notwithstanding the fact that these may have internalized
aspects of colonialist thought, our analysis often becomes non-
committal. We become hesitant to refute or to criticize. We sidestep
the issue of refutation and shift analysis solely to the understanding
of what people say and why they say it. This is a logical corollary of
the intellectual position that sees something like the Hamitic hypothesis solely as discourse and does not engage or challenge the
hypothesis at the level of fact. This is the position taken by L Malkki
in a book which, in other respects is a valuable study of the mythico-
historical constructions of Hutu refugees in Tanzania, Purity and
Exile (Malkki, 1995: 104).

Although, in some instances, this position may be justified and
may spring from a healthy scepticism of ethnocentric Western
representations of non-Western realities, it evades responsibility in
those instances where the constructs of our interlocutors have
dangerous political implications, as is the case with Hamitism in
central Africa. Rwandans and Burundians are unlikely to abandon
Hamitism on the basis of the simple assertion that it is a racist and
hegemonic model ultimately rooted in Western colonial experience.
Refutation must engage the factuality of the Hamitic hypothesis as
well, even if this means that some aspects of it may be affirmed.

Otherwise we are left with an inconsistency: a position that claims privileged critical insight where European models of history are concerned and no such insight where non-Western models are concerned. If we completely avoid engaging the latter at the level of fact as well as at the level of discourse, we may very well become unwitting handmaidens to the violence that such models may promote. This is the case with versions of history that continue to be advanced by Hutu and Tutsi extremists in Rwanda and Burundi and are accepted as truth by many of their compatriots. Yet when these histories are closely examined, what is revealed is that they are only slightly modified versions of the Hamitic hypothesis.

Tutsi extremists make use of their version of the hypothesis to claim intellectual superiority; Hutu extremists employ theirs to insist upon the foreign origins of Tutsi, and the autochthony of Hutu. No matter which side uses the Hamitic hypothesis, however unwittingly, it reproduces a colonial pattern: one that essentializes ethnic difference, justifies political domination by a single group, and nurtures a profound thirst for redress and vengeance on the part of the defavourized group. When acts of massive violence are at issue, as they clearly have been in Rwanda and Burundi, and where the possibility of violence continues, can we as anthropologists comfortably claim that the factuality – truth or falsehood – of our interlocutors' historical constructions is of little concern to us? Can we comfortably claim that our only concern is to determine what people take to be the 'truth' and why?

In this chapter I intend to examine the Hamitic hypothesis as much from a factual perspective in light of recent research concerning the peopling of east central Africa, as from the perspective of discourse. I will briefly discuss the intellectual antecedents of Hamitism in East Africa and their ideological motivation, but will not review all criticisms that have been levelled at the hypothesis, which by now are quite numerous (Evans, 1980: 15-43). I will, however, attempt to point out which aspects of the hypothesis can be refuted at the level of fact and which cannot, given the present state of knowledge. Then I will attempt to explain the local persistence of Hamitic notions in central Africa by showing how these have become incorporated in local models of ethnic identity and difference. I will discuss examples of Hamitic notions in use by central African intellectuals and politicians that have entered the public record, as well as examples that I personally encountered among Rwandan acquaintances during my most recent field research

in Rwanda from October 1993 until April 1994, when the genocide
began.

European Origins of the Hamitic Hypothesis

In Ranger's terms, the Hamitic hypothesis bears many of the
characteristics of an 'invented tradition' (Hobsbawm and Ranger,
1983), and approaches the lay, non-scientific understanding of the
term 'myth', in the sense of a story woven from half and less than
half truths. European colonialists used this hypothesis in contradictory ways. At times the so-called Hamites, taken to be all black
Africans, were denigrated; at other times, as in East Africa, Hamites
were perceived to be quasi-Caucasian and thus superior to other
Africans. This latter pattern characterized early historical writing
about Rwanda and Burundi and influenced the development of a
colonial administrative system in which a minority of Tutsi were
favoured at the expense of Hutu and Twa. As Prunier states, 'There
are probably few instances, in Africa or elsewhere, of a country that
became the subject of myth to the extent that Rwanda was in the
late nineteenth and early twentieth centuries,' (Prunier, 1995: 346).

Three strands of nineteenth-century European thought contributed to the weaving of this story: theology; biology, and anthropology. The name 'Ham' comes from the Old Testament, after Noah's
son who failed to avert his eyes in shame upon seeing his father
drunk and naked. For this lapse in respect, Noah, upon awakening
from his drunken stupor, cursed Ham's son Canaan. Canaan and
his descendants were destined to become the slaves of Shem and
Japheth, two other sons of Noah. As Evans points out, the story
makes little sense unless understood as myth. Not only does Noah
seem to have overreacted, but he punishes Ham's son, Canaan,
rather than Ham himself (Evans, 1980: 15–16). In apocryphal
versions of the same story, which grew up during the Middle Ages,
this sin had not been Ham's first. Having allegedly disobeyed his
father's command to observe sexual abstinence while on the Ark,
Ham was cursed with a black skin (Fenton, 1996: 7). In other stories
he and his descendants were banished from the Promised Land
and commanded to go to the south, where they would become
'hewers of wood' and 'drawers of water'. To the Boers of South
Africa, the Biblical story of Ham justified the enslavement of
Africans. From Calvinist theology came the Boer belief that they

themselves were the 'elect,' while all black Africans as Hamites were 'damned.' God had condemned Ham's descendants to lives of perpetual servitude.

Elsewhere, theology joined with biological determinism and early anthropology to produce the Great Chain of Being theory. According to this theory, human races followed a ranked order in terms of moral and intellectual capacities. Later in the nineteenth century it was thought that this ranking could be demonstrated quantitatively – one needed only measure the internal volume of the skull. Not surprisingly, the largest skull volumes were observed among the researchers' own racial group: white, northern Europeans. Smaller volumes were observed among native Americans, Asians, and sub-Saharan Africans. For that reason, so-called civilization had attained its highest level among Europeans.

Something of a contradiction to the theory was posed when voyages of discovery and exploration revealed complex state systems, metallurgy, and other highly developed arts elsewhere on the globe. This was especially troublesome in sub-Saharan Africa where small-brained specimens could not have been expected to develop anything approaching 'civilization'. Interlacustrine African state systems and iron smelting in these areas had to be explained away. Perhaps the first to offer an explanation along these lines was the explorer, John Henning Speke, in his book *Journal of the Discovery of the Source of the Nile* (1863). According to his theory, superior races inevitably conquered inferior races. If Hamites were doomed to inferiority in southern Africa, in interlacustrine Africa they became, for Speke, the superior, conquering race. Despite their black skins, these Hamites were said to be almost Caucasian. According to Speke, Hamites moving out of the Middle East became the Galla and Oromo in Ethiopia. Ethiopian Galla-Hamites migrating southward became the Hima in Uganda and the Tutsi in Rwanda and Burundi (Prunier, 1995: 7). Later in 1902 Sir Harry Johnston embellished upon Speke's theory claiming that the idea of the state and the institution of sacred kingship in interlacustrine Africa had been brought by pastoral invaders called the Bacwezi (Prunier, 1995: 10). The Tutsi king of Rwanda was thus of non-autochthonous origin; he was a Hamite-Bacwezi Tutsi from Ethiopia.

Speke's evidence for his theories derived from his reading of the Bible and from visual observation of East African peoples. Johnston added to that a superficial look at East African oral traditions concerning the mythical Bacwezi. Despite their flimsy scientific basis, Speke's and Johnston's theories quickly achieved the status of received wisdom. Subsequent explorers, historians, missionaries, and anthropologists took the Hamitic hypothesis more-or-less as dogma, modifying it only slightly. Hamites became, variously, the descendants of Egyptians, a lost tribe of Israel, descendants of the Magi kings, immigrants from Tibet, Melanesia, or Asia Minor. All of the early writers appeared to agree on several things: the Hamites were not Negroes, they were more intelligent than other Africans, and they were physically more attractive. Prunier cites Father van den Burgt's comments on the Tutsi from Burgt's French-Kirundi dictionary:

> We can see Caucasian skulls and beautiful Greek profiles side by side with Semitic and even Jewish features, elegant golden-red beauties in the heart of Ruanda and Urundi.
>
> (Prunier, 1995: 9)

Tutsi were intelligent and attractive, but rather frail; they were destined for governance. Hutu were stocky, coarser featured, but not overly intelligent; physical strength made them suited for agricultural labour. Very close to Speke's theory was a statement by Charles G. Seligman who, after the First World War, became a champion of African racial theories and was one of E.E. Evans-Pritchard's former mentors:

> Apart from relatively late Semitic influence...the civilizations of Africa are the civilizations of the Hamites, its history the record of these peoples and of their interaction with the two other African stocks, the Negro, and the Bushman, whether this influence was exerted by highly civilized Egyptians or by such wilder pastoralists as are represented at the present day by the Beja and Somali. The incoming Hamites were pastoral 'Europeans' – arriving wave after wave – better armed as well as quicker witted than the dark agricultural Negroes.
>
> (from C.G. Seligman cited by Sanders, 1969: 521)

Had these pseudo-historical and barely disguised racist musings remained with Europeans they probably would not have caused much enduring harm. But this was not to be, as the example of Father van den Burgt shows and as other scholars have pointed out, Catholic missionaries working, teaching, and writing in Ruanda-Urundi were among the prime agents by which Hamitism was transmitted to Rwandans and Burundians (Chretien, 1997: 14).

Thus began a story that, in the retelling, took on the appearance of truth. Soon linguists were employing the terms 'Hamitic' or 'Semito-Hamitic' ('Sem' refers to Noah's other son, Shem) to refer to languages now known as Afro-Asiatic. As an ethnonym the label was used to refer to various East African pastoralist peoples: Ethiopian Galla and Oromo, Somali, Ugandan Hima, Rwandan and Burundian Tutsi, Southern Cushitic speakers (Iraqw) found in Kenya and Tanzania, and even Nilotic speakers, such as the Nyoro in Uganda, or the Maasai in Kenya and Tanzania. Besides the fact that the Hamitic hypothesis was obviously racist and Eurocentric, it conflated three things better left separate: race, language, and culture.

Subsequent scholarly judgement of the Hamitic hypothesis has been almost universally negative. In reaction to its extreme primordialism, most students of Rwanda and Burundi have taken a constructionist position insisting upon the socially and historically contingent nature of the ethnic categories in Rwanda and Burundi and their varied use by interest groups in specific social, political, and economic circumstances. In more general terms, with regard to the question of African ethnicity in other contexts, historical constructionism is the position taken by Comaroff in his essay 'Totemism and Ethnicity' (1995). Although I would agree with much that characterizes this position, it must be recalled that no group constructs anything *ex nihilo*. There is always an antecedent reality upon which any construction is based, and obviously not all aspects of it change at the same rate; some things can remain relatively stable. Furthermore, the degree to which subsequent constructions are credible or not is influenced by the elements retained from earlier positions and not all of these elements can be expected to enjoy equal plausibility. Finally, the assertion that something is a socio-historical construction is not, in itself, proof of its falsity. The apparent distance, then, between primordialism and constructionism may lead us to overlook all that lies in between. Is it logically possible, for example, to sustain the hypothesis that many of the people who comprise Hutu, Tutsi, and Twa had separate biogenetic and geographic origins, while also admitting the socially and historically constructed nature of the categories, Hutu, Tutsi, and Twa, as identities? Might there be some truth to the Hamitic hypothesis if we divest it of its Eurocentrism and racism?

Let us take the question of race first. Racial arguments, based on vaguely defined and determinist notions of biology and the Great

Chain of Being theory, have almost always been used to advance the political claims of one group against the claims of other groups. Clearly this ideological use of race has predominated for much of the last century and much of this one in Europe and the United States. Transplanted to Rwanda by Europeans, this notion of race has characterized Rwandan thinking in the post-colonial era. The use of the French term *ethnie* or the Kinyarwanda term, *ubwoko,* marked upon Rwandan citizens' national identity cards was inspired by similar ideological motives. First used during the colonial era (1930s) by Belgian administrators in order to favour the Tutsi, ethnic identification on ID cards was later retained by post-colonial Rwandan governments in order to favour the Hutu. Whether *ethnie* or *ubwoko,* the terms were in essence synonyms for 'race' in the biologically determinist sense (Franche, 1995). Today, after the Rwandan Patriotic Front's victory in 1994, new Rwandan identity cards no longer bear mention of a person's ethnicity, but whether ethnicity has been eliminated as a prime determinant of one's chances in life is far from clear. Keeping in mind the above caveat about race, it is important not to discredit all biology. While discarding 'race' or *ethnie* as the primary concept by which to understand human diversity in Rwanda and Burundi, it is useful to consider the biological characteristics of interlacustrine peoples and, to this end, the work of physical anthropologists who have studied gene frequencies and distributions in Africa. Not all biology is biological determinism; molecular biology can serve a useful function in both history and in anthropology. Such data, used in conjunction with archaeological, cultural, and linguistic information, can help to shed light on historical factors such as the movement of peoples, their subsistence techniques, and their interactions with others.

Excoffier, Pellegrini, Sanchez-Maras, Simon and Langaney (1987) summarize much of the available data. According to these authors, gene distributions of Rhesus factor, gamma-immunoglobulins (the Gm system), and HLA genes show clusterings that correlate well with the major African language families. In other words the peoples who constitute the four major African language families (according to Greenberg) – Niger-Kordofanian, Nilo-Saharan, Afro-Asiatic, and Khoisan – tend to share biological as well as linguistic affinities (Excoffier et al., 1987: 151). This stands to reason. People who speak together, tend to intermarry with one another and to share genes. When the genetic indicators are considered for interlacustrine Tutsi and Hima, however, they are something of an anomaly. Although they speak Bantu languages (Kinyarwanda, Kirundi, Rukiga, and Runyankole), their genetic markers show them to be more closely related to peoples who live in northeastern Africa and who are Afro-Asiatic speakers (Excoffier et al., 1987: 182). This finding supports one of the assertions of the Hamitic hypothesis and allows a non-racist interpretation of it – that interlacustrine Hima and Tutsi may have descended from or intermarried with north-east African groups.

One could raise various objections to this study. In subscribing to a view which sees Hutu and Tutsi as genetically related to Afro-Asiatic speakers, are the authors naively reiterating pre-1960s received wisdom? The answer seems to be no, for they critically examine the Hamitic theory in some detail (Excoffier et al. 1987: 156). They are aware of the misuses of the Hamitic hypothesis and of the controversies which it has continued to engender. One could raise other objections: who were the Tutsi and Hutu that blood samples were taken from? Were the people self-defined as Hutu and Tutsi, or did others define them and if so, how? Were the sample sizes used by Excoffier et al. sufficiently large? How were the samples taken? If the findings of Excoffier et al. can be upheld, what they demonstrate is that Tutsi and Hutu may well have had ancestors who came from northeast Africa. Their findings neither address nor support those aspects of the Hamitic hypothesis that claim the Tutsi were an intellectually superior 'race,' that they conquered large portions of interlacustrine Africa, that their presence in interlacustrine Africa post-dates that of Bantu speaking cultivators, or that they brought the institutions of the state and sacred kingship with them from Ethiopia, Egypt, ancient Israel, or Asia. In short, their findings do not address the ideological corollaries of Hamitic racial theory.

Turning to language and culture, evidence from historical linguistics and archaeology indicates that interlacustrine Africa and areas adjacent to it acted as something of a 'melting pot' in terms of bringing together peoples of varied geographic origins, different languages, and diverse subsistence types. Because of the area's ecological diversity, various groups of people were able to practise a wide array of subsistence techniques in scattered micro-environments relatively close to one another. Where language is concerned, there is strong evidence that Afro-Asiatic languages, Tale Southern Cushitic in particular, were spoken in areas to the west and northeast of Lake Victoria and to the east of present day Rwanda and

Burundi as early as the first millennium before Christ (Schoenbrun, 1990; Ehret, 1974). Tale Southern Cushitic speakers, according to Schoenbrun, 'had to have been already living there when Great Lakes Bantu communities began moving in toward the end of the last millenium B.C.' (Schoenbrun, 1993: 16). At about this same time, to the north of Rwanda, in areas to its west, as well as in western Burundi, Central Sudanic (Nilo-Saharan family) languages were spoken (Schoenbrun, 1993: 16). Sog Eastern Sudanic (Nilo-Saharan family) languages were spoken in areas to the south of Rwanda and to the east and west of the Ruzizi River at about this time (Schoenbrun, 1993: 15). Towards the end of the last millenium before Christ, proto-Great Lakes Bantu (Niger-Kordofanian family) speakers were also present in areas that are now Rwanda and Burundi and in contact with these other groups.

From loanword sets and from the results of soil pollen analysis, Schoenbrun reasons that the various peoples in the interlacustrine region interacted with one another considerably and that sub-sistence techniques were often borrowed along with their associated vocabularies (1993). Early Southern Cushites raised some grains, notably sorghum and millet, but were for the most part cattle herders. They herded and bred cattle and subsisted largely on their milk and blood (Schoenbrun, 1990: 174). According to Ehret, it is probable that they did not have chiefs or centralized political structures (Ehret, 1974: 9). Although the Bantu language speakers were predominantly agriculturalists, it is probable that they acquired cattle herding from interaction with Southern Cushitic speakers (Schoenbrun, 1990: 176). Indeed, some words in Kinyarwanda are of Southern Cushitic origin – for example, *ikimasa* meaning 'young bull,' from the root *masa* ('meaning bull or cow which has not produced young') (Schoenbrun, 1993: 31). Central and Eastern Sudanic speakers also lived close to the area and appear to have farmed sorghum and raised livestock, although they kept both small stock and cattle (Schoenbrun, 1990: 178). The term for 'cow' in Kinyarwanda, *inka*, appears to have had either a Sog Eastern Sudanic origin (Schoenbrun 1993: 30) or possibly a Southern Cushitic origin; it does not appear to have been formed on a Bantu root.

Eventually, Bantu speakers predominated in Rwanda and Burundi as well as in most other parts of interlacustrine Africa, but their presence does not appear to have clearly antedated Southern Cushitic speakers nor Central and Eastern Sudanic speakers. Those Southern

Cushitic speakers who were not absorbed into Bantu-speaking communities were pushed to the outside limits of the area as were Central and Eastern Sudanic speakers. To this day, two small enclaves of Southern Cushitic speakers (*Iraqw*) can be found at the eastern edge of the inter-lacustrine region in northern Tanzania near the border with Kenya. Could some Ugandan Hutu and Some Rwandan and Burundian Tutsi be the descendants of originally Southern Cushitic speakers who became linguistically assimilated to the larger numbers of Bantu speakers? This is possible judging from both the genetic and the linguistic findings. What can be affirmed, if Schoenbrun's interpretation is correct, is that non-Bantu speaking agropastoralist or pastoralist peoples more than likely preceded rather than followed Bantu speakers into the area, in sharp contrast to the Hamitic hypothesis. North-east Africa and interlacustrine Africa were not isolated from one another in geographic or cultural terms. Contacts may have been going on for millennia. People, languages, objects, and ideas flowed from north to south, and from south to north.

Although it is possible that many Tutsi and Hutu are descendants of people from north-eastern Africa, virtually nothing supports the portion of the Hamitic hypothesis that claims their ancestors conquered the Bantu speakers with whom they interacted. Nor is there any proof that they brought centralized political institutions or sacred kingship to Rwanda and Burundi. Pastoralism in general is infrequently associated with state formation, whereas the opposite is the case where agriculture is concerned. Among Southern Cushitic speakers extant today, acephalous polities are the rule (Ehret, 1974), although how far back in time this type of political organization can be extrapolated is unclear. As for the pre-colonial Rwandan state, evidence tends to support the hypothesis that it was Hutu in origin. Earlier studies of Rwandan kingship rituals, for example, point to a probable Hutu origin (D'Hertefelt and Coupez, 1964).

In 1884 when German explorers contacted the king of Rwanda, Kigeri IV Rwabugiri, they noted the kingdom's tripartite division into named categories of Tutsi, Hutu, and Twa. They also noted that Rwabugiri and many members of his court were Tutsi. From the 'conquest theory' of earlier writings, they concluded that the Tutsi must be racially superior Hamites. This influenced their decision to run the colony of Ruanda-Urundi through Tutsi. What the Germans did not correctly perceive was that many Hutu and a few Twa had positions of considerable influence and responsibility in the Rwandan kingdom under Rwabugiri. In fact, Rwabugiri may have actually favoured Hutu and Twa as soldiers and army chiefs over Tutsi (Prunier, 1995: 15). Nor did the first colonists have an accurate view of the extent and limits of the central Rwandan state's effective area of control. In some areas to the south-west and north-west, for example, independent Hutu kingdoms and acephalous polities continued to exist and to defy the expansionist ambitions of the Rwandan state until well into the twentieth century (Chretien, 1997; Newbury, 1988).

The Germans did not understand the wide variety of patron–client relations in Rwanda. For them the *ubuhake* contract between a Tutsi patron and a Hutu client was the paradigmatic relation that defined Hutu servitude to Tutsi.[2] Finally, German colonialists did not comprehend that a degree of fluidity characterized the categories Tutsi, Hutu, and Twa. If a Hutu or Twa became prominent as a soldier or army chief, or sufficiently wealthy in cattle, he might marry a woman from a well-placed Tutsi lineage. The descendants of such unions were often considered Tutsi. Sometimes an entire Hutu lineage might be elevated to Tutsi status by entering into alliance relations with a prominent Tutsi group (Newbury, 1988). Social transformations such as these occurred frequently enough to justify a specific term in Kinyarwanda, *kwihutura,* which signified 'to become Tutsi, to cease being Hutu' (Jacob, 1984: 590), but the number of people affected by it in relative or absolute terms is not known. Likewise it was possible for Tutsi to descend in social status and to be considered Hutu; according to some of my Rwandan acquaintances the term *kwitutsira* was used to signify this social descent, but this term can not be found in Jacob's dictionary of Kinyarwanda (a 2,000 page abridged version of Rwanda's National Scientific Research Institute's dictionary of Kinyarwanda in Butare, Rwanda). The meaning of the term, Hutu, 'social son, client, or someone who does not possess cattle' (Jacob, 1984: 590), and the origin of the term, Tutsi, from *gutuuka* meaning 'to enrich someone' (Jacob, 1985: 404), reinforces the interpretation that the categories were status-related, malleable, and not purely ascriptive.

Belgians who followed the Germans after the First World War, repeated their predecessors' errors, perceiving Tutsi as racially superior and favouring them in government, education, and commerce. Because they accepted Speke's, Johnston's, and Seligman's theories uncritically, the Germans and then the Belgians exacerbated ethnic divisions in Rwanda. An administrative school was established at Nyanza, for example, to prepare cadres for the indirect rule state apparatus. Over three-quarters of the students at this school were Tutsi and only Tutsi could attain the higher echelons of the local colonial state hierarchy (Chretien, 1997: 68). Concomitantly, the favourable perception that the monarchy had once enjoyed among many Rwandans was undermined as the king's redistributive and ritual functions became less and less significant under colonialism. By the late 1920s, for example, the Rwandan king, Yuhi Musinga, was no longer performing the rituals associated with kingship (Linden, 1977: 157–60). Colonialist comitment to Hamitic theories served more than a local purpose. As the latter were based upon social Darwinist assumptions, privileged Europeans could tolerate and explain away inequality both in their own countries and elsewhere in the world. Poverty and subjugation wherever they occurred were the inevitable results of an impoverished biological heritage. In shaping the Rwandan polity in accordance with the Hamitic hypothesis, and in enlisting Tutsi as the locally superior race, the Germans and Belgians were hardening the local categories into immutable realities.

Rwandan Models of Difference and Relatedness

Despite flaws in the Hamitic hypothesis that became increasingly apparent to scholars in the 1950s and 1960s, a time which coincided with Rwanda-Urundi's decolonization process, it was never really subjected to criticism nor openly debated among Rwandans and Burundians. Events at this time seemed to have transpired independently of what had been the ideological cornerstone of the colony. Shortly before independence the Belgians began to reform the indirect rule state apparatus and the places of Tutsi and Hutu in it, but for reasons unrelated to Hamitism. Out of fear that the pro-Lumumbu faction of educated Tutsi was about to gain ascendancy within Rwanda, the Belgian colonial administration supported by the Rwandan Catholic Church, rapidly set about replacing Tutsi chiefs and sub-chiefs with Hutu. At about this same time the first Rwandan political parties came into existence, all but one of which were based along ethnic lines (see Chapter 1). Events rapidly degenerated into violence and, after two years of this, the UN stepped in to oversee elections in 1961. Not suprisingly given the demographics of Rwanda, Hutu political parties won an overwhelming majority.

Hutu were now in complete control of the state, but an intellectual critique of colonialist ideology and the role of the Hamitic hypothesis in that ideology had never been allowed to develop and mature. Perhaps if it had, many Rwandans would have understood that their experience with colonialism and their responses to it had left a wide chasm between the country's two most numerous groups.

It would be an oversimplification, however, to attribute the origins of all inequality and ethnic discrimination in Rwanda to colonialism. The Hamitic myth was not the only factor that promoted inequities among Rwanda's three groups. Well before colonialism, both Tutsi and Hutu discriminated against Twa. In part this stemmed from the fact that Twa were associated with the forest and indeed some among them continued to gain their livelihood from hunting and gathering in forested areas. Over the centuries, though, as Rwanda's wooded areas disappeared, most Twa chose alternative livelihoods but were only permitted to exercise the least esteemed occupations. Many Twa became potters, for example, an occupation that was shunned by both Hutu and Tutsi because it involved direct contact with the impure earth (see below). Others became entertainers, torturers, and executioners at the court of the Rwandan king. There was thus a local model of difference that functioned in an analogous way to Hamitic ideology. In a certain sense Hamitic ideology was compatible with Rwandan social experience in areas under the aegis of the Rwandan king, because here there was a well-delineated social hierarchy predicated in part on a local form of discrimination. This local model interacted with Hamitic ideology and other colonialist conceptualizations of difference in ways that reinforced ethnic differentiation and essentialization in Rwanda.

Perhaps the most significant difference that nineteenth-century colonialist discourse posited was that which delineated colonizers from the colonized – civilization. For Europeans, it was obvious that they were 'civilized' and everyone else was less so. The dichotomy of civilized versus uncivilized was central to colonialist discourse, as can be seen from the Berlin Conference of 1884–5. Colonial powers agreed that they had an obligation, a 'civilizing mission', to help the colonized along the road to 'civilization'. In some ways the 'civilizing mission' was inconsistent with other aspects of nineteenth century thought, namely biological determinism, which asserted that the differences observed in terms of civilizational level among peoples were due to biological and thus immutable differences among peoples in terms of intellectual and moral capacities. This was a central contradiction in colonialist thought, but occulting it had ideological benefits. The doctrine of 'civilizing mission' could be used to rationalize colonialism as a humanistic enterprise.

Although many social groups ascribe the position of 'humanity' to themselves, something slightly less than 'humanity' to their closest neighbours, and 'non-humanity' to all others, in many cases the judgement of negative alterity is turned upon people within a group's own midst. This was the case in pre-colonial Rwanda, for the judgement and perception of negative difference was levelled not so much at Hutu by Tutsi or at Tutsi by Hutu, as by both groups against a third, the Twa. According to many scholars, the presence of Twa in Rwanda predates both Tutsi and Hutu, although in censuses taken at various times during the twentieth century, the Twa constitute only about one percent of the total population.

Despite their sparcity in number, Twa were significant as a group for they were locally perceived to be closer to 'wildness' than to 'humanity'. For Tutsi and Hutu, Twa were Rwanda's 'uncivilized', widely seen as uncouth and gluttonous. The polluted status of Twa could be seen in practices involving commensality. Where Tutsi and Hutu ate or drank with one another, sharing the same cooking or drinking vessels, people of either group strictly limited commensality with Twa. Although Twa might be present where Tutsi or Hutu were drinking or eating together, and they might be given food and drink, their portions were always served in separate vessels that others present would not use. It is impossible to precisely assess the historical depth of these practices, called *kuneena Batwa*, but it is probable that they date from pre-colonial times. When colonialists came to Rwanda and Burundi, they were not particularly interested in the Twa. Twa, after all, constituted a small minority with marginal political significance. Colonialist intervention in the local social arrangements did not act consciously in favour of, nor against Twa interests; it ignored them. It is therefore difficult to imagine that the practices called *kuneena Batwa* had anything but an indigenous and pre-colonial origin. Local distinctions among the three groups also operated at the level of production and consumption. Where production was concerned, contact with the earth was devalourized. Twa, as potters, had the most direct contact with the earth. Hutu, as cultivators, also had contact with the earth but this contact was mediated by tools. Tutsi, as cattle herders, had the least contact with the earth. With regard to consumption, liquid aliments were

the most highly esteemed (De Heusch, 1985). Tutsi had a diet
consisting more of liquids – milk, honey, beer, and cattle blood –
than of solids. Some claimed not to eat solids at all. Others only
ate them when they were sure not to be observed. When they ate
meat, they preferred beef first, then goat, but never mutton. Sheep
were esteemed as animals that accompanied cattle herds and kept
them calm. Hutu had more solids than liquids in their diet and
more goat than beef. Like the Tutsi, the Hutu spurned mutton.
Because they ate mutton, Twa were perceived to have the least
discriminating diet. These practices have been described by the
earliest missionary ethnographers of Rwanda (De Lacger, 1959),
but a problem remains in accurately pinpointing their exact time
of origin and their degree of generality. Once again, however, the
practices do not appear to have been the direct result of colonialism.

These ethnically differentiated production and consumption
patterns may have antedated, coincided with, or even post-dated
the process of hierarchization in central Rwanda. It is not clear
whether the practices helped to generate hierarchy or merely served
to reflect it. Once in place, however, the practices reinforced social
boundaries between the groups. As for their degree of generality,
it appears that the practices were pronounced tendencies rather
than hard-and-fast rules. Many Tutsi cultivated the land as well as
raised cattle, and many Hutu husbanded cattle as well as cultivated.
Only the Twa neither cultivated nor herded livestock. The differences were most significant in central Rwanda. Here the Rwandan
king placed Hutu in charge of collecting and preparing agricultural
foodstuffs for the royal household, Tutsi in charge of providing
milk, while Twa served the king in baser, less prestigious tasks
(entertainers, spies, torturers, and executioners). The practices did
not follow anything as rigid as caste prohibitions, although the
Rwandan social system has sometimes been compared to a caste
system (Maquet, 1954; De Heusch, 1966), but they did serve to
demarcate and perpetuate differences among the three groups. In
sum, it is difficult to attribute all social boundary formation among
the three groups to colonialism alone.

When colonialism began to transform Rwandan society, local
concepts of difference interdigitated with European ones. Hamitism,
based upon biologically determinist models of race and hierarchy,
could be integrated with Rwandan models of difference because
Rwandans already had their own 'inferior race'.[3] Within a few
decades, a hierarchy based upon presumed differential embodiment

of 'civilization' could emerge with Europeans at the top, Tutsi slightly beneath them, Hutu beneath Tutsi, and Twa at the bottom. As colonialism proceeded it was to the advantage of Tutsi to reinforce European perceptions that this hierarchy was rooted in local historical and cultural realities. Their success at doing this explains the probable origin of the so-called 'premise of inequality' (Maquet, 1954).

In Comaroff's essay on ethnicity and totemism, he criticizes those views of ethnicity that view it as primordial (1992: 49–67). The only aspect that is primordial about ethnicity, he argues, is the propensity of all societies to delineate human relations in terms of oppositions. What is not primordial is the nature of these oppositions and the level at which the opposition is used – race, culture, nation, or tribe. These factors depend on the social and historical context. In Rwanda, the colonial opposition of civilized versus uncivilized assumed importance at the ideological level of race. Grafted to the local scheme of difference, the categories, Tutsi, Hutu, and Twa, came to be considered as 'races' in the biologically determinist sense. When the Belgian colonial authority instituted national identity cards marked with the bearer's *ethnie* or *ubwoko* upon them, race was the intended meaning.

Scholarly Models of Ethnicity

Scholarly theories concerning the origin of ethnicity in Rwanda tend to be situated somewhere between two poles. One pole posits a separate geographic and biogenetic origin to each of the three ethnic groups. The other pole hypothesizes that the groups were constituted as separate races or *ethnies* only because of colonialism and the Hamitic hypothesis. According to the second theory, differences in diet and way of life over the course of generations brought about the differences in physiognomy often remarked among Tutsi, Hutu, and Twa.

Indeed, there are three ideal somatic types among the three groups: Twa tend on the average to be the shortest in stature, some closely resemble the short-statured foragers in neighbouring Zaire (once termed 'pygmies'); Hutu tend to be of moderate height; Tutsi tend to be taller on the average than Hutu, thinner, and with narrower noses. These bodily types constitute statistical tendencies; many people cannot be readily classified into one group or another solely on the basis of somatic form. Some Rwandans and Burundians say that about one third of the time they themselves can be wrong about judging someone's ethnicity on the basis of physiognomy alone. Partly this is due to the fact that intermarriages among the groups, particularly between Tutsi and Hutu, have always occurred with some degree of frequency. It is also due to the fact that, even within groups that have been endogamous for many generations, there is a range of somatic variation.

During the 1994 genocide Tutsi were killed for various reasons. Some were killed because neighbours or acquaintances had identified them as Tutsi and indeed lists had been prepared to that end. In cases where potential victims were unknown to their persecutors, the national identity card was checked. When a person was unknown to his or her captors and claimed to have lost the identity card, physical appearance spelled the difference between death and survival. Typically Tutsi features were sufficient grounds for execution. If one looked Hutu, yet did not have an identity card, one was usually spared. In Nairobi in June of 1994, I met one young man who, although classified as Tutsi because of his father, managed to pass through every roadblock because of his typically Hutu features. Another Rwandan was nearly executed because of his Tutsi-like features despite the fact that his father and his official identity were Hutu, although his mother was Tutsi. Taken to the army base in the city of Gitarama, he was released when an officer there recognized him as the son of a prominent Hutu businessman.

The two scholarly theories about Rwandan ethnicity tend to be adapted in part or in whole by various political groups within Rwanda and Burundi. The most extreme form of the separate origins hypothesis, virtually identical to the Hamitic hypothesis, can be found in the earliest missionary ethnographies of Rwanda as in the work of Pages (1933), or that of De Lacger (1939). A more cautious version of the theory of separate origins appears in Maquet (1954), probably the first serious professional ethnography about Rwanda. Maquet's version of this theory claims that the Twa, who were originally all foragers, controlled most of present day Rwanda at a time when Rwanda was largely covered with forest. Then Bantu-speaking cultivators, the Hutu, began entering the area although Maquet is unsure of the exact time. They began large-scale deforestation of Rwanda. The last to enter Rwanda were Tutsi cattle herders. Maquet guesses that their presence dates back at least four centuries. Maquet follows received wisdom in speculating that the Tutsi originated from Galla country in Ethiopia and Somalia, but here he warns readers that given the lack of linguistic evidence ('Hamitic' was still being used as a linguistic term in the 1950s) and the fact that all contemporary Tutsi speak Kinyarwanda, a Bantu language, the use of 'Hamite' or 'Hamitic' to describe them is unjustified. He prefers the terms 'Ethiopian' or 'Ethiopoid' (1954: 22–6).

Maquet's use of the separate origins theory makes no claims concerning the origins of the Rwandan state. Luc De Heusch in *Le Rwanda et la civilisation interlacustre* (1966) echoes Maquet's separate origins theory, but is quite clear in denying that the Rwandan state and the institution of sacred kingship could have had Tutsi origins. Both institutions, he claims, were operative well in advance of the presumed Tutsi arrival (1966: 14). De Heusch's model of Rwandan ethnicity resembles Maquet's in other respects. De Heusch, for example, follows Maquet's use of the notion of caste, but he defines caste more precisely than Maquet, emphasizing the central character-istics of economic specialization and endogamy. In a limited sense De Heusch is right as general tendencies, specialization and endog-amy were certainly observed among the groups during the twentieth century. If, however, we require that explicit rules of behaviour based on notions of ritual purity govern the practices of economic specialization and endogamy (the definition of caste advanced by Dumont, 1980), then the notion of caste is inaccurate for Rwandan ethnic groups.

Despite the attempts of Maquet and de Heusch to distance them-selves from the Hamitic hypothesis, the separate origins theory suffers guilt by association due to its superficial resemblance to the Hamitic hypothesis. This resemblance is superficial because claiming that the Tutsi and Hutu have separate geographic and biogenetic origins makes no assertion concerning presumed intellectual differences between the groups, nor the origin of the Rwandan state. Nevertheless, because of the resemblance many scholars have modified the separate origins theory or discarded it altogether. This position maintains that the ethnic groups in Rwanda and Burundi are colonial constructions, ideological entities that colonialists found useful in order to impose their rule on the area. This is the position advanced by Vidal (1991). The problem with this view is that it fails to explain why the earliest European visitors to the area noted the tripartite division of Tutsi, Hutu, and Twa in central Rwanda (De Heusch, 1995). It seems more probable that the division preceded the arrival of Europeans.

A somewhat less categorical departure from the separate origins theory asserts that Tutsi and Hutu (although not Twa) have similar biogenetic origins. According to this version, diet and way of life have led to differences in physiognomy; ethnic categorization in Rwanda is primarily a question of economic specialization and social class. The most fanciful rendering of this theory claims that cattle herders, because of their knowledge of breeding, were able to subtly apply selective breeding methods to themselves and to favour those genes that encoded for typically Tutsi traits such as tallness (Desmarais, 1978). Yet another theory, which ends up joining the single origins theory in terms of its practical implications, claims that both groups have multiple biogenetic, linguistic, and geographic origins. These are so complex that it makes little sense to try and unravel them.

The view advanced by Franche (1995) is akin to the above theories that question the assumption of separate origins but it goes even further by problematizing and ultimately rejecting the issue of origins altogether. Instead, he considers the question of the Rwandan groups as a question of identity in general. Franche reiterates the assertion that ethnic difference in Rwanda was something that was 'fetishized' by Europeans according to racialist preconceptions, but he rejects the notion of social class. This notion distorts Rwandan realities because it induces us to think about Rwandan social realities as if these were characterized by 'class struggle', where our ultimate frame of reference for thinking about class and class struggle is European experience (1995: 4). Franche maintains that Rwandan 'ethnies' were neither castes nor classes. Indeed, the use of the terms, Tutsi, Hutu, and Twa, as aspects of identity may have preceded the arrival of colonialists, but then other identity markers were also in use – clan affiliation (such as *abazigaba, abasinga, abanyiginya*), regional origin (*abakiga* for people from the north, *abanyenduga* for people from the south), economic activity, and so forth. Moreover, the ethnic terms (Tutsi, Hutu, and Twa) may not always have meant the same things in every region where they were employed (Newbury, 1988). The terms have to be considered in relation to the regional, historical, and social contexts in which they were used. It was only as a result of colonialism and the Hamitic myth that the terms took on meanings that approximate those of race. These racial meanings, of colonial construction, conditioned much of the interaction between the groups during the twentieth century and provided the ideological fuel used by local extremists during the tragic events of 1994 (Franche, 1995).

Franche's essay raises valid objections to the customary scholarly views of Rwandan ethnicity. He is correct in insisting upon a contextualized and historicized examination of the use of the terms Tutsi, Hutu, and Twa. He is also correct in criticizing the rapid use of European intellectual concepts and models as a means of understanding Rwandan experience with terms such as 'tribe', 'class', 'caste', or 'race'. However, in his zeal to overturn all intellectual remnants of biological determinism and the Hamitic hypothesis, he may go too far in rejecting all attempts to determine the origins of Rwanda's people. European racism was certainly transplanted to the African continent with the Hamitic hypothesis and it has indeed subtended the racial models of history used by unscrupulous Rwandan and Burundian politicians today, but not all biology is biological determinism. Physical anthropology, biology, and genetics when employed in conjunction with data from archaeology, linguistics, and socio-cultural anthropology can contribute to our understanding of African historical processes and they should not be discarded simply because some practitioners of these disciplines have either been racists or unaware of the racialism of their intellectual models. Demonstrating that there might be genetic and linguistic factors that link interlacustrine Africa to northeast Africa does not constitute affirmation of the Hamitic hypothesis nor of its corollary racism. On the contrary, much of this evidence refutes some of the more extreme Hamitic claims.

Rwandan and Burundian use of Scholarly Theories

At various times, aspects of the above theories have been employed by intellectuals and politicians in Rwanda or Burundi to advance their political aims. In early colonial Rwanda, it was to the advantage of privileged Tutsi to echo the sentiments of colonialists and claim Hamitic descent and concomitantly a separate origin from Hutu. It was also to their advantage to create 'invented traditions' along these lines in the form of oral histories and legends which clearly delineated them from Hutu, and insisted upon their intellectual, moral, and/or military superiority.

One of the most widely known examples of these oral literary creations was the story of the three sons of Gihanga (legendary first king of Rwanda): Gatutsi, Gahutu, and Gatwa (Smith, 1975: 39). According to the story, Gihanga entrusted a full pot of milk to each son, asking him to guard it during the night until his return the next morning. Quickly overcome with hunger, Gatwa drank his pot of milk and then fell asleep. Overcome with fatigue, Gahutu began to doze off and while doing so, spilled some of his pot of milk. Only Gatutsi, resisting both hunger and fatigue, remained awake and vigilant, presenting Gihanga with a full pot the next morning. Because only Gatutsi had managed to save his milk, Gihanga gave him the right to rule Rwanda and to own cattle. Gahutu would have to follow Gatutsi's orders and would only be allowed to own cattle given to him by Gatutsi. As for the hapless Gatwa, he was to be deprived of both political power and cattle ownership.

Although this version of the story admits to a common fraternity among Gatutsi, Gahutu, and Gatwa, the story extols the superior ability of Gatutsi to transcend bodily urgings and desires. As demonstrated earlier, the one perceived to be least able to control bodily cravings was Gatwa. In a sense Gatwa was perceived as outside the social contract, more a creature of the forest than of human society. As for Gahutu he was undeniably human but, like Gatwa, less able than Gatutsi to deny the body and exert self-control.

In a more erudite vein, Alexis Kagame, a Tutsi Catholic priest (1912–81) and the leading Rwandan intellectual of the late colonial era, echoes the theme of Tutsi superiority in his history of Rwandan kingship, *Inganji Karinga*, (The Victory of Karinga) (1959). Karinga was the name of the most important royal drum and the key emblem of the monarchy. In this book the vaunted superiority of the Tutsi was military in nature rather than intellectual, although the latter was certainly implied. Published between 1943–47 at the request of the Rwandan king, Rudahigwa, the book chronicles the history of the kingdom as an inexorable series of Tutsi victories over Hutu chiefs, termed *abahinza*. The book makes no concession to delicate sensibilities in its description of the tortures and humiliations meted out to the vanquished including a description of the custom of adorning the royal drum, Karinga, with the severed testicles of enemies (Franche, 1995: 21). Mirroring Hamitic themes, Kagame insists upon the Ethiopian origins of Tutsi and of virtually all Rwandan social and political institutions. Going even further than the missionary ethnographies, his version of Rwandan history admits of no institution as having had a Hutu origin.

Kagame's writings, more inspired by the early missionary view of Rwandan history than by careful research, were later used by high-level Tutsi to counter Hutu pleas for redress. In a 1957 document called the *Bahutu Manifesto*, a group of Hutu intellectuals (including Gregoire Kayibanda, see below) called upon the Rwandan king, Rudahigwa, to consider ameliorating the condition of Hutu in the country. The *Bahutu Manifesto* follows the single-origin theory, basing its appeal on the common fraternity of Hutu, Tutsi, and Twa as sons of Kanyarwanda. In response to it, twelve of the king's highest level vassals denied all relationship to Hutu or Twa on the basis that their ancestor, Kigwa, was antecedent to Kanyarwanda.

> The Bahutu maintain that Kanyarwanda is the father of Batutsi, Bahutu, and Batwa; but we know that Kigwa comes long before Kanyarwanda and that consequently Kanyarwanda lived after the three races, Bahutu, Batutsi, and Batwa, were already well in place. [. . .] We find all the detail in Inganji Karinga. Our kings conquered the country of the Bahutu, so how can they now claim to be our brothers?
>
> (Nkundabagenzi, 1962: 35)

Up to about 1958, most Tutsi politicians in Rwanda claimed separate origins whereas many Hutu politicians claimed a single origin for the two ethnic groups. When it became clear shortly thereafter that the Belgians were in favour of reforming the system and replacing Tutsi administrators with Hutu, some Tutsi nationalists began to embrace a single origin theory. If Hutu and Tutsi were a people with a single origin, why not throw out the ethnic distinctions altogether? In that way other criteria to choose administrators, such as education, would have to be used, and as Tutsi at the time were better educated than Hutu, they might be able to preserve their privileges in an apparently non-ethnic society. In fact this tactic resembles what occurred in neighbouring Burundi. While denying ethnicity at one level (no ethnic mention on identity cards for example), Tutsi supremacists in Burundi managed to gain control of the state by controlling the army (see below).

The Belgian colonial administration in Rwanda was not eager to undo the ethnic categories, however, as they were distrustful of Tutsi nationalism. Belgians deeply feared that those Tutsi who were trying to enlist Hutu in their anti-colonialist cause were leaning in the direction of Patrice Lumumba of the Belgian Congo and international communism. They accused the nationalists of being anti-Belgian and anti-Church. As a result the colonial administration moved quickly to embrace what had become the safer ethnic group and the Governor-General, Jean-Paul Harroy, proceeded to replace

Tutsi administrators with Hutu. Belgians also aided in the organization of Hutu political parties, virtually guaranteeing that these
would win in later UN sponsored elections. The Catholic Church,
for its part, and to some degree independently of the colonial
administration, changed direction and began to tilt in favour of
Hutu who comprised the majority of the Church's converts (Linden,
1977). Without Belgian and Catholic Church support, Tutsi political
dominance in Rwanda was doomed and indeed most traces of it
were undone during the revolutionary years of 1959–62. But ethnic
categorization remained unchanged. When Belgium granted Rwanda
independence in 1962, the new Hutu government under Gregoire
Kayibanda did not eliminate ethnic identification on national
identity cards nor did it attempt to attenuate the popular perception
of ethnicity, which by then was strongly racialist. In keeping ethnic
identity clearly delineated by means of identity cards, the new
government could ensure that Tutsi would be discriminated against
in employment and in school and university placements.

   Even if only a minority among them had actually benefited under
colonialism, Tutsi as a 'race' suddenly found themselves the country's
new second class citizens. Now it was Hutu politicians who were
echoing Hamitic themes and their separate origins from Tutsi. Tutsi
became 'invaders from Ethiopia'. Occasional military incursions
into Rwanda by Tutsi exile groups (*inyenzi*) based in neighbouring
countries did nothing to help matters. *Inyenzi* raids, which continued
until 1964, provoked racialist propaganda and violence against Tutsi
still living in Rwanda. Each raid precipitated new killings of Rwandan
Tutsi and new waves of Tutsi refugees who fled to Burundi, Zaire,
Tanzania, and Uganda. Kayibanda's Hutu government found that
it could exploit the raids to divert attention away from its own
failings. In the absence of raids it organized internal persecution
of Tutsi on other grounds. This period of Rwandan history established a pattern, whenever the Rwandan government encountered
internal problems, it would inflame popular resentment against
Tutsi.

   In neighbouring Burundi a different pattern emerged. Witnessing
the political changes in Rwanda, Tutsi supremacists wanted to stave
off a similar tide of events. These Tutsi managed to reinforce their
control of the government via coups, assassinations (including the
key assassination of Prince Rwagasore – the most popular Burundian
political leader of the time and one with a multiethnic following),
and a purge of Hutu from the military. Those Tutsi who assumed

power could even deny ethnic motivation, because Burundian identity cards bore no mention of whether their holders were Tutsi, Hutu, or Twa. Officially Burundi could claim that Burundians were a single people, although in reality it practised discrimination against Hutu. In response to this deliberate and disingenuous obfuscation of ethnicity, Hutu ethnic politicians began to insist upon their separate origins from Tutsi.

Separate origins in Rwanda did not require subtle measures of obfuscation, for there was the plainly marked ID card. When that was not sufficient to determine the easy scapegoat, Tutsi physical features would do. The 'events of 1973' show this. In 1973 Kayibanda, facing increasing opposition from northern Hutu, who were well represented in the army but not elsewhere in the regime, played the Tutsi card once again. Some elements in Kayibanda's coterie accused Tutsi of being overly represented in the private sector, in the Rwandan Catholic Church hierarchy, and in schools. Many Tutsi schoolteachers were fired while extremist Hutu teachers and pupils organized the persecution of Tutsi school children. Rwandans who lived through this era told me that Tutsi children would be asked to stand and identify themselves while the teacher would harangue and humiliate them in front of the other pupils. Children had their noses measured for width and their fingers for length. Many were physically abused if they were determined to be Tutsi by these means. Some Tutsi were killed and many more fled the country. Habyarimana overthrew the Kayibanda regime, promising to put an end to the disorder, and instituted a policy of regional and ethnic equilibrium.

According to the new policy, government jobs, places in secondary schools and universities, even to some extent jobs in the private sector, were to be apportioned to southern Hutu, northern Hutu, and to Tutsi on the basis of their representation in the population. The new government chose population figures of 9 per cent Tutsi, about 90 per cent Hutu, and a little less than 1 per cent Twa, figures that probably underestimated the proportion of Tutsi, at least at the time of the census. In the years after the census, many Tutsi fled and others were changing their identity classification wherever possible. Despite Habyarimana's policy, many more northern Hutu than southern Hutu received government jobs and secondary school placements and many fewer Tutsi than the 10 per cent allotment. As for the Twa, they never received even the apportioned 1 per cent of state jobs or school placements. Despite prejudicial treatment against them, many Tutsi still living in Rwanda welcomed the Habyarimana regime because it had put an end to the violence.

For the next fifteen years, Rwandan Tutsi were left relatively unmolested by the regime. Tutsi could work in the private sector, for international organizations, and some became quite successful as independent entrepreneurs. A few others worked in government jobs, but there was almost no Tutsi participation in politics. Despite this, some racially extremist Hutu complained that Habyarimana was 'too soft' on the Tutsi. In the face of lingering racism, the Rwandan Tutsi knew that Habyarimana was about the best that they could hope for and thus most of them kept their resentments to themselves. With the Tutsi silent, other serious rents in the Rwandan sociopolitical fabric could come to the fore. Before 1990 the most serious among these was that between northern and southern Hutu, for the people who benefited most from the regime were northerners. As the southern Hutu became increasingly disaffected, they attempted to form opposition political parties. True to the pattern established by Kayibanda, the Habyarimana regime and its associated political party, the MRND (Mouvement Revolutionnaire National pour le Developpement), responded to this threat and proceeded to play the Tutsi card yet again toward the end of the 1980s. This strategy received impetus from the Rwandan Patriotic Front's invasion of Rwanda from Uganda on the night of 4 October 1990.[4]

Tutsi-baiting moved into high gear in the wake of the invasion. The MRND party, whose officers dominated local government, began organizing local level massacres of Tutsi. Once again Hamitic themes such as the mythical history of Tutsi as 'invaders from the north', began to be heard from the mouths of extremist politicians. One notable example was a speech given to MRND party members near Gisenyi by Dr Leon Mugesera on 22 November 1992:

> The opposition parties have plotted with the enemy to make the Byumba prefecture fall to the *Inyenzi*. [. . .] They have plotted to undermine our armed forces. [. . .] The law is quite clear on this point: 'Any person who is guilty of acts aiming at sapping the morale of the armed forces will be condemned to death.' What are we waiting for? [. . .] And what about those accomplices (*ibyitso*) here who are sending their children to the RPF? Why are we waiting to get rid of these families? [. . .] We have to take responsibility into our own hands and wipe out these hoodlums. [. . .] The fatal mistake we made in 1959 was to let them [the Tutsis] get out. [. . .] They belong to Ethiopia and we are going to

find them a shortcut to get there by throwing them into the Nyabarongo
river [which flows northwards]. I must insist on this point. We have to
act. Wipe them all out!

(Prunier 1995: 171–2)

Mugesera's words proved prophetic. During the genocide of 1994,
thousands of bodies were thrown into the Nyabarongo River, which
ultimately empties into Lake Victoria via the Akagera River. So many
decomposing bodies collected there in May to July 1994 that Lake
Victoria fishermen had trouble selling their fish to consumers in
Kenya and Uganda, who were afraid that the fish were unhealthy.
Although this fear was probably exaggerated where the fish were
concerned, decomposing bodies on the shores of the lake in proximity to human settlements were indeed a health hazard. International aid was needed to help Lake Victoria communities remove
and bury the bodies.

In contrast to Hutu extremists like Mugesera, who was recently
on trial as a war criminal in Canada where he was employed as a
university professor, members and supporters of the RPF during
the 1990s were trying to undermine the Hamitic hypothesis and
the theory of separate origins. From a corpus of documents entitled
'La crise Rwandaise en quelques documents' that I received from
RPF supporters in Kenya in June of 1994, one notes the use of
scholarly articles that critically examine the Hamitic myth, the
separate origins hypothesis, and the colonial role in the construction of ethnicity. In effect, for the RPF it became politically advantageous either to insist upon possible shared origins with Hutu or to
insist upon the colonial construction of the 'ethnies'. One notable
article in the dossier was entitled 'Deux mille collines pour les petits
et les grands', written by Michel Elias and Danielle Helbig, which
appeared in *Politique Africaine* (June, 1991). Among other points,
the article traces a shift in discourse among 1950s Belgian colonial
administrators from talking about Tutsi as 'born rulers' and Hutu
as 'born servants,' to Tutsi as 'lazy oppressors' and Hutu as 'serfs,'
'slaves,' or 'victims'. This shift to a social class model of Rwandan
difference is dissimulating, according to Elias and Helbig, for if we
look beneath the surface of the language of 'abused peasants' and
'lazy oppressors', what we find is that the new terms are merely
synonyms for the old racial terms. A social class model has merely
been grafted onto the previous biological determinist model without impugning or altering the latter in any significant way.

Books that appeared during the 1970s and 1980s written by former Belgian colonial administrators and Catholic Church officials have also been characterized by this conflation of class and race. Tutsi in these works are described as 'Hamite invaders from the north' who 'conquer' the original Hutu inhabitants, 'colonize', and 'oppress' them. In no way is the old Hamitic interpretation undermined; all that changes are the moral valences attributed to each of the 'races'. Where the Tutsi had once been depicted as beautiful, intelligent, and almost Caucasian, they were now 'lazy colonizers' and 'foreign oppressors' of the Hutu masses. Such pandering, both to the new Hutu masters of Rwanda, whose official rhetoric claimed that the 1959 revolution was 'social' in nature rather than ethnic or racial, and to sentiments of anti-colonialism, is of course bitterly ironic given the source of the statements. We have come full circle in the valuational imagery attributed to 'Hamites', but Hamitic theory remains unassailed. Lamentable though these statements were, by the 1980s they were more reflective of local Rwandan discourse than constitutive of it. From independence to the present, it has been mostly Rwandans and Burundians who have kept the Hamitic themes alive.

Recent Local uses of the Hamitic Hypothesis

Rwanda

All that has been discussed to this point might be of academic interest only were it not for the fact that the Hamitic hypothesis has continued to serve the purposes of extremist ideologues in Rwanda and Burundi. I repeatedly heard evidence of this during my most recent period of fieldwork in Rwanda where Family Health International, a subcontractor for USAID, employed me as an AIDS behavioural research specialist. Between late October 1993, when I arrived in Rwanda, and the time when I was emergency evacuated from Kigali on 9 April 1994, I spoke with many Rwandans about the political situation in the country and was witness to its gradual slide into total disorder. When several attempts to install the broad-based transitional government, as called for under the Arusha accords of August 1993, failed because President Habyarimana and his allies managed to continually scuttle the peace plan's implementation, I saw the 'dogs of war' being slowly unleashed. Roving bands of *Interahamwe* Hutu militia became bolder in their harassment of Tutsi civilians and of Hutu known to be opponents of the Habayarimana regime. Several Hutu opposition politicians were assassinated and acts of terrorism against Tutsi and Hutu opposition party members became more frequent despite the observing presence of UN troops whose mandate prevented them from interfering to prevent violence even during acts of murder. Finally President Habyarimana's plane was shot down near Kigali airport on 6 April 1994.

Before that time I had often discussed the political situation with Rwandan friends. Some of them were supporters of the government, others were supporters of the RPF, yet others were supporters of political parties opposed both to the ruling MRND and to the RPF. From Rwandans who were supporters of the MRND and the Habyarimana regime, I often received versions of history along these lines:

> We Hutu are Bantus. Although the Twa were here first, when we arrived we lived in peace with them. We cleared the land and farmed it. They made pots or hunted in the forest. The Tutsi are Hamites. They came from the north and much later than the Hutu or the Twa. The first kings in Rwanda were Hutu, but the Tutsi say they were Tutsi. The Tutsi used their cattle to trick Hutu into doing work for them. Then the Tutsi managed to conquer one Hutu kingdom. When the Europeans came, they helped the Tutsi to conquer the rest of our lands.

I received a similar version of history from an informal conversation in May 1993 with a high ranking official of the MRND party. He added that Westerners did not realize the degree to which the RPF were guilty of human rights abuses; they did not realize that the RPF had made territorial gains only because they had attacked northern peasants killing hundreds and causing hundreds of thousands to flee southward, forcing the already strapped Rwandan government to divert manpower and resources to deal with the displaced. He claimed that the RPF would eventually turn on their supporter, Ugandan President Yoweri Museveni, and attack Uganda. The RPF's aim was to restore the monarchy and to carve out a Tutsi state comprised of parts of Rwanda, Burundi, Zaire, and Uganda. In January 1994, several months after our conversation, the same official warned one of my closest friends, a Tutsi and RPF supporter married to his wife's sister, that soon massacres were going to occur in Rwanda and that these would be worse than those

of 1959–64. In effect, he was warning my friend to leave the country
while he could.

A version of history close to the above was also exploited by the
Hutu extremist radio station in Kigali, RTLM, during 1993 and
1994. A frequently evoked scenario on this radio was the spectre
of RPF 'feudal-monarchists' returning to subjugate Hutu cultivators
as they had once been subjugated under Tutsi kings. Often the
station superficially concealed its anti-Tutsi racism by referring to
Tutsi as *sebatunzi* ('the sons and daughters of cattle herders') and
to Hutu as *sebahinzi* ('the sons and daughters of cultivators'). When
I asked Rwandan friends of mine why such overt racism was tolerated on the public airwaves one of them, a Hutu, told me, 'They
only say what everyone thinks.'

After the genocide started, in April 1994, the station exhorted
the *Interahamwe* death squads to be untiring in their 'work'. 'The
tombs are only half full', was one of their slogans in May. By late
June of 1994, with the Rwandan government forces continuing to
retreat before the RPF advance, most of the victims of the genocide
had already been killed. Along with the fleeing RGF army, the
RTLM relocated in the border town of Gisenyi (near Zaire), where
it quickly resumed broadcasting. By then the French were preparing
their supposedly humanitarian intervention – 'Operation Turquoise'.
Because the French had supported the Habyarimana regime unwaver-
ingly since the beginning of the conflict, despite strong evidence
that a genocide was in the making (Verschave, 1995), the RTLM
assumed that the French were coming to save the Rwandan interim
government. RTLM called upon the population to welcome the
French. Their appeal to young Hutu women, as I discuss later in
this work, was especially revealing of lurking Hamitic imagery (see
Chapter 4).

In contrast to the extremist Hutu position, insisting upon separate
origins of Hutu and Tutsi, the official RPF position was closer to
the single origins theory. From RPF sources that I met during a
visit to their headquarters in Kigali in March, 1994, I was told that
ethnicity needed to end in Rwanda:[5]

> Who knows where the ethnic groups came from and when, maybe we
> all came from the same place. These are things that even scholars are
> not really sure about. All you need to do is look around here [their
> encampment] and you will see that many of our soldiers and officers
> are Hutu. The tragedy of Rwanda is that no one has tried to get beyond
> ethnic politics as we [the RPF] are trying to do. Hutu and Tutsi

lived in peace before the Europeans came and we could live in peace again.

(conversation with an RPF soldier, January, 1994)

Indeed my interlocutor was correct about certain things that he told me. Perhaps as many as 20–30 per cent of their total soldiers were Hutu, according to a speech given by Alison des Forges in Washington DC, August, 1994.) As for the noble sentiments supposedly motivating the RPF to transcend ethnicity in Rwanda, this was of course debatable, especially as a year or so after the RPF takeover, many of the Hutu members of the new government had abandoned it.

Some RPF soldiers explained to me that they joined the *Inkotanyi* because of what had happened in 1990 shortly after the October RPF invasion from Uganda. One RPF officer recounted:

Like most Tutsi in Rwanda, I was not a supporter of the RPF in October, 1990. On the contrary I was against them when I learned that they had invaded the country. But then I was arrested and thrown into Nyamirambo stadium with thousands of others. Many were Tutsi, but some were opposition party members. There was almost no food and very little water. People crouched down in the morning to eat the grass and lick the dew. We became goats. They beat and mistreated us. Soldiers patrolled above in the stadium. One day they claimed that we were trying to escape and began shooting at us. Some were killed. I was right next to someone who was shot through the leg. Later the international organizations protested because of human rights abuses. The soldiers began bringing us porridge in large troughs, but we didn't have bowls or dishes to eat it with. We used our sneakers and shoes. Later they let us out. The international protest had grown too embarrassing for them. Some [former prisoners] have gone crazy. Some have never recovered their health. Some, like me, went over to the other side. That's why I am here now. That's why I became an *inkotanyi*.

(conversation with an RPF soldier, January, 1994)

But from other more extremist supporters of the RPF, I received a more mythologized version of the conflict and of their history:

We Tutsi were once the nobles in this land and the Hutu were our slaves. Hutu do not have the intelligence to govern. Look at what they have done to this country in the last thirty years.

(conversation with an RPF supporter, Kigali, February, 1994)

Several other Rwandan Tutsi who supported the RPF echoed the sentiment that the Tutsi were by nature more intelligent than Hutu. According to them, this was why Tutsi deserved to take the reins of government. Although many other Tutsi that I talked to did not concur with the myth of Tutsi natural superiority, there were certainly many who did – enough to make one realize that Hamitism was alive and well on both sides during the pre-genocide months of 1994.

In January 1994 I had a conversation with a Tutsi woman who expressed her satisfaction that, in accordance with the Arusha peace arrangements, an RPF battalion was now stationed in Kigali at the Conseil National du Developpement. The Tutsi should participate in government she explained, because they were more intelligent than Hutu. I replied to her that if she believed that Tutsi were superior to Hutu than I could equally claim as a white person, that I was superior to all black people, for this kind of thinking had the same origin. 'But we have to be more intelligent than Hutu', she replied, 'we have survived.'

Rwandan ethnic extremists on both sides were taking inspiration from a single source. They were selectively remembering the Rwandan past with whatever elements advanced their cause, but the ultimate model for their remembering was almost always the Hamitic hypothesis. Hutu extremists would recall their supposed prior arrival to Tutsi in Rwanda; they would remember Tutsi treachery and oppression. Tutsi extremists recalled the past glories of the Tutsi kingdom, its alleged larger area than the Rwanda of today, and the intelligence of its early leaders. Both strategies were extremely distressing to me, having done fieldwork in Rwanda during the mid-1980s, when ethnicity seemed to be receding as a political issue. Occasionally I would argue with my Rwandan friends, trying to explain the contradictions of racialist versions of their past. On one occasion I gave a public talk to this effect at the United States Information Service in Kigali. After the talk a Rwandan approached me and said that I had made some errors. According to him it was not true that during the events of 1959–64 northern Hutu had killed large numbers of Tutsi residing there. 'We only warned them, so they would leave on their own. After all, Hutu had been there first.' Inherent in this statement was the attitude that although it might be morally reprehensible to kill Tutsi, it was certainly not reprehensible to encourage their departure. This was a recurrent notion – one that was also expressed in Mugesera's speech cited above, that very few Tutsi had been killed during 1959–64 and that the overwhelming majority of Tutsi had been forewarned and allowed to escape. In comparison to the 1994 genocide this may have been true; nevertheless, tens of thousands of Tutsi had also been killed in the earlier massacres.

Yet not all Rwandans in late 1993 and early 1994 were simply living out the patterns established by mythologized versions of their history, there were others whose political sophistication and historical knowledge was quite impressive. One evening, in the company of my two closest Rwandan friends, two business partners, one of whom was a Hutu and the other a Tutsi, we visited someone who was a business associate of theirs, a certain Ephraim. Ephraim was a member of the PSD (Parti Social Democrate). Several of the party's leaders were present at Ephraim's home and naturally the conversation turned to Rwandan politics. One of them asked me what the typical Western view of the events in Rwanda was and I explained to him that the media in the US tended to depict events as a centuries old tribal struggle between Hutu and Tutsi. He went to great lengths to explain to me why this view was erroneous, how it was being presently exploited by the MRND, CDR, and other extremist groups allied with President Habyarimana and had been exploited by Westerners in the past. He also explained that some Rwandan political parties, like the PSD, were ethnically mixed. He took pride in the fact that the PSD had resisted all attempts on the part of Habyarimana and his coterie to splinter it into ethnic factions. Months later, in Nairobi, I met Ephraim again after he had narrowly escaped from Rwanda. He informed me that the PSD party (both Hutu and Tutsi members) had suffered enormous losses during the genocide. Practically everyone I had met that evening at his house was now dead.

More recently in the United States, I have occasionally subscribed to an Internet discussion group that consists mostly of Rwandans living in the US or Canada and others who are non-Rwandan. Most of the more vocal participants on the Internet appear less willing than the Rwandan PSD to put ethnicity behind them. Instances where subscribing Rwandans and others on the Internet refer to Tutsi as 'Hamites' and to Hutu as 'Bantus' are so frequent that it is impossible not to be struck by the persistence of these terms and their associated view of history. Only a tiny minority of subscribers object to the stereotypes, and when they voice their objections they are invariably attacked by a numerically superior chorus of voices who accuse them of being dupes of the RPF.

Burundi

Although I have had very little direct field experience in Burundi, it is clear that extremists there have employed Hamitic themes as well. However, according to some scholars of Burundi, such as Lemarchand, Hamitic mythical history never achieved the same degree of importance in Burundi as in Rwanda:

> In effect, from the 1920s on it is in Rwanda rather than in Burundi that we observe the strengthening of Tutsi hegemony under the pressure of the old shibboleths and prejudices of a 'Hamitic' view of history.
>
> (Lemarchand, 1990: 238)

Although Lemarchand would not deny that the colonial state contributed to ethnic polarization in Burundi, he cautions us not to overestimate this role and concomitantly to attenuate the degree of responsibility that post-independence Burundian politicians must bear in the tragic events of their country's recent history.

In an earlier work Lemarchand emphasizes the differences between pre-colonial Rwanda and Burundi and comments upon their implications for the emergence of ethnic consciousness (1970). In contrast to Rwanda, for example, where the Tutsi population lived in most areas of the country (with the notable exception of northern Rwanda where there were relatively few Tutsi), 80 to 85 per cent of Burundian Tutsi resided in the province known as Bututsi and very small numbers elsewhere (1970: 25). Rwanda was characterized by a greater centralization of power; only the Banyiginya lineage held the kingship. In Burundi, according to Lemarchand, there were two groups of Tutsi, 'the 'low-caste' Tutsi-Hima and the 'upper-caste' Tutsi-Banyaruguru (1970: 23). There were also 'princes of the blood' or *ganwa* in Burundi, whose power rivalled that of the king.

> This greater variety of status groups ranging from prince to commoner, is one major reason why in the past Burundi society was relatively free of racial tensions; just as the degrees of social distance within the Tutsi stratum were at times far more perceptible than between Tutsi and Hutu, the distance between them and the princely families was equally if not more conspicuous.
>
> (Lemarchand, 1970: 24).

In contrast to the above view, Chretien claims that the role of colonialist ideology and colonial administration was crucial in imparting an elan to events in Burundi from which it has not been able to extricate itself.

The fundamental political divisions from which all Africa suffers have taken the cruel form of internal racism here during the last fifty years. This was legitimated by colonial 'scientific' discourse and internalized by the first literate generations.

(Chretien, 1991: p. 460)

Instead of attempting to assess the relative degree of responsibility of colonialism as opposed to post-colonial internal politics in Burundi, for Chretien the more important facet of the problem is to keep social analysis from collapsing into racial analysis.

The core of the problem in Burundi lies in the socio-racial confusion that characterizes both analyses and grievances. [. . .] The reduction of all social problems to that of ethnicity and the conflation of the ethnic categories with social classes constitutes an ideological and political trap which has resulted in massive violence (in 1965 and in 1972), panic, and hate in Burundian society.

(Chretien, 1991: 459)

Exploring all the ins and outs of this debate would divert us from our purpose. Lemarchand is certainly correct in insisting upon the sociocultural and political specificities of Rwanda and Burundi, but it is also clear, even if this may have had less importance in Burundi, that the Hamitic stereotypes have been operative here as well. From a recent book by Liisa Malkki, *Purity and Exile*, we see that Hamitic themes emerge in the speech of Burundian refugees. During 1985–86 the author interviewed two groups of Burundian Hutu refugees who had fled to Tanzania after the predominately Tutsi army massacred over 100,000 Hutu in 1972–73. One group of refugees resided in Mishamo camp under the direction of Tanzanian authorities while the other consisted of people living in the township of Kigoma.

Hutu refugees within Mishamo camp presented an idealized version of Burundi history – one that the author terms a 'mythico-history'. In it the refugees opposed their presumed morally superior claims to Burundi based on autochthony to the morally inferior claims of Tutsi, who were said to have been more recent immigrants to the area – sixteenth century A.D. as opposed to first century

B.C. (Malkki, 1995: 60–1). The Hutu claim of authochthony acknow-
ledges the prior residence of Twa, but explains that Hutu and Twa
lived peacefully together and intermarried with one another. In
contrast to the attempt to attenuate difference between Hutu and
Twa, the Mishamo refugees insisted upon difference wherever the
Tutsi were concerned referring to them as 'imposters' or as 'a race
of foreigners' (Malkki, 1995: 60–1).

Pursuant to the strategy of emphasizing rather than obscuring
difference, one of the Mishamo refugees had an interesting interpretation of the school book version of the legend of Gatutsi,
Gahutu, and Gatwa (discussed above in reference to Rwanda).

> Kigwa and his Three Sons
> In primary school [in Burundi], we had a little book of readings. This
> book was full of lies – made by the Tutsi – [in order] to hide their
> native country which they had left, so that the Hutu would not know
> the national country of the Tutsi. [. . .] The text said: 'Once, Kigwa, a
> man descended from the sky. He had three sons: Rututsi, Ruhutu, and
> Rutwa. The first son was called Rututsi. Why? The second, Ruhutu.
> Why? The third who was the last was called Rutwa.' At that moment,
> we were obliged to read this text, and to learn it by heart – ip-so fac-to!
> I ask myself: Kigwa, he descended from the sky . . . ? This [story] was
> some of the malignity of the Tutsi so that the Hutu would not find out
> where the Tutsi came from. That they stay with their lies, these Tutsi
> coming from the sky, sons of Kigwa!
>   (Malkki, 1995: 65–6)

This legend should be considered in relation to the comments made
earlier with regard to Kigwa and Kanyarwanda. During the late
1950s in Rwanda, Hutu politicians were attempting to advance their
aims by claiming common descent of the three ethnic groups from
Kanyarwanda. High-level Tutsi monarchists and defenders of the
status quo countered this strategy by saying that their forefather
was Kigwa, that Kigwa was anterior to Kanyarwanda, and that the
three ethnic groups were already in existence by the time of Kanyarwanda. For these Tutsi, common descent was impossible.

Here, in the Burundi instance, we see a sharp contrast with the
Rwandan case. Burundian Hutu refugees discount the story of
Kigwa and common descent of the ethnic groups as a Tutsi fabrica-
tion. Although the official position of the Burundian government
in 1972 was to deny ethnicity by insisting upon a single origin of
the three groups and by making no mention of ethnic affiliation

on the national identity card, in actuality this strategy served merely
to dissimulate ethnic discrimination. By 1972 the army and the
government were largely controlled by Tutsi. It made sense in the
Burundian case for Hutu politicians to assail the single origin story,
just as, in the late 1950s in Rwanda, it made sense for Hutu politicians to support the theory of a single origin. In Rwanda or
Burundi whether one supports or denies the theory of a single
origin or the theory of separate origins depends upon the historical
circumstances.

Once again, though, it needs to be emphasized that the stories
of the Mishamo refugees echo familiar Hamitic themes and in doing
so betray probable links to Hutu extremism, a point that Malkki
overlooks. Tutsi are invaders from the north who migrate southward
along the Nile and gain political ascendancy over Hutu through
'trickery' and 'malignity' (Malkki, 1995: 68). Terms like 'trickery'
and 'malignity', which are often used by these Hutu refugees, do
not refute the Hamitic assertion of superior Tutsi intelligence, they
merely invert its moral valuation. When Tutsi gave their cattle to
Hutu, it was only to trick Hutu into servitude. 'Our ancient parents
were deceived by the Tutsi', the refugees claim (Malkki, 1995: 69).
It is as if the refugees were saying, 'Yes, the Tutsi are smarter than
us, but they use their intelligence for evil.'

Another cluster of refugee themes centres upon the body and
the sociomoral valences associated with typical Tutsi features. Here
the Mishamo camp residents describe Tutsi as being 'taller', 'thinner',
and 'of a beautiful stature' (Malkki, 1995: 79). Malkki claims that,
'It was also universally agreed that the Tutsi were more "beautiful"
than the Hutu', (Malkki, 1995: 79). Although more 'beautiful',
the Tutsi 'cannot do painful chores' (Malkki, 1995: 79). Tutsi are
depicted as 'lazy'. 'They eat our sweat', say the refugees (Malkki,
1995: 80). Furthermore, Tutsi use the beauty of their women as
another means of tricking Hutu into servitude. 'The Tutsi girls are
much more beautiful than the Hutu girls', (Malkki, 1995: 82). The
refugees explain that when a Hutu man marries a Tutsi girl, she
and her parents will trick the Hutu into working and providing for
all of them (Malkki, 1995: 83). These remarks, made by Hutu victims
of the Burundian Tutsi army, have to be considered in juxtaposition
to the remarks made by Rwandan Hutu extremists on the RTLM
radio (see Chapter 4). The alleged superior beauty of Tutsi, a trait
evoked decades earlier by Father van den Burgt in his Kirundi
dictionary, appears to be something that is concurred to by many

Burundian and Rwandan Hutu be they victims or persecutors. Of course, all ways of assessing human physical attractiveness or sexual allure are necessarily culture-bound; what is remarkable here is the degree to which the European established aesthetic has been internalized. The transferral of this aesthetic from Europeans to Burundians could obviously only have occurred through the mediation of Hamitic themes.

Malkki notes that many elements of the 'mythico-history' employed by the Mishamo refugees have European colonial origins:

> The refugees seem to have been influenced on this point ... by the old 'Hamitic hypothesis,' a long discredited academic theory which saw the centralized kingdoms of central Africa as the work of an 'advanced race' of invading 'Hamites'.

(Malkki 1995: 68)

Nevertheless, the author eschews the project of attempting to discriminate between true and false elements in Hutu mythico-histories (Malkki, 1995: 104).

It is at this point in Malkki's otherwise fascinating description and analysis of the experience of Burundian Hutu refugees that I am forced to disagree. Although the book is inspired by Foucault's interest in the 'technologies of power', one important Foucaultian point that the author partly misses is that power acts most efficiently when it acts without being seen – from the inside of our beings rather than by the external coercive mechanisms of the polity. Rwanda and Burundi offer the example of a power/knowledge nexus acting as much from within the consciousness of individual social actors as through the institutions of state power, although obviously these have acted as well. Hamitism has provided much of the psychological impetus behind the acts of violence in Rwanda and Burundi. Like racialist schemes elsewhere in the world, it has ranked groups of people according to civilizational level, intelligence, and physical beauty. It has elevated some and demoted others, dooming the latter to the perennial resentment of their presumed inferiority. One of the reasons why people in this area of the world have killed their compatriots by the hundreds of thousands is because of the enduring psychological damage that has been done to them by the Hamitic hypothesis.

Conclusion

Although Hamitic themes have been internalized almost to the point where they 'go without saying', edging ever closer to the pole of 'hegemony' and slipping away from the pole of 'ideology' (Comaroff and Comaroff, 1992: 28–9), they have not yet reached that point; they can still be subjected to argument and contestation. However difficult it may be to disabuse people of Hamitic beliefs, the attempt must be made. It is incumbent upon the scholarly community, especially those who are Rwandan and Burundian, to dissect Hamitic theories and subject them to the scrutiny of new evidence and new argumentation. But refutation will not proceed very far if it is confined to the level of discourse alone. Nor will deconstructing the concept of race put an end to racism. In the case of Rwanda and Burundi, with its persisting potential for enormous human catastrophe, we achieve nothing by refusing to challenge those among our Rwandan and Burundian interlocutors who wittingly or unwittingly mistake the facts of their history. Discredited in academic circles though it may be, Hamitism is still capable of motivating the thoughts and actions of thousands of Rwandans and Burundians.

The question then becomes how we can best go about accomplishing this objective. I find much in Franche's essay with which to agree: much depends upon what one means by the terms 'Tutsi', 'Hutu', and 'Twa'; much depends on the terms' historicity and their salience given other possible markers of identity such as clanic, regional, or economic labels. Nevertheless, in contrast to Franche, I do not believe that students of central Africa should avoid the question of biogenetic and geographic origins altogether. Doing so risks putting us back in the realm of the 'single origins hypothesis', which, far from preventing ethnic domination, has been used in Burundi to obfuscate and uphold the nature of Tutsi domination. We need to engage the biological and physical anthropological evidence. If we do not, greater is the likelihood that such findings will be selectively appropriated by Rwandan and Burundian racial extremists and put to ideological use. As scholars we can neither ignore, nor selectively use those findings of biological or physical anthropological research that suit our ideological purposes, however laudable those purposes might be. Biological determinism is the problem, not biology; 'scientism', not science. It is not the question of origins *per se* that has generated racism in central Africa

– it is the moral evaluation of people's putative origins. These are not the same things.

Even if it can be demonstrated that present day Rwandan and Burundian Tutsi manifest genetic affinities to people in north-eastern Africa who are Afro-Asiatic speakers (Excoffier et al., 1987), this does not mean that Tutsi were 'invaders from the north'. From Schoenbrun's work, one can conclude that Afro-Asiatic-speaking pastoralists preceded the arrival of Bantu speaking peoples in the general area of interlacustrine Africa. Although it is impossible to know for certain whether these early inhabitants can be considered the direct precursors of today's Tutsi, this finding certainly impugns the Hamitic assertion of Bantu speakers' prior residence in the area followed by a 'Hamitic invasion'. At any rate, when one is talking about movements of peoples that appear to have taken centuries, if not millennia, is it really possible to speak of any single group as 'invaders' or 'conquerors?'

Other evidence points to the social mutability of the categories Hutu, Tutsi, and Twa. Is it possible that the social identities associated with these terms were malleable in some instances, but yet usually transmitted from one generation to the next without much change? Is it possible that the either/or, 'achieved' versus 'ascriptive' dichotomy of an earlier sociology oversimplifies the case just as the primordialism versus constructionism dichotomy does today? It must be noted that it is logically possible for many people categorized as Tutsi to have north-east African origins while also admitting that many people so classified have been socially transformed into Tutsi and do not have north-east African origins. These possibilities are not mutually exclusive. By what criterion, other than our own ideological preferences, does it have to be all one way or the other?

Public attention to and debate over the lingering force of the Hamitic hypothesis must be encouraged in Rwanda and Burundi. Rwandans and Burundians must lead this debate. Just as in South Africa where South African thinkers, writers, and artists of diverse ethnicities examined apartheid theories, criticized them, refuted their alleged factuality, and subjected the theories to irony, so must Rwandans and Burundians examine their lingering commitment to Hamitism. To do this they need to be exposed to all the evidence regarding the Hamitic hypothesis, favourable or unfavourable. They are certainly capable of judging this evidence on its own merits. Their awareness of the various ways by which their intellectuals and political leaders have manipulated Hamitic themes and images, bringing death, exile, and misery to thousands of victims, should then become apparent. This evidence is certainly available to academics, but it has yet to be effectively disseminated to Rwandans and Burundians at the grass roots level. Media for public debate exist in the form of radio and television in central Africa, yet as far as I know this debate has never been launched.

Finally, Rwandans and Burundians, Tutsi and Hutu, have to re-examine their attitudes to the Twa. Some sources estimate that thousands of Twa also died during the 1994 genocide in Rwanda. From all indications racism against Twa is not something that was imported from Europe, yet it has probably contributed to the more virulent forms of racism between Tutsi and Hutu. As history else-where in the world has shown, it is not possible to discriminate against a single group without that racism affecting all other groups. Racism does not condemn one group and one group only to dimin-ished status, leaving all others alone. It draws moral distinctions between polar extremes and then creates as many categories between the extremes as appear locally necessary.

Ultimately Rwandans and Burundians have to assume responsi-bility for their history and for the social arrangements that charac-terize their present forms of governance. This does not mean forgetting the colonialist and all the damage that he has left in his wake. On the contrary, central Africans need to discuss colonialism in all the media that are at their disposal. Yet central Africans must also realize, and never forget, that colonialism is still among them. This colonialism no longer takes the obvious form of a white face, the obvious form of a colonial administrator, or the obvious form of a colonial office. This colonialism is more subtle and more difficult to overcome, for it is in the hearts and minds of every ethnic extremist, every Tutsi and Hutu and Twa, who imagines him or herself superior or who feels the need through the force of arms to overcome an imagined inferiority. It is this decolonization that has not yet occurred in Rwanda and Burundi and that violence can only perpetuate and never erase. It is only the decolonization of these beliefs and attitudes that will put an end to the endless cycle of see-saw killing that has characterized relations between groups. It is only through this kind of decolonization that Rwandans and Burundians will imagine and become the new species of being that Fanon calls for in *The Wretched of the Earth*. Yet it is also here that, in rejoining Fanon, I must also part company with him, for the violence in central Africa has so far not accomplished this goal and it is difficult to imagine how it ever could. Far from being psychologically liberating, far from helping to create a truly new and post-colonial human, violence in central Africa has only served to perpetuate a sense of victimization on both sides and to harden ethnic stereotypes. The next phase of decolonization in Rwanda and Burundi must come from within people's beings. It must be peaceful yet at the same time bring about a revolutionary change in the way Gatutsi, Gahutu, and Gatwa view each other. They must see that only as partners can they keep the milk pot full.

Notes

1. My translation. From *Les Damnés de la Terre*, Frantz Fanon, 1968, Paris, Librairie Francois Maspero.
2. The patron–client relationship known as *ubuhake* has been classically depicted as one where a Tutsi patron (*umushebuja*) gives a Hutu client (*umugaragu*) a cow (Maquet, 1954). In exchange the Hutu client was expected to labour for his patron or in some cases serve him militarily when called upon to do so. In addition, all female offspring of the cow were to be returned to the patron whereas the client could keep all male calves. In more recent years Maquet's description has been challenged by scholars who claim that the geographic distribution of *ubuhake* was limited in pre-colonial and early colonial Rwanda, and that there were other patron–client relationships that were more egalitarian than *ubuhake* (Newbury, 1988). Although *ubuhake* came to symbolize Hutu social inferiority to Tutsi in the waning years of the colonial regime and was often criticized by politicized Hutu, *ubuhake* may have been more an artefact of an already engendered inferiority based upon control over land rather than the generative mechanism of this inequality (Vidal, 1969).
3. It is difficult to apply the term 'racism' in the classical biologically determinist sense to this discrimination although in its effects it certainly seems to resemble it. Twa were denigrated by both other groups, although, as mentioned earlier in this text, some individual Twa may have been singled out for special attention and advantageous treatment by Rwandan kings as in Rwabugiri's case where a few Twa may have been elevated to relatively high rank and given Tutsi women as wives.
4. Although usually considered an all-Tutsi organization, according to Alison des Forges in a speech presented at the National Holocaust Musuem in Washington DC in August 1994, 20–30 per cent of the RPF's soldiers were Hutu.

5. As part of the Arusha accords, one battalion of RPF soldiers, to protect RPF political representatives, was permitted to stay in the Remera section of Kigali at the CND building. I was able to visit them in the company of two acquantances who were RPF supporters.

CHAPTER THREE

The Cosmology of Terror

Introduction

In light of recent criticism that the concept of culture has been overly reified, that no human group has ever been characterized by a single coherent set of norms, beliefs, and attitudes and that there are no such things as rules, only negotiations, much anthropological analysis of late has returned to a kind of methodological and ontological individualism. Eschewing homeostatic 'social structures' and the decoding of 'deep structures', many anthropologists have turned in the direction of analytic approaches that emphasize diverse subjectivities, multivocality, and multiple interpretation (Clifford and Marcus, 1986). These latter claim that anthropologists of intellectualist bent ignore or diminish the subject, that they depict social actors as mere bearers of their culture rather than its shapers. History, in the hands of the intellectualists, also loses its dynamism as all becomes reduced to the recapitulation of the same or very similar structures of thought. Yet, in the other camp, among those who insist upon difference, many appear bent upon abolishing the concept of culture altogether. In earlier versions of methodological individualism, as in transactionalism and rational choice theory, individuals everywhere seemed to think and to act alike. Like *Homo economicus*, social actors exercised their free will, maximizing utility, and choosing courses of action according to perceived cost/benefit ratios. Culture was additive, an aggregate generated by the sum total of individuals' choices (Barth, 1959). Although more recent individualist approaches often criticize the presumed universality of a maximizing person, culture has nevertheless become fragmented into a cacophony of multiple and conflicting discourses in which the subject often disappears in a cloud of complexity and incoherence (Ortner, 1995: 183).

99

Yet it could also be argued that, in the latter case, the notion of the subject is a culture-bound one, grounded in individualist and egalitarian assumptions that 'celebrate difference and interpretation' (Kapferer, 1989: 193). Culture according to this strain of thought has become epiphenomenal, a dependent variable, a mere instrument in the political or economic struggle rather than the ideational crucible in which these struggles find their significance. In earlier versions individualist assumptions were explicitly stated; more frequently today they are not. In either case cultural voluntarism and its more recent avatars continue to sound particularly Western in perspective.

Attempting to wend the way between an overly reified notion of culture and the concept's effective negation has presented anthropology with a formidable challenge; neither side appears to be completely right, nor completely wrong. Yet both sides are loath to consider the possibility that the analytic strength that one might derive from an axiomatically unified set of presuppositions may also be a weakness. Perhaps this is nowhere more apparent than in the domain of political anthropology where scholars like John Gledhill are insisting that, to understand the political behaviour of élites in the non-Western world, one must understand not only the varied self-interests of social actors and the multiplicity of discourses they construct, but also the cultural frameworks in which actions occur and that render these actions meaningful (Gledhill, 1994). Indeed the members of such élites are playing to win, but the parameters of the contest – its rules, its moves, its spoils, even its modes of transgression – are largely culturally determined. We cannot assume that the manifestations of power in the world are everywhere the same, for as Gledhill shows, there are profound differences in political cultures. Economic and political behaviour outside the Western context is unlikely to be understood without some sense of these differences.

Gledhill's point should also be considered in relation to similar findings made in the field of ethno-psychology and ethno-psychiatry. Individuals may make reasoned choices within frameworks of perceived punishment and reward, but the individual is always a socially constructed entity and the frameworks of perception and motivation within which he or she operates are cultural in nature (Kakar, 1982). We cannot assume, in the manner of behaviourism, that individual choices follow a universal logic within readily discernible parameters of tension reduction and pain avoidance.

Gledhill's work builds upon that of Michel Foucault, Pierre Bourdieu, and Bruce Kapferer. From Foucault, Gledhill pursues the insight that power involves not only the negative aspect of constraining the volition of others, but a positive aspect. Social actors in specific cultural and historical circumstances are constructed to think and to act in certain ways (Gledhill, 1994: 126). We need to understand the construction of the subject from the inside out in order to understand power in its fullest dimensions and this, Gledhill argues, might best be accomplished by building upon conventional anthropological studies of symbolism (Gledhill, 1994: 126). To this end, Gledhill cites the work of Pierre Bourdieu and his use of the notion of *habitus* and Bruce Kapferer and his use of the notion of ontology. It is to these theorists that I turn in this chapter in attempting to understand some of the cultural dimensions of what occurred during the 1994 genocide in Rwanda where up to one million people were killed – one seventh of the country's population. Although much of what I will concern myself with in this paper involves the politics of ethnicity in Rwanda, my major point is that we cannot make sense of the Rwandan tragedy through political and historical analysis alone, although these are certainly necessary. Indeed, something political and historical happened in Rwanda in 1994, but something cultural happened as well. The violence which occurred there, and which continues to a lesser extent today, was not merely symptomatic of a fragmented social order succumbing to externally and internally generated tensions. Beneath the aspect of disorder there lay an eerie order to the violence of 1994 Rwanda. Many of the actions followed a cultural patterning, a structured and structuring logic, as individual Rwandans lashed out against a perceived internal other that threatened in their imaginations both their personal integrity and the cosmic order of the state. It was overwhelmingly Tutsi who were the sacrificial victims in what in many respects was a massive ritual of purification, a ritual intended to purge the nation of 'obstructing beings' as the threat of obstruction was imagined through a Rwandan ontology that situates the body politic in analogous relation to the individual human body.

As I will attempt to show in this chapter, many of the representations concerning bodily integrity that I encountered in popular medicine during fieldwork in Rwanda in 1983–5, 1987, and 1993–4, emerged in the techniques of physical cruelty employed by Hutu extremists during the genocide. But there was no simple cultural determinism to the Rwandan genocide. I do not advance the argument that the political events of 1994 were in any way caused by these symbols nor by Rwandan 'culture', conceived of in a simplistic and culturalist way in the manner of Goldhagen's controversial analysis of the Nazi genocide (1996). These representations operated as much during times of peace as at times of war. The 'generative schemes' – the logical substrate of oppositions, analogies, and homologies – upon which the representations were based constituted for many Rwandans, a practical, everyday sense of body, self, and others. Because these 'generative schemes' were internalized during early socialization, they took on a nearly unconscious or 'goes without saying' quality (Bourdieu, 1990: 67–79). Although many Rwandan social actors embodied this knowledge, they never explicitly verbalized it. It could not, therefore, be ideological in any direct or simple way, despite the fact that Hutu extremists made use of political symbols that bore the imprint of the generative schemes.

The symbolic system I describe here takes root in representations that go back at least to the nineteenth century and elements of it can be discerned in the rituals of Rwandan sacred kingship practised during pre-colonial and early colonial times. In that sense much of this symbolism is relatively old. It must be emphasized, however, that neither the symbolic nor the normative structures of early Rwanda were faithfully and mechanically reproduced during the events of 1994. Clearly both manifest continuity with and divergence from the past. The context in which the symbols appeared was quite contemporary, for the discourse of Hutu ethnic nationalism with its accompanying characteristics of primordialism, biological determinism, essentialism, and racism are nothing if not modern. In that sense the ideology of Rwandan Hutu extreme nationalism bears much in common with German National Socialism and other twentieth-century sectarian extremisms and some authors have alluded to possible comparisons between the Rwandan genocide and others (Prunier, 1995). Nevertheless, beyond the similarities manifest in the various instances of massive state terror that have occurred during the twentieth century, one must also address the specificities of each event.

Other Scholarship on Violence and its Relation to Rwanda

The point that violence may be culturally or symbolically conditioned is not new. In a work edited by Nordstrom and J.-A. Martin (1992), the authors remark 'that repression and resistance generated at the national level are often inserted into the local reality in culturally specific ways' (1992: 5). Yet elsewhere in the volume the contributors seldom live up to this promise, showing more that violence and terror split communities along fault lines that can be demonstrated by social analysis rather than that violence follows culturally specific modalities. Coming closer to this point, Michael Taussig describes the narrative forms that accompanied the emergence of a 'culture of terror' in the rubber collecting regions of early twentieth-century Colombia (1984). In Taussig's book *Shamanism, Colonialism and the Wild Man*, he again takes up the subject of the Putumayo violence committed against native Americans as reported by the English investigator, Roger Casement:

> From the accounts of Casement and Timerman it is also obvious that torture and terror are ritualized art forms and that, far from being spontaneous, *sui generis,* and an abandonment of what are often called the values of civilization, such rites of terror have a deep history deriving power and meaning from those very values.
>
> (1987: 133)

Taussig analyses colonialist discourse and underscores the manichienne nature of its explicit opposition, savagery versus civilization. He unmasks the bitterly ironic process of mimesis that was at work when rubber company overseers both imagined into existence and became the savage in gratuitous acts of terrorism and torture. His point that the forms of violence practised in Pututmayo logically extended the ideological and normative patterns of colonizing culture rather than being a departure from them, is well taken, yet one is left to wonder from the pithy statement cited above whether there might be more to this claim than discourse analysis alone is capable of revealing, specific art and ritual forms from colonizing cultures that Taussig might have analysed and that tell us something about European preoccupation with the demonic, and the tendency to project fears of it onto convenient scapegoats, whether internal or external.

Rwanda, during the years leading up to the genocide of 1994, became a 'culture of terror' and there were a number of narratives in circulation that Hutu extremists used to justify violence against the Tutsi. These included narratives of the sort: 'Tutsi are invaders from Ethiopia', 'we carry the Tutsi on our backs', 'Tutsi are lazy', 'Tutsi are shrewd and conniving', 'They use the beauty of their women to seduce us into working for them', and others. Many of the narratives of Hutu extremism that I encountered in 1994 Rwanda or in earlier fieldwork during the 1980s, closely resemble the 'mythico-histories' discussed by Liisa Malki in her book, *Purity and Exile*, among Burundian Hutu refugees in a Tanzanian camp (1995). Many of the narratives take root in the early colonial histori-ography that depicted Tutsi as intelligent 'Hamite' invaders who conquered the slower-Witter 'Bantu' Hutu. The selective use of this historiography leads one to believe that the narratives, far from being recent creations, date from late colonial times and form something of a substrate for the ideology of Hutu ethnic extremism.

More germane to the purposes of this chapter, Malkki's book also describes the techniques of violence meted out against Hutu victims in Burundi during that country's genocidal events of 1972–3. These techniques included: impaling men from anus to head or mouth, impaling women from vagina to mouth, cutting foetuses from their mothers' wombs, forcing parents to eat the flesh of their children, forcing a parent and child to commit incest by roping them together in a sexual position prior to killing them (Malkki, 1995: 87–98). She raises interesting questions with regard to the forms that the violence took and the accounts about it:

> it is relevant to ask how the accounts of atrocity come to assume thematic form, how they become formulaic. [. . .] The first thing to be examined is the extent to which the techniques of cruelty actually used were already meaningful, already mythico-historical.
>
> (Malkki, 1995: 94)

> One need only inspect reports from Amnesty International and other organizations whose main purpose is to document human-rights viola-tions to begin to see that the conventionalization of torture, killing, and other forms of violence occurs not only routinely but in patterned forms in the contemporary world. Torture, in particular, is a highly symbolized form of violence. At this level, it can be said that historical actors mete out death and perpetrate violence mythically.
>
> (Malkki, 1995: 94)

Nevertheless, despite the assertion that the violence in Burundi was already 'mythico-historical' and that it was patterned – an assertion that would seem to cry out for ritual and symbolic analysis – Malkki's analysis does not pursue this avenue other than in general comments about the attempt on the part of Burundian Tutsi to humiliate and to dehumanize their Hutu victims, to render them powerless, to destroy the life of their future generations, or to reverse natural processes (Malkki, 1995: 98). While all her statements are true, my contention is that Malkki's comments leave the ontological dimension of extremist violence in Burundi and Rwanda untouched. Many of the same forms of violence, the same techniques of cruelty were encountered in Rwanda during the 1994 genocide: impaling, evisceration of pregnant women, forced incest, forced cannibalism of family members. There were also other forms of torture and terror in Rwanda that may or may not have occurred in Burundi: the widespread killing of victims at roadblocks erected on highways, roads, streets, or even on small footpaths; the severing of the Achilles' tendons of human and cattle victims; emasculation of men; and breast oblation of women.

In order to make these forms of violence comprehensible in terms of the local symbolism, it is first necessary to understand, as Pierre Clastres instructs us, that social systems inscribe 'law' onto the bodies of their subjects (1974). Occasionally physical torture is an integral part of the ritual process intended to inculcate society's norms and values. Using *The Penal Colony* by way of illustration Clastres states, 'Here Kafka designates the body as a writing surface, a surface able to receive the law's readable text'.[1] Clastres expands upon this by considering the cognitive role of the body in ritual, 'The body mediates in the acquisition of knowledge; this knowledge inscribes itself upon the body'.[2] And ritual, Clastres emphasizes, involves the mnemonics of ordeal and pain, '[. . .] society prints its mark on the body of its youth. [. . .] The mark acts as an obstacle to forgetting; the body carries the traces of a memory printed upon it; *the body is a memory*'.[3]

Although the rituals of which Clastres speaks are rites of passage, specifically, male initiation rituals in so-called 'primitive societies,' I believe that many of his insights could be fruitfully extended to the actions of modern nation-states, particularly actions of a violent and terroristic nature. It is here that Clastres presages Bruce Kapferer's work on nationalism, particularly with regard to the mythico-ritual dimensions of nationalism as these delineate an analogic space relating the body to the body politic. As Kapferer states: 'I have shown that in the myths and rites of evil, as in the legends of history, the order of the body is identified with and produced within the order of the state' (1988: 78). Kapferer shows that the passions, violence, and intolerance that characterize modern nationalism cannot be understood solely through the analysis of the associated political pragmatics. Nor can these passions be interpreted in purely psychological terms, as simply the tension-dissipating response to psychological stress generated by disorder and rapid social change. In order to understand the passions of modern nationalism, as well as the violence and terror unleashed upon the bodies of its sacrificial victims, we need to understand its ontological dimensions.

Building upon Benedict Anderson, Kapferer makes the point that, 'Nationalism makes the political religious and places the nation above politics' (1988: 1). He then proceeds to analyse Sinhalese and Australian nationalisms, which, although quite different in their specific ontologies, are both constitutive of being and personhood. Condensed within these ontologies are the 'myths, legends, and other traditions to which these nationalisms accord value' (Kapferer, 1988: 6). Further on in the book he describes the pre-reflective dimensions of ontology:

> it describes the fundamental principles of a being in the world and the orientation of such a being toward the horizons of its experience. It is an ontology confined within the structure of certain myths and, as I have shown, it is an ontology that governs the constitution and reconstitution of being in some rituals.
>
> (Kapferer, 1988: 79–80)

Borrowing from Louis Dumont's work, Kapferer describes Australian nationalism as 'individualistic and egalitarian,' that of Sri Lanka as 'hierarchical and encompassing'.[4] He also describes, in both instances, what these specific nationalisms posit as potentially destructive to the cosmic order of the state and malevolent to the person. In the Sri Lankan case, malevolence takes the form of resistance to the hierarchical, encompassing Buddhist state. Tamils may live peacefully in Sri Lanka but only as subordinated, encompassed, internal others. In the Australian case, malevolence takes the form of an arbitrary state contemptuous of, or indifferent to, issues of personal autonomy and integrity (Kapferer, 1988: 7).

Democracy and Hierarchy in Rwanda

Rwandan nationalism more closely approaches the 'hierarchical, encompassing' type that Kapferer describes, despite its frequent appeals to democratic values. In monarchical Rwanda, the state was a hierarchical and encompassing order much of whose potency was embodied in the person of the Tutsi king or *mwami*. After the 'Hutu revolution' of 1960, dictatorial power was vested in the person of the Hutu president. Nevertheless, the ideology of Rwanda's Hutu élite after 1960 emphasized democracy and egalitarianism. Of course what was implied by this ideology was tyranny of the majority – at least the tyranny of a small clique within the majority – and systematic monopolization of the state apparatus by this clique and their clients. During the political turmoil of the 1990s and before, Hutu extremist politicians made frequent use of the terms, *rubanda nyamwinshi*, meaning the 'popular mass' or 'rule by the popular mass', and all Rwandans knew that Tutsi were excluded from this group. As long as Tutsi did not object to their 'encompassed' status, which was more politically than economically prejudicial to them, they were left alone. Although they could not hold political office after 1960, they could gain wealth and status through other avenues. It was not until Rwanda's experiment with multi-party democracy, beginning in 1989, that a few Rwandan Tutsi began to hold significant political positions.

In early Rwanda, rituals of the state were conducted under the aegis of the Rwandan sacred king (*mwami*) and his college of ritual specialists (*abiiru*). After the Hutu revolution, nationalist rituals in the modern sense began to be celebrated. Although this was not my area of interest at the time, I occasionally witnessed such celebrations during my first fieldwork in Rwanda during 1983–5. The most common of these occurred every Wednesday afternoon and were called 'animation'. Virtually all Rwandans who were employed by the state and including some who were employees in private enterprises, would be excused from work and would gather together in small groups to sing or chant. Organized into *cellules* and sometimes referring to themselves as *groupes de choc,* the groups would compose and rehearse litanies about the country's development, the accomplishments and qualities of President Habyarimana, or those of the political party that he had founded, the 'Mouvement Revolutionnaire pour le Developpement' (MRND), the country's only political party between 1973 and 1989. On national holidays such as the

5 July celebration of Habyarimana's 1973 coup d'état, such groups would perform publicly competing with one another in the expression of attachment to the nation and to its leader. In these state rituals the values of democracy and equality would be extolled and the overthrow of the Tutsi monarchy and rejection of *ubuhake* would be evoked by way of substantiating the Hutu government's commitment to those values. Nevertheless, it was clear to most Rwandans that President Habyarimana held absolute power and that political and economic advancement were largely dependent upon one's proximity to the President and his coterie. Northern Hutu, especially those who were officers in the Rwandan Army, were the most favoured under the regime, although some Tutsi and southern Hutu had become prosperous in other ways. At the time of my first fieldwork in 1983–5, Rwanda was more divided by class and region than by ethnicity, as the chasm between the military/merchant bourgeoisie and the rural peasantry (95 per cent of the population) continued to grow.

Although it was ultimately along ethnic lines that the Rwandan social fabric tore asunder during the genocide of 1994, this was not a foregone conclusion. After 1990 many events orchestrated by supporters of the President and the two political parties that were most avidly racialist in ideology – the MRND and the more extreme CDR (Comité pour le Defense de la Republique) – subverted existing political alliances between Hutu and Tutsi opponents of the regime and precluded others from forming that might have prevented the genocide. Several key people who appealed to both southern Hutu and Tutsi were assassinated. One such assassination, that of Felicien Gatabazi, arguably Rwanda's most popular political leader and head of an ethnically mixed party, the Parti Social Democrate (PSD), occurred one evening (25 January 1994) so close to my home in Kigali that I heard the three bursts of automatic rifle fire that killed him. My most informed Rwandan acquaintances at the time claimed that members of Habyarimana's élite Presidential Guard had carried out the assassination. Gatabazi's party had been attempting to forge an alliance between peasants in southern Rwanda and liberal entrepreneurs and intellectuals of both ethnicities in the cities of Kigali and Butare. The party vehemently opposed the ethnic rift that the MRND and the CDR appeared bent upon deepening. Following Gatabazi's assassination the depth of anger of PSD supporters was so profound that the next day, Hutu peasants in southern Rwanda fortuitously spotted, then pursued, the leader of the extremist CDR, Martin Bucyana, in his car *en route* to Kigali from Butare. Furious over Gatabazi's murder, they eventually managed to stop the car. Then with hoes and machetes, they murdered all three occupants, including Bucyana, his brother-in-law, and the car's driver. The incident underlined the fact that many Rwandans in the south were more incensed about regional favouritism and domination by the Habyarimana clique than they were about ethnicity. For two full days after the CDR leader's death, supporters of the regime fomented violence in Kigali in which Tutsi and PSD party members were specifically targeted; virtually everyone in the city stayed home from work (*ville morte*). A few people were killed; many more were intimidated into abandoning their houses in Kigali or coerced into paying 'insurance' to *Interahamwe* militia members. On the third day after Gatabazi's death, normalcy abruptly returned as if by command; the lesson to those who did not support the ethnicist line of the MRND and the CDR had been conveyed.

Fieldwork in Rwanda

I have lived for several extended periods in Rwanda. For eighteen months, during 1983–5, I studied Rwandan practices of popular medicine. Later I returned there during the summer months of 1987 to do follow-up work on popular medicine. In recent years some of my research in Rwanda has taken an applied direction. In May of 1993, for example, I journeyed to Rwanda for a one-month period in order to serve as a consultant for Family Health International (FHI), a subcontractor for USAID. I participated in organizing an AIDS prevention project that was to be funded by USAID. It was again as an employee of FHI that I returned to Rwanda in late October 1993 to begin AIDS-related behavioural research. Although I had hoped to live in Rwanda for at least two years and to conduct research on sexual behaviour and HIV transmission, this proved to be impossible due to the renewed outbreak of hostilities that followed the assassination of President Habyarimana on 6 April 1994.

During my last period of fieldwork in Rwanda, I witnessed the country's slow but inexorable slide into chaos. After several attempts to install the broad-based transitional government failed, I became keenly aware that the Habyarimana regime and the MRND had not been serious about the peace accords signed with the Rwandan Patriotic Front in Arusha during August of 1993. Encouraged by the unwavering support of French backers, Habyarimana and his supporters were treating the accords as 'just a piece of paper'. During the five months or so that I resided in Rwanda, violence gradually escalated. Acts of terrorism became more common, *Interahamwe* militia members grew bolder in their attacks upon civilians, and there were several assassinations.

It had not been my intention to study or to witness the degradation of the political situation in Rwanda. Originally I had hoped to further my explorations into the popular perceptions of sickness and in particular, of sexually transmitted diseases. My job with FHI in Rwanda was to help adapt HIV prevention and intervention strategies to local social and cultural realities. I had been chosen for this task because FHI was aware of my previous research on popular medicine and, in particular, of my research emphasizing the importance of bodily fluids in the local cognitive models of sickness. These were obviously important because bodily fluids transmit HIV, and preventive strategies generally focus on 'barrier methods' such as condom use, which impede their passage. From previous research in Rwanda, I had advanced the hypothesis that impeding the passage of bodily fluids between partners was locally perceived as unhealthy and that this resistance would have to be overcome in culturally appropriate ways in order to promote safer sex practices (Taylor, 1989).

Rwandan Symbolism and the Body

Although the connection between local cognitive models of illness and ethnic nationalism may appear distant at first glance, their relatedness lies at the level of myth and symbol. The Rwandan body is, following Clastres, an imprinted body – imprinted with the condensed memories of history. Following Kapferer, it is only through myth and symbol that we can grasp the logic of these condensed memories and their significance to Rwandan Hutu nationalism because the latter derived much of its passionate force from a mythic logic constitutive of being and personhood:

> Broadly, the legitimating and emotional force of myth is not in the events as such but in the logic that conditions their significance. This

is so when the logic is also vital in the way human actors are culturally given to constituting a self in the everyday routine world and move out toward others in that world. Mythic reality is mediated by human beings into the worlds in which they live. Where human beings recognize the argument of mythic reality as corresponding to their own personal constitutions – their orientation within and movement through reality - so myth gathers force and can come to be seen as embodying ultimate truth. Myth so enlivened, I suggest, can become imbued with command-ing power, binding human actors to the logical movement of its scheme. In this sense, myth is not subordinated to the interests of the individual or group but can itself have motive force. It comes to define significant experience in the world, experience which in its significance is also conceived of as intrinsic to the constitution of the person. By virtue of the fact that myth engages a reasoning which is also integral to everyday realities, part of the taken-for-granted or 'habitus' [Bourdieu, 1977] of the mundane world, myth can charge the emotions and fire the passions.

(Kapferer, 1988: 46–7)

Nevertheless, in order to understand these mythic and pre-reflective dimensions of ontology, we need to move beyond Kapferer's and Dumont's categories of 'egalitarian and individualistic' versus 'hier-archical and encompassing'. We need to shift analysis to an almost 'molecular' level and to consider the structures of thought that underlie the construction of the moral person in Rwanda and that constitute a specific practical logic of being in the world. These structures must be seen both in their formalist dimension and in specific instances of their use and enactment in everyday social life. Proceeding in this fashion we may then be able to appreciate that, lurking beneath the extraordinary events and violence of the genocide, one perceives the logic of ordinary sociality.

Much of this ordinary, practical logic can be discerned in Rwandan practices related to the body and aimed at maintaining it or restor-ing it to health and integrity. From Rwandan popular medical practices that I observed during the 1980s, I have advanced the hypothesis elsewhere that a root metaphor underlies conceptualiza-tions of the body (Taylor, 1992). Basically these conceptualizations are characterized by an opposition between orderly states of humoral and other flows to disorderly ones.[5] Analogies are constructed that take this opposition as their base and then relate bodily processes to those of social and natural life. In the unfolding of human and natural events, flow/blockage symbolism mediates between physiological, sociological, and cosmological levels of causality. Popular healing aims at restoring bodily flows that have been perturbed by human negligence and malevolence. Bodily fluids such as blood, semen, breast milk, and menstrual blood are a recurrent concern as is the passage of aliments through the digestive tract.[6] Pathological states are characterized by obstructed or excessive flows and perturbations of this sort may signify illness, diminished fertility, or death.

In making the claim that a root metaphor underlies many Rwandan popular medical practices, I am not asserting that all medicine in Rwanda is characterized by a unified set of symbolic or ideational forms. Medicine in Rwanda, as elsewhere in the world, is highly pluralistic. Biomedicine exists alongside popular medicine and in recent years even Chinese medicine has taken hold in Rwanda. Clearly these diverse medical practices as well their ideational bases have become somewhat syncretized over time and there are certainly Rwandan popular healers whose therapies are idiosyncratic to a greater or lesser degree. Rwandan medicine taken as a whole is far from monolithic. Be that as it may, one cannot help but be struck by the number of disorders in popular medicine that are characterized by perturbations in humoral flows. While not every Rwandan imagines illness in the same way, nor does every healer treat it in the same way, the pervasiveness of fluid metaphors certainly seems to indicate that these symbolic patterns characterize the thinking of many people.

Fluid metaphors suffuse Rwandan popular medical practices, yet healers and their patients do not explicitly verbalize them in any local mode of exegesis. The model that I hypothesize for Rwandan popular medicine thus does not appear to be a fully conscious one. This is in sharp contrast with similar 'image schemata' (Johnson, 1987) found elsewhere in the world. For example, in some forms of Indian popular medicine, healers explicitly talk of illness in terms of interrupted flows of *kundalini* (Kakar, 1982). Similarly, in many forms of Chinese popular medicine, concern is expressed about the flow of *qi* through the body; therapeutic measures are taken to direct or unblock *qi* flow (Farquhar, 1994). Despite an apparently less-than-conscious quality in Rwanda, flow/blockage metaphors are imaged and enacted in a diverse array of domains. Although they may be most commonly encountered in popular healing, my research has revealed that similar representations are also present in myths, legends, and the rituals of sacred kingship, and that they involve potencies of various types (Taylor, 1988).

Because of the implicit quality of this symbolism, it is not possible to ascertain the degree to which Rwandans from various regions and of differing ethnicity, gender, or class have or have not internalized it. Although it may be possible in some instances to verify how many people have knowledge of a specific healing procedure or belief (see discussion below), it is impossible to affirm whether this specific knowledge, or lack of it, implies or does not imply adherence to an associated mode of thought. This means that, at a second level of understanding, attention needs to be shifted away from the study of the formal properties of the symbolism, to its various enactments in social life.

Popular Medicine

During my fieldwork in Rwanda in the 1980s, I found that illnesses were often characterized by perceived irregularities in fluid flows and that these tended to have an alimentary or reproductive symptomatic focus. Concern with ordered flows and their proper embodiment was not just implicated in illness, however; it was also implicated in health. From the very moment when a human being enters this world, these metaphors figure prominently in the cultural construction of the person. Practices associated with childbirth, for example, focus upon certain portions of the child's anatomy. Rural Rwandans that I interviewed both in northern and southern Rwanda during the 1980s recounted versions of the following practices.

After giving birth a new mother is secluded for a period of eight days (today this period is often shorter). On the ninth day, the newborn child is presented to other members of the family and local community for the first time (*gusohora umwana*). This rite of passage can only be performed after the baby's body has been examined and found to be free of anal malformations. People at this occasion receive a meal, especially the children present, who are given favourite foods. These children in turn bestow a nickname on the new-born child, which will remain their name for the child. A few months later, the parents give the child another name, but the children continue to call the infant by their name. The meal given to the children is termed *kurya ubunyano*, which means 'to eat the baby's excrement', for Rwandans say that a tiny quantity of the

baby's faecal matter is mixed with the food. This appellation celebrates the fact that the baby's body has been found to be an 'open
conduit', an adequate vessel for perpetuating the process of 'flow'.
In a sense, the baby's faeces are its first gift and the members of
his age class are its first recipients. The children at the ceremony
incorporate the child into their group by symbolically ingesting
one of his bodily products. Their bestowal of a name upon the
infant manifests their acceptance of the child as a social being.

The confirmation of the baby's body as an 'open conduit' is a
socially and morally salient image. If the body were 'closed' at the
anal end, the baby would still be able to ingest, though not to
excrete. The baby would be able to receive, but unable to give up
or pass on that which it had received. In effect, its body would be a
'blocked' conduit or pathway. In social terms, such a body would
be unable to participate in reciprocity, for while it could receive, it
could never give (see also, Beidelman, 1982). That gift-giving and
reciprocity are important aspects where Rwandan concepts of the
moral person are concerned can be discerned from the term for
'man' in Kinyarwanda – *umugabo* – for it is derived from the verb,
kugaba, which means 'to give'. The construction of the moral person
among rural Rwandans is contingent upon the social attestation
that the person properly embodies the physiological attributes that
analogically evoke the capacity to reciprocate. This entails the
capacity to ingest and the capacity to excrete, or, in socio-moral
terms, the capacity to receive and the capacity to give. Consequently,
two portions of the anatomy and their unobstructed connection
are at issue: the mouth and the anus. By analogical extension the
concern with unobstructed connection and unimpeded movement
characterizes earlier Rwandan symbolic thought about the topo-
graphy of the land, its rivers, roads, and pathways in general.

Illnesses treated by Rwandan popular healers are often said
to be caused by the malevolent actions of other human beings.[7]
Sorcerers act upon others by arresting their flow of generative
fluids; they make women sterile and men impotent. They are also
vampirish, anthropophagic beings who parasitically and invisibly
suck away the blood and other vital fluids of their victims. In other
instances sorcerers may induce fluids to leave the body in a torrent
causing symptoms such as haemorrhagic menstruation, the vomiting of blood, projectile vomiting, and violent diarrhoea. There are
thus two basic expressions to symptoms in this model: 'blocked
flow' and 'haemorrhagic flow'.

One example of *uburozi* (spell, poisoning) that is quite commonly
treated by both northern and southern Rwandan healers is that
called *kumanikira amaraso* (to suspend blood). In this poisoning, a
fluid is taken from the intended female victim: either her menstrual
blood (*irungu*), her urine, or some of the fluid exuding from the
vagina after parturition (*igisanza*). The sorcerer takes one of these
fluids, adds medicines to it, puts it in a packet and suspends the
packet from the rafters of a house, or among rocks on the summit
of a high hill where rain cannot touch it. If menstrual blood or
urine has been taken from the woman, she will be unable to conceive. If *igisanza* has been taken from the woman, she will be able
to conceive, but unable to deliver the baby. The foetus will become
turned transversally in the womb or it will move upwards toward
the heart. In both variations of this poisoning, whether the woman
is pregnant or not, the female victim's reproductive capacity is
obstructed. Another variation of this spell, sometimes called *umuvu*,
entails throwing the packet with the woman's menstrual blood or
urine into a fast moving stream. In this case the woman's menstrual
flow becomes excessively abundant or prolonged.

In effect, by suspending a woman's blood or other fluids involved
in sexuality or reproduction, the woman's reproductive functions
are also suspended. Both she becomes unable to deliver the baby
already in her womb, or her menstruation stops and she becomes
sterile. By suspending the woman's bodily fluids in a position
between sky and earth, or in a place where rain cannot touch them,
the woman's body becomes 'blocked'. When her fluids are put into
a body of fast moving water, her menses become dangerously
abundant, an example of 'haemorrhagic flow'.

Healers vary in their treatment of this poisoning. Nevertheless
these variations possess features in common. One healer has the
woman lie on her back while naked. He takes medicines and sprinkles
them in a line from the woman's forehead, over the middle of
her face, over her chest and abdomen, down to her genitals. The
logic behind this treatment appears to be that movement must be
encouraged from the top of the body to the bottom, from the
head to the genitals. Another healer, a woman named Antoinette,
uses a different method of cure, but her treatment of *kumanikira
amaraso* follows a similar line of symbolic reasoning to the previous
one.

Antoinette has the woman lie naked on the floor of her house.
Her abdomen faces upward. Someone climbs onto the roof of the

house, parts the thatch, and then pours an aqueous mixture of
medicines through the opening onto the woman's abdomen. Another
person inside the house rubs the woman's stomach with the medi-
cinal mixture. In this treatment the blockage within the woman's
body is analogically posited as a blockage between sky and earth,
for it is counteracted by someone's actually moving to the sky
position (ascending to the roof of the house), and pouring fluids
earthward. This time, however, the downward movement of fluids
includes the woman's body in the circuit of flow from sky to earth.
The cure is a virtually one-to-one homeopathic reversal of the
symbolic operations accomplished in the poisoning, which removed
the woman's body from the circuit of moving fluids by 'suspending'
her blood between earth and sky.

Yet a third healer, Baudouin, treated *kumanikira amaraso* in
a different yet symbolically comparable way. In one case that I
observed, he gave the afflicted woman, who was unable to deliver
despite being pregnant, water with a piece of hippopotamus skin
in it. In addition, he administered a remedy concocted from the
umuhaanga plant (*Kotschya aeschynomenoides; Kotschya strigosa var.
grandiflora; Maesa lanceolata*). The name of this plant comes from
the verb *guhaanga* which means: (a) to create, to restore, to invent;
(b) to occupy a place first; (c) to germinate, to blossom; (d) to
have one's first menstrual period. He also gave her a plant called
umumanurankuba, a name which comes from the words: *kumanura*,
to make something descend, or to depend on, and *inkuba*, thunder.
The full meaning of the name of this plant would be: 'to make
thunder descend, to depend on thunder' – to make rain fall.

Once again this is an image of restoring the sky to earth movement
of rainfall, and by analogy, restoring orderly flows to the woman's
body. In restoring the flow, the healer renders the woman capable
of creating, capable of blossoming. The use of the hippopotamus
follows the fact that it is an animal closely associated with terrestrial
waters.

It is difficult accurately to assess the number of Rwandans whose
thought during illness episodes conforms to the model of 'flow/
blockage'. Rwandans among whom I studied popular medicine
during my first two periods of fieldwork included Hutu, Tutsi, and
Twa of both sexes. Although I studied Rwandan popular medicine
mostly in rural areas, a small number of my interlocutors lived in
the cities of Butare and Kigali. The idea of conducting a survey to
determine the percentage of a population that subscribes to an

implicit model strikes me as absurd. What can be affirmed, however, is that the practice of *kumanikira amaraso* is encountered in southern and central Rwanda as well, and even in urban areas. During my most recent fieldwork (1993–4), a Rwandan colleague of mine, Pierre Ntereye, showed me some of his research results concerning attitudes toward sexuality, pregnancy, and contraception among urban Rwandans in the capital city of Kigali.[8] Although Ntereye had not yet analysed his results, I was struck by the number of respondents who simultaneously claimed knowledge of *kumanikira amaraso*, but yet scepticism as to its purported efficacy. Were they being sincere or were they merely trying to appear 'rational' to an educated interlocutor? Furthermore, whether sceptical or not of *kumanikira amaraso*, this does not imply internalization or non-internalization, use or non-use, of flow/blockage metaphors. A substantial number of respondents also claimed that 'suspending blood' could be used intentionally as a means of contraception and was not always a malevolent spell intended to induce sterility. A few female respondents even admitted that their mothers had 'suspended' their first menstrual blood in order to assure that they would not become pregnant out of wedlock.

Another female fertility disorder encountered in both northern and southern Rwanda and often treated by popular healers is that called *igihama*. A woman who lacks breast milk is called *igihama*, as are women who lack vaginal secretions during intercourse. The noun *igihama* is derived from the verb, *guhama*, which means: 'to cultivate a field hardened by the sun; to have sexual relations with a woman who lacks vaginal secretions' (Jacob, 1984: 437–38). Women who lack breast milk after childbirth and those who lack vaginal secretions during intercourse are similar, for in both cases their fertility is threatened. Both women lack an essential bodily fluid – in one case the fluid that will nourish a child, and in the other case, the fluid that is deemed necessary in order for the woman to have fruitful sexual relations and by consequence, to conceive.

Close to the southern Rwandan town of Butare, I elicited the following illness narrative in 1984 from a woman named Verediana who had consulted a healer named Matthew. This narrative is remarkable in that it illustrates the imagery of perturbed menstruation, perturbed lactation, reduced fertility, and interruption during the course of a journey. At the time, however, I had little idea that the events related in this woman's story were connected in any other way than that which she persistently emphasized: these were persistent misfortunes whose seriality proved that they were due to the malevolent influence of sorcerers.

Verediana came to Matthew convinced that she had been poisoned. This time she had been sick since July 1983, approximately one year before I met her. Her primary symptom consisted of prolonged, abundant menstruation. Although she had visited a hospital and received injections that stopped her haemorrhagic periods, she still felt intensely afraid. She often had trouble eating. Recently she and her husband had separated. Immediately after their separation her symptoms improved, then they began to worsen anew.

According to Verediana, it was the older brother of her husband and his wife who were her poisoners. She believed that this man afflicted others through the use of malevolent spirits. In previous years she had been suspicious of another brother of her husband, a man who was suspected of sorcery and later killed by a group of his neighbours. She also felt that her husband was in league with his brothers all of whom were eager to have her out of the way.

In recounting earlier misfortunes, Verediana explained that her third pregnancy had been interrupted by the baby's premature birth at eight and a half months. Somehow the child managed to survive despite her reduced lactation. Before this occurrence, she had lost a child. During the troubled events of 1973 – revived tensions between Hutu and Tutsi and the government's inability to deal with the situation had led to a military coup – she was being transported to the hospital in labour. She recalls that there were numerous roadblocks and barriers erected on the roads. Despite these barriers, she finally arrived safely at the hospital. Her child was born alive, but died the next day. When I suggested to her that her difficulty in reaching the hospital may have had more to do with national events in Rwanda than with actions of her persecutors, she replied, 'Yes, but why did I go into labour at just such a time?'

Matthew's diagnosis was that Verediana was suffering from *amageza* affliction, a spirit illness that can cause excessive blood flow from the vagina.

Notice that in this narrative, Verediana speaks of disorderly bodily flows: haemorrhagic menstruation, premature birth, and diminished lactation. She also mentions physical obstructions encountered while *en route* to the hospital in 1973. The background to this incident, the political events of 1973, constitutes a moment when political relations between Rwanda's two most numerous ethnic groups, the Tutsi and the Hutu, had degenerated into violence.

Many of the details that Verediana employs in her narrative are images of incompletion, partial arrest, or obstruction: difficulty in eating, diminished lactation, barriers on the roads, a child who dies soon after birth, or a baby who was born prematurely – that is, it left her womb before it had been completely formed by the process of intensified mixing of husband's semen and wife's blood that is supposed to occur during the final stages of pregnancy (*gukurakuza*). Other details are images of excessive flow: menstrual periods that are prolonged and haemorrhagic.

She implicates several domains of problematic social relations that merge together in her story: difficulties with her husband in the context of a polygynous household, relations with her affines, political conflict between Tutsi and Hutu during 1973. This woman's story is remarkable in touching so many levels at once. While the symptomatic focus is her body, an analogy is constantly being drawn between it and other domains of social life: her relationship with her husband, her relationship with her affines, even the relations between Tutsi and Hutu at the national level. Her narrative moves from her body, to the household, to the extended family, to the nation in a seamless series of symbolically logical leaps, for all are posed in terms of bodily and social processes whose movement or obstruction are causes for concern.

Rwandan Sacred Kingship

If flow/blockage symbolism can be discerned in the narratives of individual patients and in the therapeutic means employed by healers, it is logical to ask if similar symbolism can be found, as Verediana's narrative suggests it might, at the level of representations of the polity as a whole.

Although it is difficult to find clear evidence of this symbolism for the post-colonial Rwandan state and its rituals of nationalism (although it may exist), there is indeed strong historical evidence for it before independence at the time when Rwanda was a sacred kingdom. Here, the principal sources of symbolic material are texts of the royal rituals performed by the king and his college of ritualists, dynastic poetry, and popular narratives recounted about Rwandan kings.

In the pre-colonial and early colonial period the king's ritual specialists memorized the ritual texts. Later during the 1940s and 1950s, when it appeared that knowledge of the rituals might be lost forever as the last generation of royal ritualists begin to die off, the texts were transcribed by Rwandan and European scholars. In 1964, M. d'Hertfelt and A. Coupez published Kinyarwanda texts and French translations of seventeen of the royal rituals in a book entitled, *La royaute sacrée de l'ancien Rwanda.*

Although Coupez and d'Hertefelt do not attempt to precisely date their versions of the ritual texts, it is quite likely that they go back at least to the pre-colonial times of the nineteenth century. The last Rwandan king who presided over the enactment of the rituals, the last king who could be truly described as 'sacred' in terms of local perceptions, was Yuhi V Musinga whose reign (1896–1931) straddles the end of the nineteenth century and the early period of Catholic evangelization. Musinga and his *abiiru* performed the rituals until the late 1920s, at which time they began to be neglected for fear certain ritual practices might offend European and Catholic sensibilities. Despite Musinga's concession, Belgian colonial authorities deposed Musinga in 1931 and replaced him with his mission-educated son. In the texts published by d'Hertefelt and Coupez, there are procedures in the rituals that Europeans would have found difficult to accept: ritual copulation on the part of the king and his wives, human sacrifice, ritual war, and adornment of the royal drum with the genitals of slain enemies.

As for the ethnic origin of the rituals, although the central Rwandan monarchy was dominated by a Tutsi king and many of his closest associates were Tutsi, many scholars claim that similar rituals were being performed in Hutu polities prior to the central kingdom's existence (d'Hertefelt, 1971: 32). It is probable that the existence of the state in central Rwanda preceded its becoming a Tutsi-dominated institution. Therefore the rituals and their attendant symbolism cannot readily and simply be ascribed to later Tutsi dominance. In addition, although the Rwandan king was Tutsi, the rituals he enacted had to address the preoccupations of the Hutu majority, particularly the concern for orderly rainfall and an abundant sorghum harvest. Moreover, in material terms the king performed a redistributive function, concentrating wealth then redisbursing it.

Careful reading of the ritual texts indicates recurrent preoccupation with maintaining orderly fluid flows and implicitly that of *imaana*. The term, *imaana*, although often translated as 'God', only occasionally referred to a supreme being. More frequently, *imaana* was a generalized creative or transformative force or as d'Hertefelt and Coupez have translated the term, a 'diffuse fecundating fluid' of celestial origin. Gaining access to the powers of *imaana* and keeping the fluids of production, consumption, and fertility in movement were arguably the most important ritual functions of the Rwandan king (*mwami*). The *mwami* was the ultimate human guarantor of the fertility of bees (for honey), cattle, women, and land. In times of drought, famine, epidemic, or epizootic, he could be deposed or called upon to offer himself (or a close relative) as a sacrificial victim (*umutabazi*), so that the shedding of his blood would conjure away collective peril. The king mediated between the sky and the earth. He was the most important rainmaker for the kingdom. He received the celestial gift of fertility and passed it downward to his subjects. In some instances this beneficence was conceptualized as milk, as is expressed in this dynastic poem:

> The King is not a man,
> O men that he has enriched with his cattle . . .
> He is a man before his designation to the throne . . .
> Ah yes! That is certain:
> But the one who becomes King ceases to be a man!
> The King, it is he *Imaana*
> And he dominates over humans . . .
> I believe that he is the *Imaana* who hears our pleas!
> The other *Imaana*, it's the King who knows him,
> As for us, we see only this Defender! . . .
> Here is the sovereign who drinks the milk milked by *Imaana*,
> And we drink that which he in turn milks for us!

(From *La poésie dynastique au Rwanda*, cited by A. Kagame (in French) in *La philosophie bantu-rwandaise de l'être*, 1956: 15. My translation.)

The Rwandan king, *mwami*, could be compared to a hollow conduit through which celestial beneficence passed. He was the kingdom's most giving or 'flowing' being. The image of his body as conduit can be discerned in a legend that is sometimes recounted about Ruganzu Ndori, one of early Rwanda's most important kings. A certain Augustin, the gardener at the Institut National De Recherche Scientifique in Butare during my fieldwork there, related this particular version of the story to me in 1987. Here fertility is restored to the earth by first passing through the *mwami*'s digestive tract.

> Ruganzu Ndori was living in exile in the neighbouring kingdom of Ndorwa, to the north of Rwanda. There he had taken refuge with his father's sister who was married to a man from the region. In the meantime, because an illegitimate usurper occupied the Rwandan throne, Rwanda was experiencing numerous calamities. Rain was not falling, crops were dying, cows were not giving milk, and the women were becoming sterile. Ruganzu's aunt encouraged him to return to Rwanda and retake the throne and in this way, to save his people from catastrophe. Ruganzu agreed, but before setting forth on his voyage, his aunt gave him the seeds (*imbuto*) of several cultivated plants (sorghum, gourds, and others) to restart Rwandan cultures. While en route to Rwanda, Ruganzu Ndori came under attack. Fearing that the *imbuto* would be captured, he swallowed the seeds with a long draught of milk. Once he regained the Rwandan throne, he defecated the milk and seed mixture upon the ground and the land became productive once again. Since that time all Rwandan kings are said to be born clutching the seeds of the original *imbuto* in their hand.

The image of the king's body as exemplary of a flowing process is implied in the verb *kwamira*, from which the noun *mwami* is derived. *Kwamira* has both a formal sense and a popular one. Its formal meaning is 'to make, to create, or to render fertile', but another meaning is 'to lactate' (Vansina, personal communication). In some parts of interlacustrine Bantu-speaking Africa the sacred king was called *mwami*. In many other parts, such as Bunyoro, the sacred king was termed *mukama* from the verb, *gukama*, which means 'to milk'. Sometimes even the Rwandan king was referred to as *mukama*. When the Bunyoro Mukama died, a man would ascend a ladder, pour milk onto the ground and say, 'The milk is spilt; the king has been taken away!' (Beatty, 1960: 28). The terms *mwami* and *mukama* thus encompasses several semantic domains that are central to Rwandan symbolic thought: production, reproduction, the labour associated with extracting the aliment of highest esteem, milk, and their metaphorization in the popular imagination as a flowing process, lactation.

The assertion that the *mwami* was supposed to be the most 'flowing being' of the kingdom, a hollow conduit through which fluids passed, is how I depict the concern on the part of traditional

Rwandans that the *mwami* keep the rain falling regularly, the cows giving milk, the bees producing honey, and the crops growing. Of the seventeen royal rituals recorded and annotated by D'Hertefelt and Coupez, two concern rainfall, one concerns the production of honey, another conjures away cattle epizootics (assuring the production of milk), and one celebrates the sorghum harvest (most sorghum was brewed into beer). One of the most important rituals, 'the watering of the royal herds', which was only accomplished once every four reigns and which was intended to renew the dynastic cycle, deploys virtually the entire gamut of fluid symbols including those concerning the two most important rivers of the kingdom, the Nyabugogo and the Nyabarongo – rivers that delineated sacred time and sacred space.[9]

The person of the *mwami* embodied flow/blockage imagery with regard to his physiological processes as well, for every morning the king imbibed a milky liquid called *isubyo*, which was a powerful laxative (Bourgeois, 1956). While the ostensible purpose of this matinal libation was to purge the *mwami*'s body of any poison he might have absorbed, the reasoning behind the custom goes deeper than that, for the *mwami*'s enemies were depicted as the antithesis of 'flowing beings'; they were beings who interrupted production, exchange, and fertility. They were 'obstructing beings'. When seen from this perspective, the practice of *kurya ubunyano* (discussed above with regard to new-born children) makes eminent sense.

The Rwandan mythical archetype of the 'blocking being' was a small old woman (*agakeecuru*). A legend recounts how Death, while being pursued by the *mwami*, Thunder, and God, sought refuge with this *agakeecuru*, while she was gathering gourds in a field. The tiny old woman sheltered Death 'in the fold at the front of her dress' (her vagina and uterus) where he remained to subsist on her blood (Smith, 1975: 132). Later, in eating with her descendants, the *agakeecuru* communicated Death to them and they, in their turn, to the rest of the world. In this tale we see that Death is associated with beings whose fluids do not or no longer flow, for old women do not menstruate. The origin of Death is also the origin of sorcery, for the old woman passes the contagion of Death on to others by eating with them.[10]

One of the *mwami*'s responsibilities was to eliminate beings who lacked the capacity 'to flow'. Two such beings included girls who had reached childbearing age and who lacked breasts, called *impene-bere*, and girls who had reached child-bearing age and who had not yet menstruated, called *impa* (D'Hertefelt and Coupez, 1964: 286). In both cases, the girls were put to death for want of the apparent capacity to produce an important fertility fluid, in one case, blood, in the other, milk. Obstructed in their perceived capacity to reproduce, the girls were thought to be potential sources of misfortune and aridity to the entire kingdom.

Although it might appear that the person of the *mwami* catalysed flows and eliminated symbolic obstruction, in fact, he embodied this metaphor in its entirety. While he was extolled as the being who 'milked' for others, the being who acted as the conduit of *imaana*, the being who embodied the powers of both genders as a 'lactating' male, the king was as much a 'blocking being' as a 'flowing' one. He was not simply a passive conduit through which beneficence passed – he was an active agent who possessed the power of life and death over his subjects. He could enrich his followers with gifts of cattle and land or he could impoverish them. Like a sorcerer who impedes fertility or inflicts death upon victims by invisibly sucking away their blood, the manifestation of the king's power was more likely to be felt in all those ways by which the king could obstruct human movement, economic processes, life, and human reproduction. This aspect of Rwandan sacred kingship was given less elaboration in ritual, poetry, or popular narratives, although there are aspects in the ritual texts in which the obstructive function of kingship can be discerned, albeit indirectly. This connectedness of the well-being of the polity with processes that can be promoted or inhibited can be discerned in the rituals associated with sacred kingship.

First let us take the Kinyarwanda ritual lexicon and examine the use of the term 'flow'. In the 'path of the watering', the royal ritual performed only once in every dynastic cycle of four kings and intended to revivivfy the entire magico-religious order of Rwandan kingship, there were several instances when a group of eight cows, representing all the deceased kings of the two previous dynastic cycles, along with one bull, were presented to the living king. Occasionally this group of eight cows was referred to as *isibo* ('a flow') (D'Hertefelt and Coupez, 1964: 142).[11] Examining the full meaning of the term *isibo*, we see that in other contexts it was used to designate: (a) a group of cattle rushing towards a watering trough; (b) (in war poetry) a flow of living beings, a swarming multitude; (c) force, elan, flight, impetuosity, as in *guca isibo* (especially when speaking of the *intoóre* [warriors] dances), which means, literally, 'to cut the flow' in the context of dance – to jump very high while dancing (Jacob, 1985: 169). However, the verb from which *isibo* is derived, *gusiba*, means: 1) to plug, to fill up, to obstruct, to fill a hollow or empty space; 2) to clean, to erase; 3) to decimate, to eliminate, to make something disappear; 4) to hoe the earth without taking care to remove weeds; 5) to reduce an adversary to silence by an irrefutable argument; 6) (when speaking of mammary glands) to be obstructed; 7) (when speaking of a path) to become covered over with plants. Other usages include: *gusiba inkaru* - to do grave harm to someone; and *gusiba inzira* - (literally 'to block the path'), to lose one's daughter through death (Jacob, 1985: 167).

Notice, therefore, that the noun *isibo* and its root verb *gusiba* appear to encompass two apparently contradictory meanings. One field of meaning seems to centre on the idea of living beings in movement. Another set of meanings seems to crystallize around the ideas of obstruction and loss. A single verbal concept in Kinyarwanda thus appears to encompass the idea of flow and its opposite, the idea of blockage. Furthermore, in this second instance, the notion of 'blockage' is related to the idea of doing harm to someone, as in *gusiba inkaru*, as well as to the idea of losing one's daughter, as in *gusiba inzira*. With regard to *gusiba inzira*, an analogy is drawn between 'blocking the path' and 'losing one's daughter'. In effect, when one loses a daughter, death blocks the 'path' between one's own family and that of another family – the alliance relationship that could have resulted from the gift of one's daughter to a man from another family is pre-emptively extinquished. With regard to *gusiba inkaru*, an analogy is drawn between the action of 'blocking' and the action of doing serious harm to someone – an idea that comes very close to Rwandan notions of sorcery.

This apparent antinomy between the fields of meaning denoted and connoted in the words *isibo* and *gusiba*, might appear illogical to someone situated outside the context of Rwandan social action. Within this context, this contradiction was nothing less than an ineluctable corollary to the workings of social life itself. It was its internal dialectic. Just as *imaana* could 'flow' or be 'blocked,' just as the sky could yield its fertilizing liquid in the right measure and at the right time, so could the body flow properly in health or improperly in illness. The words *isibo* and *gusiba* embody part of this recognition – the recognition that one cannot have 'flow' without 'blockage,' just as one cannot 'milk' (*gukama*) without incurring the risk of depleting the environment, and one cannot give to some without withholding one's gifts from others. Power in early Rwanda grew as much from the capacity to obstruct, as from the capacity to give.

It was through obstruction, impoverishment, strangulation, murder, and sorcery that the Rwandan king manifested the coercive aspect of his power over subjects and adversaries. The pre-colonial Rwandan polity, through its king, unabashedly proclaimed its expansionist intent in the five royal rituals directly concerned with warfare. In one such ritual, *Inzira yo Kwambika Ingoma* ('the path of adorning the drum'), the genitals of important slain enemies were ritually prepared in order to be placed within containers and then hung upon 'Karinga' (the most important royal drum). Early Rwandan warriors carried a special curved knife that was used to remove the genitalia of slain enemies. During this ritual the king and his ritualists would shout:

Ngo twahotor Uburundi kuu ngoma
N'amahang adatuur umwami w'Irwanda
Twayahotora kuu ngoma
(D'Hertefelt and Coupez, 1964: 176)

May we strangle Burundi's drum
And all countries who do not pay tribute to Rwanda's king
may we strangle their drums.

Women were also victims of mutilation in earlier times. In disputes between rival 'houses', for example, it was common for the victors to cut off the breasts of women belonging to the vanquished group, although these were not used in the above ritual.

The Rwandan monarchy manifested its control over flowing processes – rainfall, human fertility, bovine fertility, milk, and honey production – through its ritual capacity to catalyse or to interdict them. Kings thus encompassed the qualities of both 'flow' and 'blockage' and in that sense, were ambiguous, 'liminoid' beings, the embodiment of evil as well as good. At times of dire calamity to the polity as a whole, the king became the ultimate repository of ritual negativity, the ultimate 'blocking being' and in these instances, it was his blood that had to be sacrificially shed to reopen the conduits of *imaana*. According to Rwandan dynastic legends, many kings were said to have died as ritual sacrifices. Indeed, the events leading up to and including the 1994 genocide incorporate many elements of the 'mythic logic' of king sacrifice.

Ritual, Power, and Genocide

Issues of personhood and the body, all of which are generally implicated in nationalistic expressions of violence, do not follow a universal logic. Likewise, this logic is not limited to the common exigency to eliminate as many of the regime's adversaries as possible. State-promoted violence persistently defies the state's attempts to 'rationalize' and 'routinize' it. The psychologically detached, dispassionate torturer does not exist; the acultural torturer who acts independently of the *habitus* that he or she embodies does not exist. Nor can the interposition of killing machines or technology efface what Kafka so perceptively recognized in *The Penal Colony* – that societies 'write' their signatures onto the bodies of their sacrificial victims. As Foucault shows, power constructs human subjects and a certain homology obtains between the quotidian disciplinary practices employed by social institutions like the army

Figure 3.1 *Bodily mutilations as political language*
(Kangura, *February 1994, no. 56, cover*)
The RPF: Bravo Twagira!
Twagiramungu: And you said I'd never get you! Who will you lead without your arms?
Agathe Uwilingiyimana: It's not me who's cut your arms. It's the Arusha accords.

or the school to produce 'docile bodies', and the more coercive measures employed against criminals and enemies of the state (1979). Taking this observation further, one might ask: why the French once used the guillotine, the Spanish the garrotte, the English the rope, while Americans electrocute, gas, or lethally inject those in its midst whom it wishes to obliterate from the moral community? Among the numerous forms of state cruelty that Edward Peters examines in *Torture*, he notes that 'there seem to be culturally-favoured forms of torture in different societies' (1996: 171). Not all methods are used everywhere. In Greece, for example, there appears to be a preference for *falanga* (the beating of the soles of the feet), a torture that is absent from Latin America and where electrical shock predominates. In Rwanda of 1994, torturers manifested a certain proclivity to employ violent methods with specific forms. These forms betrayed a preoccupation with the movement of persons and substances and with the canals, arteries, and conduits along which persons and substances flow: rivers, roadways, pathways, and even the conduits of the human body such as the reproductive and digestive systems.

Controlling Flows

Rivers

In other work I have analysed the ritual and symbolic importance of Rwanda's rivers in light of the generative scheme of flow versus blockage. In the kingship ritual known as the 'path of the watering', for example, the Nyabugogo and Nybarongo Rivers served to revivify the magico-religious potency of the dynasty by recycling and reintegrating the ancestral benevolence of deceased kings (Taylor, 1988). While in the post-colonial Rwandan state these rivers appear to have lost their previous ritual significance, Rwanda's rivers were conscripted into the genocide. This is apparent in statements made by one of the leading proponents of Hutu extremism, Leon Mugesera.

Well in advance of the genocide, Rwandan politicians made statements indicating that elements in the President's entourage were contemplating large-scale massacres of Tutsi. One of the baldest pronouncements in this regard came from the Mugesera, an MRND party leader from the northern prefecture of Gisenyi.

On 22 November 1992, Mugesera spoke to party faithful there. It was no accident that a venue in Gisenyi prefecture had been chosen for such an inflammatory speech, because this was the regime's home turf. Gisenyi solidly backed the Rwandan government and its president. For following Habyarimana's coup d'état in 1973, the region always received more than its allotted share of state jobs, secondary school placements, and so forth. Mugesera's words were not falling on deaf ears:

> The opposition parties have plotted with the enemy to make Byumba prefecture fall to the *Inyenzi*. [. . .] They have plotted to undermine our armed forces. [. . .] The law is quite clear on this point: 'Any person who is guilty of acts aiming at sapping the morale of the armed forces will be condemned to death.' What are we waiting for? [. . .] And what about those accomplices (*ibyitso*) here who are sending their children to the RPF? Why are we waiting to get rid of these families? [. . .] We have to take responsibility into our own hands and wipe out these hoodlums. [. . .] The fatal mistake we made in 1959 was to let them [the Tutsis] get out. [. . .] They belong in Ethiopia and we are going to find them a shortcut to get there by throwing them into the Nyabarongo river [which flows northwards]. I must insist on this point. We have to act. Wipe them all out!
>
> (Text cited from Prunier, 1995: 171–2)

Shortly after this occurrence, Mugesera repeated the same speech in other Rwandan venues and several violent incidents in which Tutsi were killed can be directly traced to its instigation. Although the then Minister of Justice, Stanislas Mbonampeka, charged Mugesera with inciting racial hatred and gave orders to have him arrested, Mugesera took refuge at an army base where police dared not enter (Prunier, 1995).

In this speech there are several important elements, some of which are more apparent and others less so. That Mugesera is calling for the extermination of all enemies of the regime and especially Tutsi seems clear. The old theme of Tutsi as originators from Ethiopia or 'invaders from Ethiopia' has also resurfaced in this speech. The theme of Ethiopian origins, used during the late colonial era by apologists of Tutsi domination (cf. Kagame, 1959) has become in the hands of Hutu extremists, a means of denying Tutsi any share in the patrimony of Rwanda. Yet also present in this speech is the first explicit post-colonial reference that I know of, to the Nyabarongo River as a geographic entity with symbolic and political

significance. In this speech the Nyabarongo has become the means
by which Tutsi shall be removed from Rwanda and retransported
to their presumed land of origin. Here, it should be emphasized,
the river is again to play an important restorative and purifying
role – that of sanitizing the nation of its internal 'foreign' minority.
In the months of June, July, and August of 1994, when allegations
of a massive genocide in Rwanda were just beginning to be taken
seriously in the international media, thousands of bodies began
washing up on the shores of Lake Victoria; bodies that had been
carried there by the Nybarongo and then the Akagera Rivers.

Rwanda's rivers became part of the genocide by acting as the
body politic's organs of elimination, in a sense 'excreting' its hated
internal other. It is not much of a leap to infer that Tutsi were
thought of as excrement by their persecutors. Other evidence of
this is apparent in the fact that many Tutsi were stuffed into latrines
after their deaths. Some were even thrown while still alive into
latrines; a few of them actually managed to survive and to extricate
themselves.

Gusiba inzira, 'Blocking the path'

Among the accounts of Rwandan refugees that I interviewed in
Kenya during the late spring and early summer of 1994, there was
persistent mention of barriers and roadblocks. Like Nazi shower
rooms in the concentration camps, these were the most frequent
loci of execution for Rwanda's Tutsi and Hutu opponents of the
regime. Barriers were erected almost ubiquitously and by many
different groups. There were roadblocks manned by Rwandan
Government Forces, roadblocks of the dreaded *Interhamwe* militia,
Rwandan communal police roadblocks, roadblocks set up by neighbourhood protection groups, opportunistic roadblocks erected by
groups of criminals, and even occasional roadblocks manned by
the Rwandan Patriotic Front in areas under their control. For people
attempting to flee Rwanda, evading these roadblocks was virtually
impossible. Moreover, during the genocide, participation in a team
manning a roadblock was often a duty imposed upon people by
local Rwandan government or military officials.

Several Hutu informants who escaped Rwanda via an overland
route explained to me that they had had to traverse hundreds of
roadblocks. One informant estimated that he had encountered one
barrier per hundred metres in a certain area. Another counted forty-

three roadblocks in a ten kilometre stretch on the paved road between Kigali and Gitarama.

Leaving major highways was no solution, for one would encounter barriers erected across dirt roads and footpaths manned by local peasants. At every barrier fleeing people were forced to show their national identity card. Since the ID card bore mention of one's ethnicity, distinguishing Tutsi from Hutu was no problem and almost always, fleeing Tutsi, said to be *ibyitso* or 'traitors', were robbed and killed. When a refugee claimed to have lost the ID card, his or her physical features were relied upon as ethnic identification. It was to one's advantage to look Hutu (to be of moderate height and to have a wide nose).

In order to traverse these barriers, even as a Hutu, it was often necessary to bribe those who were in control. One prosperous Hutu businessman that I had known in Kigali and who surely would have been killed because of his political affiliation (PSD) had he been recognized, told me that he had paid a total of over five thousand dollars in bribes.

Barriers were ritual and liminal spaces where 'obstructing beings' were to be obstructed in their turn and cast out of the nation. The roadblocks were the space both of ritual and of transgression, following an ambivalent logic that Bourdieu underlines, 'the most fundamental ritual actions are in fact denied transgression' (1990: 212). There were scenes of inordinate cruelty. Often the condemned had to pay for the quick death of a bullet, whereas the less fortunate were slashed with machetes or bludgeoned to death with nail-studded clubs. In many cases victims were intentionally maimed but not fully dispatched. Beside the line of motionless corpses awaiting pickup and disposal lay the mortally injured, exposed to the sun and still writhing, as their persecutors sat by calmly, drinking beer.

One refugee who had made it to Kenya by the circuitous route of fleeing southward to Burundi, told me that he and everyone else in his company had been forced to pay an unusual toll at one barrier. Each had been forced to bludgeon a captured Tutsi with a hammer before being allowed to move on. Some in the party had even been made to repeat their blows a second or third time for lack of initial enthusiasm. The reasoning behind this can be clarified by considering the logic of sacrifice and the stigma that inevitably accrues to the sacrificer, the person who actually spills the victim's blood. As Bourdieu puts it:

The magical protections that are set to work whenever the reproduction
of the vital order requires transgression of the limits that are the
foundation of that order, especially whenever it is necessary to cut or
kill, in short, to interrupt the normal course of life, include a number
of ambivalent figures who are all equally despised and feared.

(Bordieu, 1990: 213)

Requiring those who were being spared at the roadblocks to kill a
hapless captive may seem unnecessary and purely sadistic, yet it
served a useful psychological function from the point of view of
the genocide's perpetrators: that of removing the ambivalence of
the sacrificial act and the stigma of the sacrificer/executioner by
passing these on to everyone. The ritual obfuscated the boundary
between 'genocidaires' and those who were otherwise innocent
Hutu. Not only were Tutsi and Hutu 'traitors' being killed at the
barriers – innocent Hutu were being forced to become morally
complicit in the genocide by becoming both 'sacrificer' and 'sacrifier'
(Hubert and Mauss, 1964) and shedding Tutsi blood.

Several Hutu refugees that I met in Kenya explained that they
had used elaborate ruses to avoid, or to be excused from 'barrier
duty'. One of them, Jean-Damascene, told me that he had been
obliged to spend two full days and nights at a barrier before being
allowed to return to his nearby home. As he would have been re-
summoned for additional duty, Jean-Damascene and his wife concocted a persuasive alibi. Because she was already more than seven
months pregnant and visibly so, his wife might be able to feign the
onset of difficult labour. After less than twenty-fours of rest, Jean-
Damascene returned to the barrier with his groaning, agitated wife
and asked for permission to take her to Kigali hospital. The youthful
Interahamwe in charge of the barrier seemed convinced by the
charade and let them proceed, but only after Jean-Dmascene left
his wristwatch as a guaranty.

From there the couple walked a few kilometres to the centre of
Kigali and to a large modern building where Jean-Damascene
ordinarily worked. Gaining entrance into the building through
doors that had been forced open by looters, the couple spent several
nights sleeping on the floor of an upper story corridor. During
the day Jean- Damascene ventured outside to procure food and to
ask people with vehicles if they were headed in the direction of
Cyangugu (a city located on the southern edge of Lake Kivu and
very close to the border with Zaire). Finally he found someone who

was going to Cyangugu and who was willing to take him and his wife. Once in Cyangugu, the couple crossed the border into Zaire. In Bukavu (Zaire) they met a friend who gave Jean-Damascene enough money to buy a plane ticket to Nairobi. When I met Jean-Damascene in Nairobi he was staying in the Shauri-Moyo YMCA, a place where many Rwandan refugees were being temporarily housed by the UNHCR. While in Nairobi Jean-Damascene managed to raise enough money from family and friends to buy a plane ticket for his wife who was still in Bukavu.

Hutu who were fleeing Rwandan government violence and that of the *Interahamwe* might traverse the barriers as long as they were not well-known opposition personalities who might be recognized. For Tutsi escape was next to impossible. Most Tutsi refugees that I met in Nairobi had fled from Rwanda by other means. Several had made their way to Kigali airport during the week or so of time following President Habyarimana's assassination when Belgian and French troops were evacuating their citizens via Kigali airport. A few Rwandan Government Army officers had even aided several in their escape. Those who were saved this way were extremely lucky, for only some Belgian and some Senegalese troops made much of an attempt to save threatened Tutsi. French troops, allies of the genocidal regime, cynically abandoned Rwandan Tutsi to their fate – even those who had been former employees of the French embassy or the French Cultural Centre.

One Tutsi man that I interviewed in Nairobi, a certain Viateur, recounted that he, his wife, three of his children, and several other Tutsi employees of the French Cultural Centre, had been denied evacuation by French troops who remained at the Centre for several days before abruptly deciding to depart.[12] Later Belgian troops occupied the Cultural Centre and agreed to evacuate them; the Rwandans were placed among Westerners on Belgian Army trucks. Obliged to traverse several roadblocks *en route* to the airport, the Tutsis hid beneath benches upon which Western evacuees were seated. Once at the airport they were flown out of Rwanda on Belgian transport planes.

Although the barriers that fleeing Rwandans had to contend with were effective as a means of robbing and killing many of them, roadblocks were next to useless as a means of halting the slow but inexorable RPF advance. In fact, the barriers defied military logic. Proliferated in all directions, they were counterproductive in any tactical sense, for they diverted manpower that could have been deployed in the field and they decentralized resistance to the RPF. Rwandan Government Forces and their associated *Interahamwe* militias were like a headless tentacular beast expending its rage against Tutsi civilians and Hutu moderates while doing little to confront its real adversary. Even from the point of view of the military and militia who controlled the barriers, their utility defied ordinary logic. With roadblocks so closely placed to one another – as close as one hundred meters in some instances – most were clearly redundant. Downstream barriers had little hope of catching people who had not already been stopped and fleeced of their money and belongings.

On 9 April 1994, as part of the US Embassy's overland evacuation from Rwanda, I had the opportunity to traverse many RGF barriers. At several roadblocks, soldiers could be seen openly drinking beer or whisky; there was a palpable sense of their frustration and disorientation. Yet they were very menacing. Soldiers paced suspiciously up and down the long line of stopped cars, peering into them and asking questions whenever they saw a black face. Later that day and following it, subsequent evacuation convoys fared very badly at their hands. Suspected Tutsi or Hutu opposition party members were pulled from cars and summarily shot. Simply looking Tutsi was sufficient grounds for execution. A Mauritanian friend of mine had two of his children pulled from his car and threatened because of their facial features. Only tense negotiation and the showing of every possible identity paper convinced the soldiers that the children were not Tutsi but Mauritanian. Expending so much energy against the perceived internal enemy virtually assured defeat for the Rwandan Government Forces and their allied militias, for while they wasted their time trying to stop fleeing civilians, the RPF methodically pressed its offensive, capturing one military base after another, one city after another.

If the movement of people could be obstructed with barriers, it could also be hindered by directly attacking the body. The parts of the body most frequently targeted to induce immobility were the legs, feet, and Achilles' tendons. Thousands of corpses discovered after the violence showed evidence of one or both tendons sectioned by machete blows. Other victims later found alive in parts of Rwanda where humanitarian organizations were able to intervene had also sustained this injury. Medecins Sans Frontieres, when it entered eastern Rwanda in late June of 1994, declared in presentations to televised media that this injury was the one most frequently encountered in their area. While MSF managed to save many lives among those so injured, the organization warned that in practically every case, costly surgery would be needed to restore some capability of movement to the foot. This injury, known in medieval France as the 'coup de Jarnac', has sometimes been attributed to the influence of French troops and their alleged training of *Interhamwe* militia members (Braeckman, 1994). I have no evidence to refute this in this specific instance, but Braeckman's assertion does not explain why the technique was used before in Rwanda during the violence of 1959–64 and in 1973. Moreover, in previous episodes of violence as well as in 1994, assailants also mutilated cattle belonging to Tutsi by cutting the leg tendons. Although many cattle in 1994 were killed outright and eaten, and others were stolen, a large number were immobilized and left to die slowly in the field.

This technique of cruelty has a certain logic to it where human beings are concerned. In the presence of a large number of potential victims, too many to kill at once, *Interahamwe* might immobilize fleeing victims by a quick blow to one or both of the Achilles' tendons. Then the killers could return at their leisure and complete their work. This makes sense, yet it does not explain why many who sustained this injury were children too young to walk, elderly people, people who were crippled or infirm, and people in hospital beds incapable of running away. It is here that the pragmatic logic of immobilizing one's enemies and the symbolic logic of 'blocking the path', which are not contradictory in many cases, are in conflict. Why obstruct the immobile? As with barriers on paths and road-ways, there is a deeper generative scheme that subtends both the killers' intentionality and the message inscribed on the bodies of their victims, even though these techniques of cruelty also involve a degree of improvization. Power in this instance, in symbolic terms, derives from the capacity to obstruct. The persecutor 'blocks the path' of human beings and impedes the movement of the material/symbolic capital necessary to the social reproduction of human beings – cattle. Even when it is apparently unnecessary to arrest the movement of the already immobile, the assertion of the capacity to obstruct is none the less the claim and assertion of power.

The Body as Conduit

In addition to the imagery of obstruction, numerous instances of the body as conduit can be discerned in the Rwandan violence of

1994. This imagery tends to centre on two bodily foci: the digestive tract and the reproductive system. For example, after spending several days in Bujumbura, Burundi following our land evacuation from Rwanda, my fiancée, a Rwandan Tutsi, and I took a plane to Nairobi, Kenya. When we arrived at the airport on 15 April 1994, we were surprised to see a group of about fifty or so Rwandans, mostly Tutsi, who had been stranded there for days. The Kenyan government, allied to the former Rwandan regime and already sheltering thousands of refugees from other countries in UNHCR camps, had given instructions to immigration personnel to refuse entry visas to all Rwandans. Having been deposited in Nairobi by Belgian or UN evacuation planes, the Rwandans found themselves with nowhere to go and nowhere to return. As my fiancée and I were also denied entry visas for several hours until we received help from the US Embassy in Nairobi, we had ample time to talk to the stranded Rwandans. Virtually all of them had lost numerous family members, or spouses, lovers, and friends. All were suffering from their confinement at Nairobi airport. Unable to bathe, shower, or change clothes, all looked haggard and unkempt. Their only permitted amenity was sleeping at night in tents put up by the UNHCR just outside the terminal building. We were also surprised to learn that most of them also complained of constipation.

In effect the Rwandans were somaticizing their ordeal. Having narrowly escaped death, the refugees now found themselves at the end of whatever affective, familial, and economic life they had led in Rwanda and at the beginning of a new life as yet undefined in terms of where they would live or what they would do. None at the time had much confidence that the situation in Rwanda would be quickly resolved. Most were resigned to the probability that they would never return to Rwanda and that all the other members of their family were dead. In practically all ways that one can envision human existence, whether in social or psychological terms, the lives of these refugees had reached an impasse. Coupled with this state of suspended animation was the fact that the Rwandans were virtual captives at the Nairobi airport, anxiously awaiting the results of delicate negotiations between the UNHCR and the Kenyan government. It was thus appropriate that their bodies express these various modes of obstruction through symptoms that made sense in terms of Rwandan cultural experience.

The image of the body as conduit was not only discernible in modes of somaticizing psychological distress on the part of victims;

it could also be seen in the techniques of cruelty used by the perpetrators of violence. Perhaps the most vivid example of this during the genocide was the practice of impalement. Recalling Malkki's observation above concerning the 1972 violence against Hutu in Burundi, Rwandan Tutsi men in 1994 were also impaled from anus to mouth with wooden or bamboo poles and metal spears. Tutsi women were often impaled from vagina to mouth. Although none of the refugees that I interviewed in Nairobi spoke of having witnessed impalement, it was reported in Kenyan newspapers that I read during the summer of 1994. More recently it has been cited in an African Rights report entitled 'Rwanda: Killing the Evidence' as a means by which perpetrators of the genocide still living on Rwandan soil terrorize surviving witnesses (Omaar and De Waal, 1996). For example, the report cites the case of a certain Makasi, a resident of the Kicukiro suburb of Kigali, who several months after the genocide found a leaflet shoved under his door threatening his life and that of several others:

> You, Makasi are going to die no matter what. And it will not only be you. It will be Bylingiro as well. Let your wife know that she will be killed with a pole that will run from her legs right up to her mouth. As for Charles' wife, her legs and arms will be cut off.

> (Omaar and De Waal, 1996: 15)

Even before the genocide, impalement was occasionally depicted in the popular Rwandan literature of Hutu extremism as one of the preferred means of torture used by the RPF and other Tutsi to dispatch their Hutu victims.

Notice that in the cartoon depicting Melchior Ndadaye's death,[13] in addition to impalement, there are two other aspects that also require analysis: castration and crucifixion. As explained in the above section about Rwandan sacred kingship, one of the royal rituals involved adorning the royal drum, Karinga, with the genitals of slain enemies. This is what is depicted in this scene as the captions show:

An onlooker:	Kill this stupid Hutu and after you cut off his genitals, hang them on our drum.
Ndadaye:	Kill me, but you won't exterminate all the Ndadayes in Burundi.

Figure 3.2 *The assassination of Ndadaye, reinterpreted according to the fantasies of extremist anti-Tutsi propaganda (*La Medaille-Nyiramacibiri, *November 1993, no. 17, p. 10).*

Kagame (prominent RPF general, now Vice President and Defence Minister of Rwanda):

The drum:

Kill him quickly. Don't you know that in Byumba and Ruhengeri we did a lot of work. With women, we pulled the babies out of their wombs; with men, we dashed out their eyes.

Karinga of Burundi.

There is perhaps no other pictorial image in the annals of Rwandan Hutu extremism in which so much violent imagery is condensed. At one level we see a clear reference to the often-repeated charge of Hutu extremists that the RPF were 'feudal monarchists' intent upon restoring the king and the royal rituals, including the monarchy's principal emblem – the drum named, Karinga. Another ideological claim is advanced in depicting Hutu victims of the RPF as Christlike martyrs, for Ndadaye is not just impaled, he is crucified. Yet at another level a complex synthesis has been forged. Specifically Rwandan symbols with deep historical and ontological roots have merged with those that are the more recent product of Christian evangelization.

In pre-colonial and early colonial times Rwandans impaled cattle thieves. The executioners inserted a wooden stake into the thief's anus and then pushed it through the body, causing it to exit at the neck or the mouth. The pole with its agonizing charge was then erected, stuck into the earth, and left standing for several days. Dramatically gruesome and public, this punishment carried a clear and obvious normative message intended to deter cattle thievery. In a more subtle way, the message can be interpreted symbolically. Because cattle exchanges accompany, legitimize, and commemorate the most significant social transitions and relationships, most notably, patron-client relations, blood brotherhood, and marriage, obviating the possibility of such exchanges or subverting those which have already occurred by stealing cattle removes all tangible mnemonic evidence of the attendant social relationships. Diverting socially appropriate flows of cattle by means of thievery is a way of *gusiba inzira*, or 'blocking the path' between individuals and groups united through matrimonial alliance, blood brotherhood, or patron–client ties. It is symbolically appropriate, therefore, that people who obstruct the conduits of social exchange, have the conduit that is the body obstructed with a pole or spear.

Quite obviously between the pre- and early colonial times, when Rwandan executioners impaled cattle thieves and 1994 when genocidal murderers impaled Tutsi men and women, many things have changed. Clearly the more recent victims of the practice were not cattle thieves. Were they in some sense like cattle thieves in the minds of those committing the atrocities? My feeling is that they were, although the more recent terms used in Hutu extremist discourse to describe Tutsi only occasionally make reference to actual actions of which they might be guilty, such as theft. Instead 'Tutsi are invaders from Ethiopia', 'cockroaches', 'eaters of our sweat', or 'weight upon our back'. The Tutsi, much like the archetypal *agakeecuru* discussed above, exert their malevolent influence on the social group not so much by what they do, than by inherent qualities which they supposedly embody. In that sense they approach 'blocking beings', the mythical nemeses of Rwandan tradition – the *agakeecuru, impenebere,* or *impa* and like these figures, they possess fearful powers. In this case they were obstructers of the cosmic unity of the nation as this unity was imagined by the Hutu extremist élite: a purified nation with a purified, reified 'Hutu culture' expunged of all elements of 'Tutsi culture' and rid of all who would resist the encompassing powers of the state. The torturers not only killed their victims – they transformed their bodies into powerful signs which resonated with a Rwandan *habitus* even as they improvised upon it and enlarged the original semantic domain of associated meanings to depict an entire ethnic group as enemies of the Hutu state.

Other Violence

Among other violence reported during the Rwandan genocide, there were frequent instances of emasculation of Tutsi males, even those too young to reproduce. Attackers also slashed off the breasts of Tutsi women. These techniques of cruelty were also employed during earlier periods of Rwandan history. Both emasculation and breast oblation manifest a preoccupation with the reproductive system and specifically with parts of the body that produce fertility fluids. In both cases, the symbolic function interdigitates with and reinforces the pragmatic function, but the symbolic function can not simply be reduced to the pragmatic one of destroying the future capacity of a group to reproduce. The torturers were assaulting specific and diverse human subjects as well as attacking a group's capacity to reproduce. In order to convince themselves that they were ridding the polity of a categorical enemy and not just assaulting specific individuals they had to first transform their victims' bodies into the equivalent of 'blocked beings'. A logic, *a posteriori,* was operative – reclassify through violence bodies that do not, *a priori,* manifest the imagined inadequacy. Reconfigure specific bodies through torture in order that they become the categorical abomination.

In other instances Tutsi women were taken captive and repeatedly raped by RGF soldiers or *Interahamwe* militia members before being killed.[14] Some Tutsi women were referred to as 'wives' by their rapists who kept them as sexual slaves and even brought them into the refugee camps in Zaire after the RGF was defeated. Among Tutsi women who escaped their captors, many became pregnant and then subsequently sought abortions in Catholic Rwanda where abortion is illegal. Today in Rwanda there are many children who are the products of these rapes. In many cases these children have been rejected by their mothers and are now in orphanages run by international relief organizations (Boutros-Ghali, 1996: 67).

There were also cases of forcing adult Tutsi to commit incest with one of their children before killing them (Boutros-Ghali, 1996: 67). Here the image of misdirected flows is quite clear, for incest causes blood and semen to flow backward upon one another in a closed circuit within the family rather than in an open circuit between families. Not only were the victims brutalized and dehuman- ized by this treatment – their bodies were transformed into icons of asociality, for incest constitutes the pre-emption of any possible alli- ance or exchange relation that might have resulted from the union of one's son or daughter with the son or daughter of another family.

Other Metaphors of Violence

Not all of the violence or the metaphors associated with it that occurred during the genocide followed the symbolism that I have outlined above. Many of the explicit metaphors used by promoters of the violence actually show little overt relation to this symbolism. I do not see this as problematic; as I have stated elsewhere, there were many levels to the genocide, some quite conscious, others less so.

For example, the killers' frequently made reference to the violence as *akazi kacu* or 'our work'. In my opinion, this reference addressed more the killers' psychological discomfort with their unenviable social condition of unemployment and under-employment than any covert aspect of Rwandan *habitus*. Just by becoming an *Interahamwe* and executing Tutsi, one could elevate oneself to the status of 'state employee'. One could even expect eventual compensation from the state for one's services and indeed this was sometimes given and much more frequently promised.

The 'genocidaires' also frequently employed horticultural imagery. Hutu citizens were instructed to clear away the 'tall trees', an indirect but easily understood reference to the physiognomic stereotype of Tutsi height. In other cases the nation-state became a garden, as

Hutu extremists called upon their followers to cut down the 'weeds'. Following this metaphor, promoters exhorted their followers to take care not just to remove the 'tall weeds' (adults) but to remove the 'shoots' (children) as well.

The symbolization of Tutsi malevolence also drew upon other cultural sources. Some of the Hutu extremist theories, for example, show the probable influence of Nazi theories. Was this a coincidence or was this a conscious appropriation of anti-Semitic imagery? For example, the differing physiognomies of Hutu and Tutsi were said to have moral implications and particular attention was paid to the nose. (It should be recalled that in Nazi Germany posters depicted various forms of the so-called Jewish nose.) One extremist theory that I heard in Rwanda made the claim that the degree of human goodness that one possessed was directly proportional to the width of one's nose. Hutu stereotypically have wider noses than Tutsi.

In other instances the styles affected in the improvised uniforms of the *Interhamwe* militia, their gestures and body language showed the influence of James Bond, Bruce Lee, Rambo, and Arnold Schwarznegger films, all of which were readily available and popular in pre-genocide Rwanda. Violence, it would appear, has its fashions and its styles and these are partly transnational in origin.

The Rwandan Genocide and Historical Transformation

Although I believe that the imagery of flow and obstruction was pervasive during the genocide, it would be wrong to conclude from the above argument that Rwandan culture is simply a 'machine a tropes' constantly replicating the same structures and hermetically sealed off from all influences arising from within or beyond its borders. As Bourdieu maintains, people tend to reproduce the 'structured and structuring logic' of the *habitus*. Nevertheless, although older generations subtly inculcate this logic to their juniors, the socialization process is never perfect nor complete (1977, 1990). Transformed objective circumstances always influence socialization. The tendency to reproduce a structured logic thus should not be seen as simple and volitionless replication. There is always improvization and innovation even if many of the basic patterns retain their saliency.

In the Rwandan instance, colonialism and concomitant transformations in economic and political conditions influenced the
perception and depiction of evil. Because of these changes, the
symbolism of malevolent obstruction could be applied to an entire
ethnic group. This was a radical departure from the past. During
pre-colonial times the image of the menacing 'blocking being' was
confined to a limited number of individuals. These included: *impa*
– women who had reached childbearing age and had never menstruated; *impenebere* – women who had reached childbearing age and
had not developed breasts; individual enemies of the Rwandan king,
and sorcerers. All these malevolent beings were mythically presaged
in the legend about the *agakeecuru* and the origin of death. Occasionally, in the rituals associated with sacred kingship, such individuals
were publicly sacrificed to rid the polity of their potentially nefari-
ous influence.

It was not until Tutsi and Hutu ethnic identities had become
substantialized under colonialism and then privileges awarded by
the colonial rulers on the basis of these identities, that an entire
group of people could be thought of as a source of obstruction
to the polity as a whole. Tutsi could be easily assimilated to the
category of 'invaders' because of their alliance with German, then
Belgian, outsiders and the colonialists' reliance on Hamitic theories.
When Belgians quickly shifted their allegiance to Hutu in the late
1950s, supporting the 'Hutu revolution', Tutsi were left to fend for
themselves while retaining their substantialized identity. Tutsi
assimilation to the imagery of malevolent others, 'blocked' or
'blocking beings', was facilitated by the fact that a minority among
them had indeed been favoured socially and economically under
the colonial regime. Where once there had been a sacred king
whose actions were thought to assure a religious and material
redistributive function – the downward flow of celestial beneficence, wealth, and prosperity – under colonialism popular credence
in the ritual and pragmatic functions of kingship was undermined.

In its place a privileged class of Tutsi, Tutsi administrators in
the colonial state apparatus, were perceived by other Rwandans to
have become rich by subverting the redistribution process, or, in a
symbolic sense, by impeding the flow of *imaana*. The 1959–62
revolution in Rwanda was not anti-colonial; Belgians were not
endangered or forced to flee the country – Tutsi were. Nor were
Belgian economic and cultural interests seriously threatened in the
country. Belgians continued to enjoy privileged status in Rwanda

until some time after 1990 when Belgium withdrew its military support for the Habyarimana regime. The symbolism of obstruction is indeed pre-colonial in origin, but its application to an entire group of people is a thoroughly recent, modern application reflecting transformed consciousness of the polity and of the people comprising it.

Secondly, many of the actual and symbolic forms of violence became syncretized to Euro-American or transnational forms. This is apparent in the cartoon depicting Melchior Ndadaye's death, and in other juxtapositions of transnational images and those of local vintage. Clearly the violent imaginary looks for inspiration to all possible sources. According to Jean-Pierre Chretien in Rwanda: *Les medias du genocide* (1995) Nazi symbols were attributed to the RPF by Hutu extremists. The French government's habit of referring to the RPF as 'Khmers noirs' followed in this pattern and echoed their Hutu extremist allies. Nevertheless, it was Hutu extremists who were more Nazi-like and Khmer Rouge-like in actual practice.

Conclusion

Methodological individualists might very well object that atrocities occur in all violent conflicts and that they are at their worst in fratricidal disputes and civil wars. The Rwandan atrocities would then seem to have followed an empirical, rationalist logic centred on maximizing the number of one's enemies killed, or maximizing the psychological effect by the sheer horror of atrocity. Such an explanation might concur with what the authors of the atrocities themselves might claim was the reasoning behind their acts. Although such an explanation is accurate, it is incomplete. It cannot explain the depth of passion that clearly lay behind the Rwandan violence, nor the fact that it assumed specific forms. But one type of logic to the cruelty does not preclude all others; pragmatism and symbolism in a general way are not necessarily conflictual (cf. Sperber, 1975). Killing one's adversaries while communicating powerful messages about them and oneself are not mutually exclusive. Pragmatic explanations alone, however, cannot account for the sheer number of roadblocks that refugees reported to me that they encountered. There was certainly a point of diminishing returns where adding new barriers was concerned, and it would appear that this point had been more than surpassed. Nor was impalement the only way of making one's victims endure atrocious and exemplary suffering. Did it make sense to sever the Achilles' tendons of those who had very little chance of running away? Did it make sense to castrate pre-pubescent boys? Did it make sense to cut the leg tendons of cattle rather than killing them outright?

This is where pragmatic logic alone does not fully explain the Rwandan violence. Many forms of the violence encountered here were enracinated in Rwandan ways of bodily experience and bodily predispositions lurking beneath the level of verbalization and rational calculation. Although these predispositions were political in the sense that they influenced thought and action where power was concerned, they were certainly not political in the ordinary and instrumental sense of symbols consciously used by one group to advance its claims in opposition to another group and its symbols. This symbolism was logically prior to its instantiation in a political form and not the other way around.

Moreover, the use of the symbolism was ultimately contradictory. The power of the sacred king in pre-colonial and early colonial times emanated as much from his capacity to interdict flows as well as to catalyse them, but he was usually depicted as a 'flowing being' rather than a 'blocking' one, even to the point of being represented as a lactating male. Similarly, it made symbolic sense during the 1994 violence to make the claim of power, when power was no longer clearly defined, no longer in the hands of a single hierarchical authority, when power was diffuse and in the streets, to make the claim of power by eliminating all who would subvert the encompassing order of the Rwandan state. This entailed obstructing the obstructers, sacrificing the malevolent 'blocking beings' in the nation's midst as these latter represented both potential pathology to individuals and a threat to collective order. Sacrifice took the form of interdicting the flight of Tutsi, obstructing the conduits of their bodies, impeding their bodies' capacity for movement, subverting the ability of Tutsi to socially or biologically reproduce, and in many instances turning their bodies into icons of their imagined moral flaw – obstruction. Yet it led the murderers into a paradox: in order to parry the imagined obstructer, they were forced to obstruct.

From a purely pragmatic viewpoint, one might object that the imagery of obstruction and its relation to power is quite general, even cross-cultural. A petty bureaucrat manifests his/her power over petitioning citizens by impeding the passage of papers and forms through the administrative conduits. But the same argument can be made for many, if not most other symbols. Many symbolic forms are universal. Nevertheless, universality of 'image schemata' does not really detract from the assertion that the Rwandan violence should be understood in terms of its cultural specificity, for the question that really should be asked is not whether a certain symbolic image is cross-cultural or specific, but what degree of elaboration and use a specific group makes of the image. That Rwandans make extensive use of 'flow/blockage' imagery in relation to the body seems clear from a study of popular medicine. That these images would reappear in the context of the genocide makes sense in light of Kafka's *The Penal Colony* and the comments of Pierre Clastres, for it is the human body that serves as the ultimate tablet upon which the dictates of the state are inscribed.

The Rwandan genocide was certainly about power, but not all aspects of power are of the same nature. While most of the events leading up to and during the genocide involve power in its overt ideological manifestation, something that was openly discussed and contested, there were other potencies at work, those that social actors possessed less conscious awareness of. These potencies were not of the kind that competing factions could argue about or readily explicate. On the contrary, it is likely that many people in this conflict, whether they were *Interahamwe* extremists or RPF soldiers, whether they were Hutu or Tutsi, shared some aspects of a similar *habitus* and at least some of the same ontological predispositions. This is also why many Burundian forms of violence perpetrated by Tutsi against Hutu in 1972, resemble Rwandan forms perpetrated by Hutu against Tutsi in 1994. It is also why Hutu extremists depicted forms of violence that Hutu would presumably suffer at the hands of Tutsi 'feudal-monarchists', yet actually represented what Hutu extremists envisioned doing to Tutsi. As for the representations themselves, they constituted at one level the expression of one group's attempt to dominate another, but one should not conclude from this that dominant symbols are simply and necessarily the symbols of the dominant group. These were not Hutu symbols any more than they were Tutsi symbols. This was a system of representations that permitted Rwandans to cognize potencies of diverse sorts, potencies that include political power, but yet are not confined to it. The symbols cannot be reduced to simple surrogates for political action and struggle, but must be seen as largely autonomous.

Notes

1. 'Kafka designe ici le corps comme surface d'ecriture, comme surface apte a recevoir le texte lisible de la loi' (Clastres, *La Société Contre l'Etat*, 1974: 153).

2. 'Le corps mediatise l'acquisition d'un savoir, ce savoir s'inscrit sur le corps,' (Clastres, *La Société Contre l'État*, 1974: 154).

3. [. . .] '[L]a société imprime sa marque sur le corps de jeunes gens. [. . .] La marque est un obstacle a l'oubli, le corps lui-meme porte imprimees sur soi les traces d'un souvenir, *le corps est une memoire*' (Clastres, *La Société Contre l'État*, 1974: 157).

4. Kapferer is cognizant of the criticism often levelled at Dumont's scheme as reminiscent of unilineal evolutionism with its accompanying dichotomization of tradition and modernity. Kapferer responds by explaining that both egalitarian and hierarchical forms are equally modern, but that the contrast is justified in that the two incoporate different notions of the state, nation, society, and the person. 'In Foucault's sense the two ideologies articulate rather different discursive "technologies of power"' (Kapferer, 1989: 165).

5. This opposition is certainly not the only one that characterizes Rwandan popular medicine; there are others such as purity versus pollution, hot versus cold, and wet versus dry. However, the flow/blockage opposition appears to be the dominant one in healing and may also be dominant in other domains of Rwandan symbolic thought. Its analysis has nevertheless been neglected in the earlier ethnographic writing on Rwanda.

6. Francoise Heritier's work among the Ivory Coast Samo is quite germane here. Her work addresses some of the same concerns that I encountered in Rwanda: female sterility, amenorrhea, and analogies between human bodily states and natural phenomena such as aridity and drought. While her work emphasizes the opposition between 'hot' and 'cold', this does not preclude other oppositions such as 'flow' versus 'blockage'. Similar overall concerns are likely to be encountered elsewhere in sub-Saharan Africa but with varying symbolic expressions. Among the Samo the hot/cold opposition may be the dominant metaphor but among Rwandans and others in central Africa (cf. De Mahieu, Devisch) the flow/blockage opposition may be dominant.

7. The distinction between witchcraft and sorcery is not applicable in Rwanda. The Kinyarwanda verb *kuroga* refers to the introduction of poisons or other harmful substances into a victim's food or drink, or to the performance of ritual actions intended to harm another person.

8. Pierre Ntereye and I were just about to begin qualitative research in Kigali on the local perception, conceptualization, and treatment of sexually transmitted diseases when Rwanda exploded into violence in

April 1994. Unfortunately, Pierre, his wife, and children were all killed in the massacres that followed.

9. The Nyabarongo River eventually joins the Akagera River that forms Rwanda's eastern boundary with Tanzania. The Akagera then empties into Lake Victoria, which is where the Nile River begins. In 1994 Rwanda's rivers served as disposal points for thousands of bodies, which then began to collect on the shores of Lake Victoria creating a health hazard. The importance of these rivers during the genocide in an ideological and symbolic sense will be discussed below.

10. Mystical harm in Rwanda is never an innate, congenital potentiality as it is among some African peoples; instead it is always 'sorcery' involving the idea of the ingestion of harmful substances (even when no substances may have actually been ingested by the victim). 'Les Rwandais sont obsédés par les effets néfastes de l'alimentation qui exige mille précautions, d'autant plus que la sorcellerie est toujours conçue comme un empoisonnement' (Smith, 1975: 133). (Rwandans are obsessed by the possible harmful effects of eating, which demand the observation of a thousand precautions, even more so because sorcery is always conceived of as poisoning.)

11. It is interesting to note that among the news and political magazines that came into existence in the 1990s, there was one called *Isibo*. Politically speaking *Isibo* was an opposition magazine representing the viewpoint of southern and central Hutu allied to the Twag-iramungu faction of the MDR and opposed to the MRND and the Habyarimana regime (Chretien, 1995: 383). Although I have been unable to determine the significance of the magazine's title to its promoters and readers, it does seem to indicate that the term *isibo* retains cultural and political significance in the modern context and possesses associations that go beyond that of sacred kingship.

12. During the several days that French troops controlled the Centre, Viateur had occasion to speak with the Centre's director twice on the phone. When Viateur explained that he and other Rwandan employees marooned at the Centre had nothing to eat, she suggested that they take the plantains from trees growing on the Centre's grounds. (None of the plantain trees were bearing fruit at the time.) When Viateur expressed his anxiety about the unwillingness of the French troops to evacuate him and others, she told him that maybe the RPF would rescue them. (The RPF did not take this section of Kigali until almost two months later.)

13. Melchior Ndadaye was Burundi's first democratically elected president and first Hutu president. Elected in June of 1993, Ndadaye was taken prisoner in late October and then executed (not by impalement) by Burundian Tutsi army officers in a coup attempt. Almost univers-ally condemned by other nations, the coup eventually failed, but not before it had provoked reprisal killings in which thousands of Tutsi

civilians died and counter-reprisal violence in which thousands of Hutu were killed. The coup and Ndadaye's death served the cause of Hutu extremism in Rwanda quite well and extremists lost no time in exploiting it. Unfortunately the extremists' point that the Tutsi could never be trusted as partners in a democracy gained enormous credibility in Rwanda in the wake of Ndadaye's tragic death.

14.   Violence against women also characterized another recent fratricidal conflict where genocidal acts occurred – that of Bosnia. Where the logic of violence against Tutsi women in Rwanda appears to have been aimed at subverting the reproductive capacity of an entire group there seems to have been an additional logic in Bosnia, though it is also of a cultural nature. Among Mediterranean societies character-ized by strong notions of 'honour' (cf. Pitt-Rivers, 1977), much is invested in the perceived sexual purity of a group's women. Rape, as long as it is unavenged, is not just an act that violates an individual; it is an act which subverts the honour of a family.

CHAPTER FOUR

The Dialectics of Hate and Desire: Tutsi Women and Hutu Extremism

Introduction

In the past few decades sociocultural anthropology has expanded its purview beyond the confines of the classic community study to that of the nation state, the region, and the world. In the attempt to address the cultural nature of phenomena that both affect and transcend isolated localities, anthropologists have had to come to grips with the phenomenon of nationalism (Anderson, 1983, 1991; Birch, 1989; Eriksen, 1993; Handler, 1988; Hobsbawm, 1990; Kapferer, 1988). Some of these studies have attempted to understand nationalist violence (Anderson, 1991; Hinton, 1996, 1997; Kapferer, 1988). Others have integrated more classical anthropological topics such as race and ethnicity (Barth, 1959; Comaroff, 1992; Eriksen, 1993). Anthropological approaches to nationalism, ethnicity, and violence are all important in understanding the Rwandan genocide of 1994. Yet these aspects clamour so much for attention that they obscure other dimensions such as regionalism, class, and gender. Of these three, perhaps the least remarked to date has been gender. Nevertheless, as I will attempt to show in this chapter, gender considerations are potentially capable of elucidating many of the psychological and affective dimensions of the genocide, helping us to understand the violent sentiments that were unleashed during the tragic events of 1994. In exploring gender what we will see is that the genocide was about power relations between men and women perhaps as much as it was about power relations between groups of men. Gender issues figured prominently in the social construction of boundaries between ethnic groups and in local cultural notions of racial purity.

In classic studies of ethnicity and ethno-nationalism, the point has been made that the creation of boundaries and their maintenance is of crucial importance to the process of ethnogenesis (Barth, 1956; Eriksen, 1993). Thomas Eriksen, for example, shows that boundaries between groups become more strictly demarcated as the dichotomization of identities that characterizes ethnogenesis proceeds. He also remarks that the boundaries that develop between groups are first and foremost of a social nature. Other scholars have taken a more cultural tack and have attempted to explain the deeply passionate, quasi-religious aspect to nationalism (Anderson, 1983, 1991; Kapferer, 1988). Nationalist movements seem to offer a kind of surrogate transcendence to those who embrace them. At one level, nationalism feeds on the imagery of death, celebrating the martyrdom of torture victims and fallen heroes. Yet at another level nationalist movements invoke symbols of death's denial – fallen heroes live on in myth, legend, and ritual. To paraphrase Benedict Anderson, fatality becomes transformed into continuity (Anderson, 1991: 11). Although clearly different in some respects, at the core of both nationalism and religion lie rituals of sacrifice. In defence of the nation, people willingly kill others and, if necessary, sacrifice their own lives out of sentiments of 'metaphoric kinship' (Eriksen, 1993: 12; Yelvington, 1991: 168) with fellow members of the 'imagined community' (Anderson, 1983).

In order for sentiments of 'metaphoric kinship' to become crystallized into ideologies of political action, they must be socially salient. According to Eriksen, the social dichotimization of groups usually precedes their cultural differentiation and the latter may not even be a necessary condition of ethnic division (Eriksen, 1993: 4). In the Rwandan case, this observation applies, for there was really very little of a linguistic, religious, or cultural nature that distinguished Hutu from Tutsi. Despite this, as the dichotomization of ethnic identities proceeded during the 1990s, Hutu extremists set to work trying to methodically delineate 'Hutu culture' from 'Tutsi culture'. Rwanda's national radio station, for example, ceased airing traditional folk songs in honour of cattle, deeming these to be reminiscent of the time when Rwanda was ruled by pastoralist 'feudal monarchists' – as Tutsi came to be labelled by Hutu extremists.[1] More importantly, for our purposes, extremists attempted to purify a progressively more reified version of 'Hutu culture' biologically as well. They began to discourage sexual and conjugal relationships between Hutu men and Tutsi women.

Following the examples of Linda Basch, Cynthia Enloe, Mary Moran, and Constance Sutton, all of whom have worked on the question of gender and its relation to militarism in other ethnographic contexts (Sutton, 1995), it is necessary to understand the 'gendered workings of power' where the Rwandan genocide is concerned. While the proclivity to see the genocide as purely ethnic in nature is understandable and is in part justified by local Rwandan social realities, we risk falling into the trap of extremist ideology (whether Hutu or Tutsi) if this is all we can see. Both Hutu and Tutsi extremists believe and would have others believe, that the conflicts in Rwanda and Burundi are purely racial in nature. Understanding only the ethnic dimension, however, blinds us to other social imbalances and inequities that cannot be amended by concentrating on ethnicity alone.

Where gender is concerned, this is a glaring oversight. Where there is violence, sex is usually not too far away, and where there is sex, there is always gender. This component helps explain the highly impassioned and sadistic nature of the violence, which if catalyzed politically, socially, and culturally, had to have been profoundly felt within the hearts and minds of many social actors. Despite this, it would be wrong to conclude that Rwandans are culturally prone to violence and genocide. Rwandans have no more such proclivities than any other group of people on the planet. The genocide occurred in 1994; it could not have occurred in 1991, just a few months or even one year after Rwanda was invaded from Uganda by soldiers associated with the Rwandan Patriotic Front. While small, localized massacres did occur in the wake of the RPF invasion, these were organized by MRND party notables and there is little evidence that they were manifestations of generalized popular anger against Rwandan Tutsi (Chretien, 1997). Genocides occur at specific historical junctures and the social and psychological circumstances under which they occur require elaborate preparation in advance. To that end Hutu extremists put an enormous propaganda machine into operation; one that employed all local media (Chretien et al., 1995) – radio, news magazines, television, and an ever churning rumor mill.

Gender on the Warpath

In the months leading up to the genocide violent sexual imagery of both males and females abounded in the iconography of Hutu extremist literature while acts of actual sexual violence against Tutsi women occurred with increasing frequency.

During the genocide itself, women were important as both agents and symbols and this can be seen in several different ways. As agents women played important roles on both sides during the conflict. In the Rwandan Government Army, for example, there were many female Hutu soldiers.[6] Although no woman to my knowledge was involved in actual combat operations against the Rwandan Patriotic Front, in the Hutu extremist militia groups there were women who engaged in the killing of Tutsi civilians. Other extremist women acted as neighbourhood informers keeping note of Tutsi individuals and families who resided in their section. After the onset of the violence on 7 April 1994, these informers indicated where Tutsi families lived to bands of Hutu extremist youth, the *Interahamwe*. Informers of this sort were often rewarded with the property of their victims. On the other side, the side of the Rwandan Patriotic Front, composed of about 70 to 80 per cent Tutsi (7), women were active in fund-raising activities and in the preparation and dissemination of RPF literature. I do not know whether there were women in the military organization of the RPF. The fact that Tutsi women were killed during the 1994 genocide in numbers equal to, if not exceeding, those of men bears witness to the fact that they were not perceived as innocent non-combatants. This fact should be seen in contrast to earlier incidents of ethnic violence in Rwanda, in 1959 to 1964, for example, and again in 1973, when women were not killed in numbers comparable to men. Yet the violence against Tutsi women in 1994 can not simply be attributed to the fact that some Tutsi women were involved in, or supported, the RPF cause. There was a deeper level of motivation to the violence against them and this differed from earlier incidents of violence in Rwanda's history.

The genocide aimed at reasserting the cosmic order of the Hutu state as this was imagined through an idealized, nostalgic image of the 1959 Hutu revolution which brought an end to the Tutsi monarchy and to Tutsi dominance. The only perceived blemish of the revolution, repeated frequently in the days leading up to the genocide, was its failure to purify the country entirely. Extremists regretted that they had not gone far enough in 1959, that the revolution had failed to rid Rwanda of its polluting internal other once and for all. As a corollary to this image, though less overtly stated, extremists aimed at reclaiming the lost ground of patriarchy

Figure 4.1 *Blood and sex. The horrors of war attributed to the RPF* (Kamarampaka, *7 April 1993, no. 15, p. 14) The* Inkotanyi *(FPR) at work in Ruhengeri.*

and re-asserting a male dominance that had probably never existed in Rwanda's actual history.[8] Tutsi women were pivotal enemies in the extremists' struggle to reclaim both patriarchy and the Hutu revolution, because in many respects they were socially positioned at the permeable boundary between the two ethnic groups. It was much more common in pre-genocide Rwanda, for example, to find Tutsi women married to Hutu men than to find Hutu women married to Tutsi men. As official ethnic identity (marked on everyone's national identity card) was determined by the father in pre-genocide Rwanda,[9] a Hutu man married to a Tutsi women produced offspring who were legally Hutu. Intermarriage between Hutu men and Tutsi women thus conferred the full benefits of Hutu citizenship to progeny who were perceived by many as racially impure.

As the social dichotomization process advanced during the 1990s, ambiguous ethnic identities became less and less tolerated. This applied not only to the progeny of Hutu–Tutsi unions but also to the progeny of European–Rwandan and Asian–Rwandan unions, as many such people told me. The negative portrayal of Tutsi

women in Hutu extremist literature owed much to the fact that
Tutsi women were potential mothers of ethnically anomalous
children, for more Tutsi women than Hutu women married men
of other ethnicities. As the ideology of Hutu extremism developed,
racial purity came to be seen as a necessary component of Hutu
identity. Miscegenation between Hutu men and Tutsi women began
to be viewed with hostility. Yet, at the same time, many Hutu men,
including some who were extremists, either had Tutsi wives or Tutsi
mistresses with whom they had sired children. Clearly a great deal
of psychological and social ambivalence characterized the relation
between Hutu men and Tutsi women before the genocide. In order
to understand it and its consequences, we need to understand the
history of inter-ethnic marriages in Rwanda and the colonial ideology
of Hamitism, which depicted Tutsi as racially (and intellectually)
superior to Hutu, and Tutsi women as more beautiful than Hutu
women. Conjugal unions between Hutu men and Tutsi women were
not all that uncommon in the 1970s and 1980s, even if they were
not the norm, but by the 1990s the negative perception of such
unions had become much more pronounced. During the genocide
itself, Hutu men with Tutsi wives were often forced to kill their
spouses themselves in order to prevent their own deaths and a more
gruesome death for their wives.

As the dichotomization process intensified in the years leading
up to the genocide, Tutsi women came to occupy a socially liminal
position. As 'liminoid beings' (Turner, 1977), Tutsi women were
capable of undermining the categories 'Hutu' and 'Tutsi' altogether,
although it is doubtful that most individual Tutsi women possessed
much cognizance of this fact. In marriages or long-term sexual
liaisons with Hutu men, they were giving birth to children who
were *de jure* Hutu but *de facto* 50 per cent Tutsi. By logical extension,
the perpetuation and proliferation of Hutu-Tutsi unions threatened
the categorical boundary between Hutu and Tutsi. In many cases
children of mixed marriages could have typically Tutsi physiognomies, but yet be officially classified as Hutu on their national
identity cards. One such woman, whose father was Hutu and whose
mother was Tutsi, told me that in March 1992 the bush taxi that
she was travelling in was stopped at a military roadblock. The soldier
examined everyone's identity card; when he got to hers, he scoffed
at the fact that the category 'Hutu' had been checkmarked. With
an insult he threw the card onto the roadway where she was forced
to pick it up.

It is here that we need to examine the role of women as symbols and to consider the nature of the representations that were associated with them. These representations, discernible in Hutu extremist literature, foreshadowed the degree of sadism perpetrated by extremists on the bodies of their victims. To many Rwandans gender relations in the 1980s and 1990s were falling into a state of decadence as more women attained positions of prominence in economic and public life, and as more of them exercised their personal preferences in their private lives. Complex sexual politics preceded the genocide and were manifest in it. Many of the bitter ironies and contradictions of ethnicity were played out in sex and gender terms.

Women as Symbols

First let us consider some of the more overt manifestations of gender politics in the events leading up to the genocide. The gendered aspect of pre-genocide violence was far from apparent to me until I had a conversation with a Tutsi woman in late November 1993, about a month or so after my arrival in Rwanda. From her I learned of a special precaution that she and other Tutsi women took to avoid being raped by Hutu extremists. In the months leading up to the genocide, in late 1993 and early 1994, it was not uncommon for Tutsi of both genders to fall victim to acts of terrorism and intimidation. Tutsi women, for example, were often subjected to sexual harassment by Hutu extremists and many had been raped in the two years before the genocide began. It should be emphasized that, in more peaceful times, Rwanda is not characterized by a high incidence of rape – quite the contrary. After the 1990 invasion of Rwanda by soldiers associated with the Rwandan Patriotic Front, and the subsequent anti-Tutsi propaganda effort mobilized by the Habyarimana regime, the country became more violent in general. The incidence of rape and other crimes increased dramatically. A higher level of aggression was apparent to me in 1993 in ordinary social interactions that I observed between Rwandans, especially as someone who had lived in Rwanda in the more peaceful times of the 1980s. Greater tension and distrust, for example, marked everyday interactions between strangers. Drivers on highways and streets were ruder and more pugnacious; serious accidents had to have increased. Robbery, assault, and murder all had become more frequent. Within the circle of my acquaintances virtually everyone that I knew, whether Tutsi or Hutu, had been robbed at least once or beaten up by soldiers, by *Interahamwe*, or by common criminals merely taking opportunistic advantage of the heightened social tension. Agents of the Rwandan government, in their effort to assimilate all Rwandan Tutsi to the RPF invaders and to turn the Hutu majority against them, had begun a propaganda war. Later, these same elements recruited unemployed youth from cities like Kigali to commit acts of terrorism against Tutsi and selected Hutu opponents of the regime. In doing this it opened a Pandora's box of extremism and criminality that it could hardly control. The increasing disorder of civilian life was exacerbated by reverses on the battlefield and the deteriorating morale of Rwandan government soldiers. Many of the latter deserted the front and in the general atmosphere of lawlessness that had become regnant in the cities, began to sustain themselves by robbery or by selling arms. The victims of these robberies were often, but not always, Tutsi. In Rwandan marketplaces before 1993, it was not uncommon to see grenades on sale for less than $5 each.

As a Tutsi, however, and particularly as a Tutsi woman, one was particularly vulnerable to the regime's terrorists. I heard frequent stories of rape and attempted rape. According to my interlocutor, she and others, in order to increase the bother that a potential rapist might incur, had taken to wearing tight nylon panty hose over their underwear when they went out in public. When I suggested that such a measure was hardly a lock and key, she explained to me that it was more of a deterrent than a measure of absolute prevention. It would take a rapist more time to disrobe her, she explained, and in those added seconds she might find a way to defend herself or to escape

Another very telling incident with regard to the gender politics of pre-genocide Rwanda was the death of a woman that occurred on 22 February 1993. I lived in the same neighbourhood as this woman and both heard and felt the shock wave, of the grenade explosion that killed her. The murder of this woman, named Emilita, occurred just a day after two important Rwandan politicians had been murdered. One of the latter was Felicien Gatabazi, the leader of the Social Democratic Party, Rwanda's most ethnically mixed party and most anti-ethnicist in ideology. Gatazabazi, a Hutu from southern Rwanda, was one of the country's most popular politicians. As a possible rival to President Juvenal Habyarimana in elections scheduled in two years time (according to the Arusha peace agreement), and clearly a thorn in the regime's side because of his regional origin and anti-ethnicist views, Gatabazi had been a marked man ever since he had taken the reigns of the Social Democratic Party (PSD).

On the evening of 21 February 1994 Gatabazi was gunned down at his doorstep as he was returning home from a political meeting of the PSD. As I was home that evening and Gatabazi lived in my neighbourhood, I heard the three bursts of automatic rifle fire that killed him. A few days later Rwandan acquaintances told me that his killing bore the imprint of President Habyarimana's élite force, the Rwandan Presidential Guard. The next day supporters of Gatabazi in southern Rwanda accidentally spotted Martin Bucyana, a northerner like Habyarimana and leader of the most extreme anti-Tutsi party, the Committee for the Defence of the Republic or CDR. Pursuing Bucyana's car on foot, they managed to force him off onto a side road where they caught up with him and killed him and two others in the car with hoes and machetes. The assailants were angry at the northern-dominated regime and in search of a suitable victim to compensate for the loss of Gatabazi. An aspect of this incident, however, that was seldom remarked was the fact that Bucyana, most of Bucyana's assailants, and Gatabazi were all Hutu. To many southern Hutu, neither the RPF nor Tutsi in general were the principal enemy; northern Hutu supporters of Habyarimana were. After these two murders, one clearly a planned political assassination and the other an impromptu response to it, an atmosphere of disorder reigned in the capital city of Kigali keeping frightened citizens away from work for two days. It was in this atmosphere of deteriorating social order that Emilita herself was killed when a grenade was thrown into her bathroom while she was taking a shower.

Emilita had not been a politician. Part, but not 100 per cent, Tutsi, Emilita was a singular person in many respects. First of all, she was a Seventh Day Adventist, a Protestant in Rwanda where the majority was Catholic. She was also fairly prosperous by local standards, exercising a profession that many Tutsi men practised – she was a taxi driver. Under the regime's policies of 'regional and ethnic equilibrium' in place since Habyarimana came to power in 1973, state bureaucratic jobs, secondary school and university placements were based on group proportion in the total population. According to the figures, Tutsi were allotted about 9 per cent of the jobs and placements, Twa 1 per cent, and Hutu all the rest. In

Figure 4.2 *Money and scatology: PSD party's Felicien Gatabazi, being ridiculed* (La Medaille-Nyiramacibiri, April 1993, no. 13, p. 11). *A mother of a family: Gatabazi was caught naked. He stole the refugees' money.*

actuality many fewer Tutsi than the allotted 9 per cent received jobs and school placements, and virtually no Twa. Among Hutu, northerners received a disproportionate share of the advantages. Because little education was required, driving a taxi was thus a job that attracted a high number of Tutsi men. Emilita may have been singled out for murder because of her partly Tutsi background and her religion, but it is also likely that she was singled out as a woman exercising a man's profession and doing it very well.

Emilita was quite successful as a driver. Among her clients were visiting dignitaries, high level NGO employees, and other affluent foreigners. Her success may have been due to the fact that she was a good driver, a good mechanic, and clearly quite intelligent and affable. She spoke fluent English, fluent French, owned her own vehicle, her own house, and was about to purchase a second vehicle when she was murdered. In addition to her financial success, she was physically striking. Tall and muscular she habitually wore blue jeans, sneakers, and a rakish hat. Although most people that I talked to liked and admired her, she clearly transgressed Rwandan stereotypical gender norms and did this with a certain panache. This in itself was perhaps bad enough but the fact that she was financially successful to boot and preferred by rich foreign clients also made her the object of resentment and envy. There were some female business people in Kigali, and some who were quite financially successful, but as most of them were directly or indirectly tied to men in the regime, none of them flaunted the local codes for female conduct and dress with anything like the insouciance that Emilita showed. After her death some rumours had it that she had taken her own life because of a love affair gone sour, but that seems highly unlikely. According to her closest friends, it was impossible. She derived too much joy from life. Although no one was formally accused of the crime and no group took credit for it, it is likely that Hutu extremists had killed her.

Emilita's death had not been the first time in the history of the Habyarimana government that elements within it had acted against women visibly and publicly. Over 10 years earlier, under the guise of measures intended to improve public morality, there had been a particularly brutal campaign against single urban women. I read of this campaign in the summer of 1983, shortly before I travelled to Rwanda for the first time, in an article in *Le Monde* entitled 'Liaisons Dangereuses'. In another French newspaper, *Liberation*, given more to satire than *Le Monde*, an article describing the same incident was entitled, 'Touche pas a l'homme blanc!' Both articles described a wave of repression against young urban Rwandan women who either dressed too stylishly or had European boyfriends. Many of these women had been openly intimidated and assaulted by soldiers and police on the street. When I arrived in Rwanda in the summer of 1983, women told me that some of them had literally had the clothes cut off their bodies with bayonets and then had been forced to stand in the street nearly naked until a truck would come and take them to a detention centre. Charged with 'vaga-bondage' and prostitution, hundreds of Rwandan women were incarcerated in rural detention centres called *ingorora muco*, from the verb *kugorora* (to straighten) and *umuco* (customs, mores, morality). Closely approaching the Kinyarwanda in translation, this could be rendered as 'morals straightening-out centres'.

Most of the women incarcerated in early 1983 were Tutsi and many were quite attractive. Many had been badly mistreated by their captors; some had been raped. Although a few may have been prostitutes, the vast majority were not. Most were single women employed in respectable jobs and financially self-supporting; many were highly educated. Several weeks into this wave of repression, it came to an abrupt halt. Female employees at several Western

embassies had also been arrested and the corresponding ambass-
adors had vehemently protested against this. The whole affair had
become an embarrassment to the Habyarimana government and,
later, the official who had instigated the crackdown was summarily
dismissed. Nevertheless, many of the laws that had accompanied
the repression remained in effect. Women unaccompanied by men
were not allowed to enter bars at certain hours, for example, and
the terrorizing effect on young Tutsi women lingered. Virtually all
of them exercised extreme caution in their public behaviour and
avoided frequenting public places in the company of European or
American men. One Tutsi woman told me that several months after
the end of the crackdown, she had encountered the Prefect of Kigali
while walking on the street. Seeing that she was wearing sandals
and that her toe nails had nail polish on them, he warned her that
the last time he had seen a woman dressed like that, she was in
prison. The most enduring consequence of the repression was to
plant the idea in the minds of many Rwandans that single Tutsi
women were likely to be prostitutes. This image would resurface
with a vengeance in the years before the genocide.

The atmosphere of puritanical morality affected by the Habyarimana regime during the 1980s characterized several years of its
reign. Public morality was enforced by agents known popularly as
maneko, men who usually stuck out like sore thumbs in bars and
discotheques for they were usually overdressed and invariably would
wear a small campaign button with the President's photo in the
centre. Once in 1985 while I was in a discotheque with several
Rwandan friends, I noticed one such character staring intently at
me and at the rather short woman I was dancing with, the sister of
a close friend of mine who had accompanied several others and
me to the discotheque. Rather than asking the woman directly, the
maneko came over to me and asked me a question whose officious-
ness can only be seized in the French, 'Votre cavalière,' he queried,
'est-elle majeure?'[10] She was obliged to quickly fetch her purse and
identity cards and to prove to him that she was indeed over twenty-
one years old. It was not really under-age drinking that he was
worried about; it was the possibility that the woman in question
and me might be sexually involved.

Rwandan soldiers were also agents of public morality during the
mid 1980s. Shortly before midnight on Friday nights, they would
enter bars and discotheques and make sure that everyone left
promptly by midnight. Rwanda was a tightly controlled police state

and the marked puritanism of the regime added a moral flavour to its paternalism. To many, this moral aspect imparted a certain legitimacy to the government. Habyarimana himself tried to cultivate an image of religious piety and indeed many people were appropriately impressed. When visiting him at his home in Kanombe (near Kigali's airport), foreign dignitaries were often invited to pray with him in his private chapel. The international organization of Christian Democrat parties looked favourably on Habyarimana's party, the MRND, and regularly invited Rwandan delegations to its international congresses. Very close to Habyarimana, and an avid supporter of him, the Rwandan Catholic Church hierarchy benefited from a privileged status in the country that can only be described as a state within a state. To all these moralistic trappings was associated an attendant patriarchy and naturally, a great deal of hypocrisy. Although Habyarimana himself may have been faithful to his Hutu wife, many of his high level associates had mistresses, including Tutsi mistresses, although most were married to Hutu women.[11]

Tutsi women were not the only women against whom the regime directed moralistic wrath and sexual innuendo. At the outset of the genocide, one of the first victims was an extraordinary Hutu woman, Rwanda's Prime Minister at the time, Mme Agathe Uwiringiyimana. She was killed by Rwandan government soldiers in an exemplary fashion just hours after they learned of Habyarimana's death. Mme Uwiringiyimana was a southern Hutu and one of the most influential members of her overwhelmingly Hutu party, the Mouvement Démocratique Républicain or MDR. Although the MDR was ostensibly a new Rwandan political party, in reality it was quite old (see below). In this context it owed its existence to the Western-backed democratization initiative. In 1989 President François Mitterrand of France persuaded many leaders of Francophone African countries to open their countries to greater democracy. Rwanda's leader, Juvenal Habyarimana, a personal friend of Mitterrand, reluctantly heeded his protector's words; France, after all, was one of regime's major financial backers.

With the political opening of Rwanda that came about as a result of the initiative, several opposition political parties quickly came into existence, especially in southern Rwanda. One of these was the MDR – a direct descendant of PARMEHUTU. In the 1960s PARMEHUTU's leader, Gregoire Kayibanda, became the first Hutu president of Rwanda. This southern Hutu party had little love for

Habyarimana; in 1973 he and a coterie of northern military officers deposed Kayibanda in a coup d'état.[12] Shortly after the coup, PARMEHUTU was disbanded and Habyarimana inaugurated the Mouvement Revolutionaire pour le Développement, or MRND, and established one party rule in Rwanda. In the wake of the democratization initiative, PARMEHUTU came back as the MDR while the MRND became 'Mouvement Revolutionnaire pour le Développement et la Democratie', keeping the acronym, MRND.

Agathe Uwiringlyimana had had a stellar career before joining the MIDR. She had earned advanced degrees in chemistry and had taught at Rwanda's National University in Butare. Later she became active in politics and in a few years was named Minister of Primary and Secondary Education. While in this post, she acted to make access to education in Rwanda more equitable, particularly where women were concerned. In the months leading up to the genocide, Mme. Uwiringiyimana criticized Habyarimana and his party for failing to respect and implement the accords it had signed in Arusha, Tanzania, guaranteeing peace with the RPF and a more representative form of government for the country as a whole. The Arusha accords would have retained Habyarimana as president for two more years, although with seriously attenuated powers. Furthermore, had free and fair elections ever been allowed to transpire, parties well represented in central and southern Rwanda would have probably gained the majority of parliamentary seats.

Uwiringiyimana threatened the regime as an anti-ethnicist, a southerner, and as a highly educated and articulate person, but the fact that she was also a woman potentiated all these factors. In the months leading up to the genocide, extremist Hutu cartoonists obscenely depicted her in their literature (Chretien, 1995: 368). They also depicted male Hutu opposition politicians in sexual poses, but particular venom was reserved for Agathe Uwiringiyimana whom they referred to as 'Kanjogera'.[13]

Sometime on 7 April, just a few hours after President Habyarimana's plane had been shot down, Rwandan government soldiers surrounded Mme. Uwiringiyimana's house and took her prisoner along with the ten Belgian UN soldiers guarding her. They brought her to the location in Kigali where the UN command and its soldiers were lodged. There, in plain view of the UN contingent, and all passers-by, they executed her in the street. As for the ten Belgian soldiers, they were brought to a Rwandan army base and murdered.

The complexities of gender politics do not end with the Rwandan

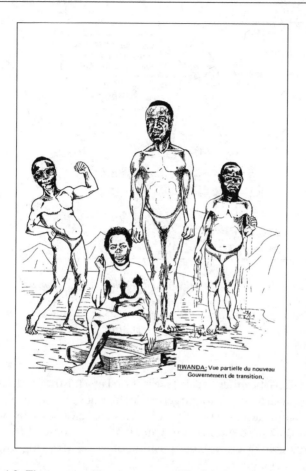

Figure 4.3 *The new transition government ridiculed obscenely.* (Kangura-Magazine, *May 1992, no. 10, cover). Ministers Boniface Ngulinzira, Agathe Uwilingiyimana, Dismas Nsengiyaremye, Pascal Ndengereho.*

regime's killing of extraordinary women. It is here that they begin, for the more we examine them, the murkier they become. One domain that was particularly complex in this regard was the area of sexual relations between Hutu extremist men and Tutsi women. According to Jean Marie Vianney Higiro, a Hutu journalist and pre-genocide director of Rwanda's National Information Office, who managed to escape to Nairobi although he was an intended target of the Rwandan regime, many high-level Hutu extremists in

Figure 4.4 *Faustin Twagiramungu and Agathe Uwilingiyimana in a pornographic situation* (Kangura, *January 1994, no. 55, cover*).
Twagiramungu: How's it going, little girl?
Agathe: It'll be just fine if you make me a minister in the transitional government.

the CDR party either had Tutsi wives or Tutsi mistresses. Ironically, in the days leading up to the genocide this put some Hutu extremists in the contradictory position of loving, at least sexually, women whom they were supposed to hate. It also put some of these men in the ideologically dubious position of siring offspring who were less than 100 per cent Hutu.

In the years before the genocide, official concern was occasionally though never overtly expressed by the regime with regard to the ethnic purity of certain people in presumably sensitive positions. In the early I 980s, for example, the Rwandan Army had deemed it necessary to purge officers suspected of having either partial Tutsi ancestry or Tutsi wives. When I did fieldwork in Rwanda in 1983–5, I personally met one such officer, a former major who had been eager to take on the politically favoured ethnicity. For a time he had succeeded. He had even managed, while still under commission, to change the ethnic classifications of many in his extended family from Tutsi to Hutu. I had even seen the national identity card of one member of the family and her card was indeed marked 'Hutu', although it was clear from her physiognomy and to all the

Figure 4.5 *Faustin Twagiramungu and Agathe Uwilingiyimana, passionate lovers according to the extremist press (*Kangura, *February 1994, no. 57, p. 5)*
Radio: February 28, 1994. The ceremonies that were supposed to occur today in the House of Deputies will not take place due to the absence of Twagiramungu and Agathe.
Agathe Uwilingiyimana: Heh! Get up, we're late. Let's go!
Twagiramungu: Little girl, let's have fun, those savages don't know what they're up to, we'll have time to put together a government.

Rwandans that I asked about her that she was Tutsi. The policy of keeping anyone suspected either of Tutsi ancestry or of having a Tutsi wife out of the army persisted until the genocide and was closely enforced by the Rwandan Army.

Going further back into the past, to pre-colonial and early colonial times, taking a Tutsi wife was often perceived as a sign of social advancement on the part of a Hutu man. In order to obtain such a wife, one had to become wealthy in bovine capital. The children of such unions were usually considered Tutsi. (This, by the way, was in sharp contrast with the late colonial and post-colonial era where the father determined ethnicity.) In effect it was possible, as a Hutu in the late nineteenth and early twentieth centuries, to have one's descendants become Tutsi by acquiring wealth in cattle and inter-

Figure 4.6 *"Agathe and Rugenera want to get their share while they're in power": two ministers being animalized (*Kangura*, February, 1994, no. 56, p. 6) Director of the National Bank: You eat what belongs to others. As for me I'm going to put a stop to it. I'm going to bash in your heads! Rugenera (Minister of Finance): What shall we do, dear?*

marrying with Tutsi. Tutsi hypogamy was justified on their part for they would often absorb rich Hutu into their lineages in this way. Practices such as these occurred often enough to justify a word in Kinyarwanda, *kwihutura*, meaning 'to cease being Hutu, to become Tutsi'. When the Rwandan monarchy and the system of Tutsi dominance that had characterized the colonial era came to an end with the Hutu revolution of 1959–62, it would have been logical for such intermarriages to decline in frequency. As Tutsi in general were now relegated to second-class status, there could be little advantage in establishing matrimonial alliances with them. Nevertheless, the practice continued.

After the revolution Hutu men still occasionally married Tutsi women, especially in southern Rwanda. It was even widely rumoured that Rwanda's first Hutu president, Gregoire Kayibanda, had had a Tutsi wife, although he was never above instigating or permitting anti-Tutsi violence whenever it was politically expedient. Although it must be admitted that certainly some Tutsi-Hutu unions after 1960 were the result of individual preference and romantic love, one has to wonder why mixed Hutu-Tutsi unions in Rwanda almost always involve a Hutu man and a Tutsi woman. Rarely does the opposite occur – a Tutsi man married to a Hutu woman. I personally knew of only one such case, although doubtless there were others.

Concerning the persistence of Hutu–Tutsi unions, it might seem that a colonial and precolonial practice simply continued into the post-colonial era. This hardly seems likely, for the social logics of these marriages are opposed, depending upon which historical era one is talking about. In colonial times where some Hutu men married up into Tutsi families, in post-colonial times we see them marrying down and gaining very little apparent social advantage by doing so. If the practice were simply a holdover from the past, one would have to explain this complete shift in social logic. Another possible explanation of the post-colonial marriage form is that it reflected a temporary relaxing of ethnic boundaries in marriage. Although there may be some truth to this hypothesis where southern Rwanda was concerned, it cannot be the whole story for then we would also expect to see an equal number of Tutsi men marrying Hutu women and this was not the case.

The question defies straightforward logic. In the past, and to a certain degree more recently, Rwandan parents exerted a high degree of control in their children's selection of a spouse. In the last few decades, young people have had greater latitude in manifesting their personal preference of spouse. Despite this, parents usually pressure their children to marry within their own ethnic group unless there are compelling reasons to do otherwise. Such pressure may be more binding where males are concerned as the husband's family must provide bridewealth to the wife's father. If a male does not have his father's agreement in a matrimonial decision, he will have to earn the bridewealth himself and even then he may encounter the prospective bride's family's objection to the marriage. Where women are concerned, the wealth or social power of the prospective husband might outweigh preference for someone from the same ethnic group. These two factors explain partly, but not completely, why there were more male Hutu married to female Tutsi than female Hutu married to male Tutsi. In effect, these explanations ignore possible motivation on the part of Tutsi women.

Where they are concerned, it is understandable that after 1960 they might perceive advantages to marrying Hutu men. Having a Hutu husband would imply some degree of protection for a Tutsi woman and her extended family in the event of ethnic troubles or violence. This, by the way, was true in all previous instances of violence in Rwanda, but was not true in 1994. Having a Hutu husband also meant that the woman's children would be more likely to receive an education as they would be considered Hutu. However, the advantages to a Hutu male in a union with a Tutsi woman are far from obvious. After the Hutu Revolution of 1959, all Tutsi had been relegated to the status of second-class citizens. Many Tutsi had lost large portions, if not all, of their personal fortunes in land, cattle, and money. What possible social advantage would accrue to a Hutu man by marrying a Tutsi woman? There would seem to be little or none. Nevertheless, the practice continued and often in the face of subtle and not so subtle obstacles that the regime placed in its path.

Besides the example of the Rwandan Army, high-level government officials were strongly discouraged from having Tutsi wives. Going against this unwritten directive did not help one's career. Having a Tutsi mistress on the other hand appears to have been tolerated. Habyarimana' s brother-in-law, Protais Zigiranyirazo, the prefect of Ruhengeri, a member of Habyarimana's inner sanctum called *Akazu*, and a member of the infamous *Reseau Zero*, which was instrumental in organizing the genocide, reportedly had a Tutsi mistress with whom he had had children, but there were some in Habyarimana's entourage who went beyond this. Habyarimana's personal physician, who was accompanying him in his plane at the time of his death, had a Tutsi wife.

Hamitism and the Politics of Beauty

It is at this point that we encounter one of the regime's thorniest contradictions. Despite all measures to discourage the practice, it found that it could not keep Hutu men from being attracted to, and occasionally establishing long-term sexual relationships with, Tutsi women. Widely reputed by Europeans to be more beautiful than Hutu, Tutsi women were even said to be more beautiful by many Hutu as well. I frequently heard statements to this effect in the 1980s during my first period of fieldwork in Rwanda. Malkki also discusses it in her book about Burundian Hutu refugees (1995). Two of the 'mythico-histories' that she analyses are entitled *Beautiful Tutsi Women as Bait into Servitude* and *The Death Trap of Tutsi Women's Beauty* (Malkki, 1995: 82–7). The gist of these stories is that Tutsi use the beauty of their women to trick Hutu into marriage. Once ensnared, the unfortunate Hutu man is said to become the virtual slave of his wife's Tutsi parents. It may be argued that, beyond readily apparent and standard determinants of beauty, the question of beauty is largely a political one. The dominant aesthetic standards of human beauty in any given social system, such an argument would assert, are the standards of the dominant class.

Such an explanation seems dubious in Rwanda where it was the women of the dominated group who were said to be more beautiful than those of the dominating group. The belief in the beauty of Tutsi women has a long precedent. Nineteenth-century European explorers, following the received wisdom of the Hamitic hypothesis, believed that the Tutsi were a quasi-Caucasian rather than a negroid race. As such the Tutsi were deserving of all the attributes of putative biological superiority – higher intelligence and greater physical beauty (see Burgt's comments p. 60).

Yet it would seem that the Hutu revolution might have overturned all that once and for all. Apparently it had not. The aesthetics of physical beauty associated with European colonialism, pitting one group against the other, persisted in Rwanda and Burundi well after 1960. In part this was reinforced by the fact that Europeans who entered into romantic involvements with Rwandan or Burundian women, or who married them, more frequently did so with Tutsi women. Unfortunately, because of their high visibility, such marriages contributed to the impression that the sexual and matrimonial destinies of beautiful Tutsi women were determined more by the laws of the market place than by Rwandan social norms. The marriages also incited resentment and jealousy among Hutu extremists. Some of the latter might have wished that Hutu women would also be chosen by Europeans; others might have resented the fact that the most beautiful Rwandan women often spurned marriage with Rwandan men and sought husbands from Europe or North America. In 1982–3 sentiments such as these had led to the imprisonment of scores of Tutsi women. In the years shortly before the genocide, the image of the alluring Tutsi woman appeared once again. In extremist literature, Hutu cartoonists depicted Tutsi women as prostitutes capable of enlisting Western support for the RPF cause through the use of their sexual charms. One cartoon shows Canadian General Romeo Dallaire, the head of the United Nations peacekeeping force in Rwanda before and during the genocide, in an amorous embrace with two Tutsi women. The

Figure 4.7 *Tutsi women, the reason why whites took the side of the FPR.*
(Kangura, February 1994, no. 56, p. 15)
General Dallaire and his army have fallen into the trap of fatal women.

caption on the cartoon reads: 'General Dallaire and his army have fallen into the trap of fatal women' (Chretien, 1995: 274).

Another cartoon shows three Belgian paratroopers in various sexual acts with two Tutsi women (Chretien, 1995: 366). This cartoon merits further commentary. In 1983 and 1984, I had occasion to discuss the 1982–83 repression against young urban women with Rwandan men. Many of my interlocutors expressed dismay that the Western press seldom printed anything at all about Rwanda and when it did, as in 1983, it chose to cast the country in a bad light. One of them asked me how I expected Rwandan parents to raise morally upstanding daughters, if the children had the example before them of prostitutes grown rich from their escapades with European men. Another man expressed disgust at the type of sexual practices that he claimed were being transmitted to Rwandan women through contact with Europeans. Specifically he mentioned anal intercourse, cunnilingus, and fellatio. In this cartoon, not only are these acts pictured, but they are also being done in a group, something foreign to Rwandan sexual norms. Similar to food taboos, perceived differences in the sexual practices between one group

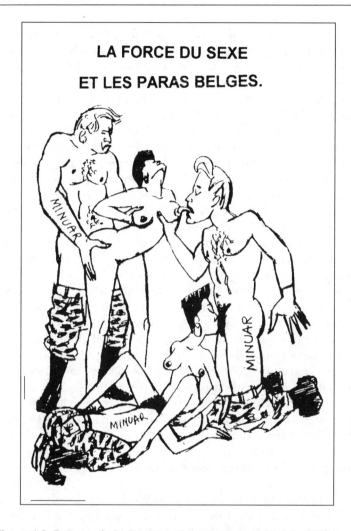

Figure 4.8 *Propaganda leading up to the assassination of Belgian blue helmets on 7 April 1994 (Power, December 1993, no. 2, p. 12) The 'power of sex.' Tutsi women and Belgian paratroopers of the UN force.*

and another are important in delineating the boundaries between the goups. Sexual practices are also, of course, highly invested with emotion. In this cartoon, Hutu extremists are by implication distinguishing their own sexual practices, procreative and moral, from European and Tutsi practices, non-procreative and immoral.

At the same time, Hutu extremists appear to be attempting to purge their ambivalence toward Tutsi women via symbolic violence, even as they project their own erotic fantasies upon them. At one level they were certainly aware that to preserve the racial purity of Hutu, they had to categorically renounce Tutsi women as objects of desire. At the same time they also knew that they themselves were not free of the forbidden desire. They were not impervious to the allure of Tutsi women and indeed they knew that many of the most prominent among them had succumbed to the temptation. If the choice between Hutu and Tutsi women were non-problematic for Hutu extremists, narratives to the effect that Tutsi use the beauty of their women to ensnare Hutu would be unnecessary. One can only speculate about the possible cognitive dissonance in the minds of many Hutu extremists where the question of Tutsi women was concerned. What is most important for our purposes is the fact that these sentiments received social expression.

For example, in December 1990 the Hutu extremist magazine, Kangura, printed what is perhaps the most succinct statement of Hutu extremist ideology – the infamous 'Hutu Ten Commandments'. Although this document has been quoted often and widely discussed by scholars who have written about the genocide (Prunier, 1995; Chretien, 1995), no one to my knowledge has pointed out that gender preoccupations were clearly very much on the minds of the extremists. Hutu extremists had to have accorded high priority to the question of relations between Hutu men and Tutsi women, for the first three of the Ten Commandments concern this subject and this subject alone.

Here are the first three commandments:

1. Every Muhutu [Hutu male] should know that wherever he finds Umututsikazi [a female Tutsi], she is working for her Tutsi ethnic group. As a result every Muhutu who marries a Mututsikazi, or who takes a Mututsikazi for a mistress, or employs her as a secretary or a protégéé is a traitor.
2. Every Muhutu should know that our Bahutukazi [female Hutu] are more worthy of, and conscious of their roles as woman, spouse, and mother. Are they not pretty, good secretaries, and more honest!
3. Bahutukazi [Hutu women], be vigilant and bring your husbands, brothers, and sons back to the path of reason.

(Chretien, 1995: 141 [my translation])

Would it have been necessary to recall all Hutu men to order in this way, if the women of the opponents' group had not exerted such compelling attraction? Why was it necessary for the extremists to assert that Hutu women are pretty, unless there were doubts to the contrary? The third commandment is also very telling: Hutu men cannot be expected to resist the attractions of Tutsi women alone; they need their Hutu wives, sisters, and mothers to call them back to reason!

Another commandment, the seventh, declared that the Rwandan Army must remain Hutu, but added to that an additional warning against Tutsi women. Apparently Hutu extremists were so preoccupied by this issue that no amount of redundancy or overemphasis could ever be deemed excessive.

7. The Rwandan Armed Forces must be exclusively Hutu. The experience of the October 1990 war teaches us this. No soldier should marry a Mututsikazi.

> (Chretien, 1995: 142 [my translation])

Beneath this ambivalence one cannot help but sense lurking Hamitic imagery – a tragic yet unacknowledgeable sense on the part of the extremists that, when all was said and done, early Europeans had indeed been correct in depicting Tutsi as 'golden-red beauties' and Hutu as inferior (and less attractive) negroids. The 'Hutu Ten Commandments' are not the only evidence of this type of sentiment. In June 1994 after months of inaction on the part of the United Nations and the international community, the French decided to intervene in Rwanda through 'Operation Turquoise'. Too little, too late, the operation saved few threatened Tutsi and may have actually facilitated escape into Zaire for the beleaguered remnants of Rwandan Government Forces and their allied extremist militias. Perceived as 'friends' by the latter, the Hutu extremist radio, Radio Television Libre de Mille Collines (RTLM), called upon the population to welcome the French. Their appeal to young Hutu women was especially revealing:

> You Hutu girls wash yourselves and put on a good dress to welcome our French allies. The Tutsi girls are all dead, so now you have your chance.

> (Prunier, 1995: 292).

The beauty of Hum women, it would seem, could only be expected to shine in the absence of competition from Tutsi women. As Prunier points out in a footnote in his book, such evidence of a lingering inferiority complex may partly account for the degree of sadism unleashed by Hum death squads against Tutsi.

Indeed, special measures of terrorism were reserved for Tutsi women by the extremists. Many Tutsi women suffered breast obla-tion, or were raped before being killed. Others were impaled with spears from vagina to mouth. Many were forced to commit incest with a male family member before being killed. Pregnant women were often eviscerated. Yet other Tutsi women were spared and taken as 'wives' by their persecutors and brought into the refugee camps of eastern Zaire. There they became sexual slaves to their captors. In the events that transpired in eastern Zaire during the last days of the Mobutu regime, some of these women managed to escape and to return to Rwanda pregnant and seeking abortion in a Catholic country that prohibits it.

Conclusion

The Rwandan genocide cannot be understood solely in ethnic terms. Although recent theoretical contributions to the study of ethno-nationalism are obviously of great importance in compre-hending this tragedy, they tend to accord little weight to gender, if they deal with it all. Gender issues interacted with ethnic ones in complex ways involving the demarcation of social boundaries and local notions of racial purity. Although these notions of racial purity were ultimately of nineteenth-century European origin and were associated with the Hamitic hypothesis, they became internalized by many Rwandans and were later used ideologically by ethnic extremists in both Rwanda and Burundi.[14] Many of the sterotypes of Tutsi women that one observes in pre-genocide Hutu extremist literature owe their existence to pre-existing Hamitic models.

The Rwandan genocide of 1994 differs from earlier incidents of massive violence in the country's history in that women were targets of violence as much as, if not more than, men. This was especially the case where Tutsi women were concerned, but was not confined to them. The conflict in Rwanda involved reasserting an imagined past condition of patriarchy as well as the perpetuation of Hutu dominance. This is why female Hutu opposition politicians, such as Agathe Uwiringiyimana, were also targeted by extremists.

Tutsi women, however, suffered the brunt of extremist violence. Hutu extremists harboured enormous psychological ambivalence toward Tutsi women. On one hand Tutsi women were despised for their potential subversive capacity to undermine the categorical boundary between Tutsi and Hutu. On the other hand, many Hutu extremist men were unable to completely shed feelings of attraction toward Tutsi women. Of colonial origin, the representation of Tutsi women as superior in intelligence and in beauty to Hutu women appears to have plagued the psyches of Hutu extremists. Envy and resentment are perhaps the most social of emotions. When these emotions concern traits like intelligence and physical beauty, they are not easily expunged.

One can seize the wealth and power from those that one envies, but one cannot seize another's intelligence and beauty. When Hutu took control of Rwanda in 1959, their revolution did nothing to reverse the ethnic stereotypes inherited from colonialism. The reason for this is that a critique of colonialism and its effects on people's categories of perception was never allowed to develop and mature in Rwanda. Although this critique is not the only measure needed in order to bring about reconciliation in Rwanda, Rwandans must start here. They must acknowledge, then question, then criticize the enduring effects that colonialism has had on their own minds.

Notes

1. Until 1960 Rwanda was ruled by a Tutsi king under the tutelage of the Belgian colonial administration. In the 1950s, educated Hutu sought a greater role in the Rwandan government and became politically active and vocal. Their movement, aided by the Rwandan Catholic Church and later supported by the Belgian colonial administration, culminated in the replacement of Tutsi administrators with Hutu under Governor General Jean-Paul Harroy. Shortly thereafter, the Tutsi king was overthrown as well as the system of Tutsi dominance. The violence of this transition between 1959 and 1964, claimed the lives of tens of thousands of Tutsi and many more thousands emigrated to neighbouring African countries, creating a diaspora. During the 1980s the sons and daughters of the original refugees sought to return to Rwanda. When their overtures to the Habyarimana government met with little

substantive action in their favour, they decided to return to Rwanda by force. Composed of about 70 to 80 per cent Tutsi, the RPF invaded Rwanda from Uganda in October 1990. Peace accords ending this war were signed in Arusha, Tanzania in August 1993 and gave the RPF most of what it had fought for. Implementing the accords, however, proved to be another matter. Hostilities between the two sides resumed on 7 April 1994 and resulted in an RPF victory by July 1994. In the intervening period approximately one million Rwandans lost their lives, mostly Tutsi, although many Hutu opponents of the regime were also killed.

2. According to most students of Rwandan politics and history such as Gerard Prunier (1995), Habyarimana's plane was shot down by elements within his own coterie who were even more extreme in their anti-Tutsi racism than him. This seems likely. With the bulk of their forces concentrated in northern Rwanda, several days away from Kigali, it is unlikely that the RPF would have acted so brashly. As for the extremists, they could hope for an angry, generalized Hutu response against Tutsi due to Habyarimana's death. Although many Hutu did not have such a response, clearly many others did. Due to the genocide's careful planning and organization probably somewhere between 60 and 80 per cent of Rwanda's resident Tutsi population died in about one hundred days.

3. Formerly called Mouvement Révolutionnaire pour le Développement.

4. The impotence of UN peacekeeping forces became apparent within weeks of their arrival in Rwanda in late 1993. On several occasions Hutu militia members openly harassed or attacked people in full view of the UN forces. Because the UN peacekeepers did not have the mandate to intervene, they would observe such incidents and photograph them. On 7 April 1994 ten Belgian soldiers associated with the UN peacekeeping force were captured and later killed by Rwandan Government Forces. This prompted Belgium to order its troops out of Rwanda. Other countries quickly followed suit and the way was clear for an unopposed genocide.

5. The term *Interahamwe* comes from the verb *gutera* – 'to throw, to attack, to launch' and *hamwe* – 'together.' *Interahamwe* were the youth wing of the MRND party. Along with 'Hutu powa' factions from other parties and the *Impuza mugambi* of the most extreme Hutu party, the Comité pour la Défense de la République or CDR, these youths were probably responsible for the majority of the deaths that occurred during the genocide. Their weapons of choice were the grenade, the machete, and the nail-studded club.

6. Under the Habyarimana government Tutsi were not allowed to serve in the military. Some Tutsi, however, who had managed to fake Hutu ethnic identity, managed to enter the military. Most were later found out and purged during the 1980s.

7. According to Alison des Forges in a talk presented at the Washington DC Holocaust Museum in August 1994.

8. As many Rwandan kings assumed this function at a tender age, in reality the king ruled in conjunction with a queen mother. Rwandan queen mothers were often politically prominent, prompting some early European explorers to speak of Rwanda as a territory ruled by a queen. One of the most famous queen mothers in Rwanda's history was Rwabugiri's favourite wife, Kanjogera. After Rwabugiri's death, Kanjogera managed to engineer a *coup d'état* at Rucunshu (circa 1896) and put her own son, Musinga, on the throne in place of Rwabugiri's personally designated successor. Biographical sketches of women whose lives straddled the pre-colonial and early colonial period are also indicative that women's lives did not improve under colonialism (see Helen Codere, 1973).

9. During the 1920s Belgians instituted administrative reforms. Shortly thereafter they began the practice of censuring Rwanda's population and having the people carry identification cards marked with their ethnicity. From this time onward, children took the ethnic classification of their father. As Belgians followed the earlier German colonial precedent of indirect rule through Tutsi, it was necessary to know who was Tutsi, who was Hutu, and who was Twa. According to early census figures, Tutsi comprised about 10 per cent of the population, Hutu about 90 per cent, and Twa about 1 per cent. This figure, later used by the Habyarimana government in its policy of 'regional and ethnic equilibrium' probably underestimated the actual proportion of Tutsi as the criterion for being classified as Tutsi was number of cattle owned. Many Tutsi reported fewer cattle than they actually owned in order to avoid higher taxes.

10. 'Your dancing partner, is she of legal age?'

11. Locally, the institution of keeping a mistress was referred to as 'deuxième bureau' or 'second office'.

12. The last Tutsi king of Rwanda abdicated and fled the country in 1960. Later, in UN sponsored elections, the PARMEHUTU party won an overwhelming majority and Gregoire Kayibanda, the party's leader, became Rwanda's first Hutu president. Two years after Habyarimana's *coup d'état*, Kayibanda died under mysterious circumstances. Local rumour has it that Habyarimana's agents slowly poisoned him.

13. See note 8. Uwiringiyimana embodied many of the qualities that patriarchal extremists bated to see in women – power, intelligence, and the courage to speak and act. These were all qualities that, according to legend, Kanjogera had possessed.

14. I treat this subject in detail in Chapter 1.

Conclusion

In the preceding pages of this work I have discussed personal experience, history, politics, symbolism, and gender. I was a witness to many of the events leading up to the Rwandan genocide, witness to the first sixty hours of violence, and because so many of the genocide's victims and perpetrators were once friends and acquaintances of mine, these events have obviously affected me in a profoundly personal way. It has become fashionable in recent years to 'blur the genres' and to write more personalistic ethnographies. Such methods can add to our understanding of massive human tragedies and Clifford Geertz's recent book, *After the Fact*, is an excellent example of this, but it is not for the sake of fashion that I have begun this work in that way, for all too often highly personal ethnographies rapidly turn in the direction of self-indulgence, telling us more about the author than the people he or she claims to be describing. I have tried to resist that tendency, but I have also been concerned to convey a sense of what it was like to be caught in the midst of *anomie*, something that most ethnographers never experience, that graduate training never prepares us for, and that, at the time, I barely understood. It has taken me several years to move beyond the grief, the anger, and the bewilderment that I felt looking back on Rwanda when once again I set foot on American soil returning to the cocoon of ignorant security and complacency that most of us in this country and elsewhere in the West call 'peace' and take as our God-given right. Yet how often our peace seems predicated on someone else's misery.

It has not been a pleasant experience to write this book. There are only villains in this story, only pain and suffering to be dissected with the anthropological scalpel. I also fear that this work may give the impression that there was no one during these tragic events who acquitted himself or herself with dignity. That, of course, is not true. In what I hope will be a future work, I will relate some of the stories that I heard in Nairobi about Rwandan Hutu and others who resisted the genocidal juggernaut up to the end and risked their lives in many cases to save fellow human beings. Heroism is eminently more satisfying to write about than human perfidy. Nevertheless, we need to understand human malevolence in all of its ramifications, for it seems that otherwise we are doomed, as happened in Rwanda, to let history repeat itself. Consider the historical context of the 1948 Geneva Convention: the self-congratulatory triumphalism, the assurance that evil had been defeated, the bold pronouncements against genocide. All that came to naught in Rwanda. To paraphrase Alison des Forges, Rwanda was simply too little, too far away, too poor, and too black for the 'developed' world to care about. I have offered an anthropologist's perspective on these events, but there are others. In a sense this book had to be written. As a distinguished senior anthropologist admonished me, 'You have a moral obligation to write this book.'

I have chosen to employ the analytic tools of classic anthropology. I have chosen to do this because I remain convinced that classical anthropology has not outlived its usefulness in helping us to understand an event like the Rwandan genocide. Such methods do not exhaust or preclude all other types of understanding, but they remain necessary if we are to progress beyond reasoning that simply recapitulates evenemential history. One of the central concerns of the literature on ethno-nationalism, for example, is the question of social boundaries. During the months of 1993 and 1994 that I lived in Rwanda, I became sadly aware of the degree to which the organs of disinformation could create new boundaries and exacerbate old ones and gain purchase on people's psyches. Yet I doubt to this day that the shibboleths and modes of thought that provided ethnic extremists with ideological fuel have been seriously challenged. Unless this disinformation is refuted and convincingly so in the public fora that exist in central Africa, their future potential for harm will remain. It is here that an anthropologically informed reading of history has something to say.

I am also convinced that classical anthropology's focus on the concept of culture, despite the wave of attacks that it has sustained in recent years, can lead us to a more profound understanding of mass violence. Terror is both ritualized and characterized by highly specific forms and these are amenable to cultural analysis. The culture of terror does not depart radically from the culture of ordinary sociality. It is the same only more so. The concept of culture can help elucidate events like genocide, but it has to be concretely anchored and directly related to what is the ultimate source and destination of terror, the human body. Terror, if we are to understand why it is so seductive and so compelling, must be analysed at its most fundamental level, and this means grounding it in the body.

Bodies in central Africa continue to be torn asunder. At the time of writing (February 1999) the prospects for lasting peace in central Africa appear dim. Violence persists in both Rwanda and Burundi, where anti-government groups wage guerrilla warfare and extremist ethnic ideologies continue to be mobilized. In the neighbouring Democratic Republic of Congo (DRC), Laurent Kabila's government is presently under attack from some of the same elements that helped put him into power in 1996. These include, among others, *Banyamulenge* from the eastern regions of the Congo. Many of the latter are Kinyarwanda speakers, ethnic Tutsi who emigrated from Rwanda well before there were colonial states in central Africa. Because of their association with the Rwandan Patriotic Front and later the Rwandan Patriotic Army, *Banyamulenge* are now being subjected to much of the same racist propaganda in the DRC that Tutsi were subjected to in Rwanda. 'Hate radio' has resurfaced in the DRC along with anti-Tutsi violence in Kinshasa and elsewhere. Nor have some of the Tutsi rebel forces shown themselves to be above genocidal acts; they have also committed massacres in the eastern DRC. Complicating matters is the fact that Angola and Zimbabwe have sent air and ground forces into the DRC to help prop up the Kabila regime, while Rwanda and Uganda have intervened on the side of the rebels against Kabila. The prospect for a generalized regional war in central Africa cannot be discounted. That new genocidal violence might be triggered by this unrest cannot be ruled out.

It is because of the continuing high potential for violence in the region that the Rwandan genocide requires multifaceted understanding. Historical analysis, gender analysis, and symbolic analysis can all contribute to this even if some levels have more immediate practical implications for policy makers than others. I have tried to address these different levels as fairly and honestly as possible in this work and have paid particular attention to where all of them converge on the theme of the body. Representations of the body can be seen to underlie much of the politics and the violence that has occurred in Rwanda and in neighbouring regions. At an ideological level, for example, we witness the enduring force of nineteenth century European pseudo-scientific models, using some fact and much fiction, to classify bodies into those with brains and those with muscle, those with beauty and those without. This has had enduring psychological repercussions. To this day possessing the wrong physiognomy in central Africa can get a person killed, not by Europeans, but by other central Africans.

But not all of the violence during the Rwandan genocide can be explained by a politics of the body or a calculus of the body politic. Although much of the politics and the political history of the last forty years can be understood as the actions of calculating subjects operating under the assumptions of Hamitic ideology, there is much that cannot be understood in this way. At a pre-ideological and largely unconscious level, attention needs to be paid to the ontological and cosmological implications of the malevolent body, depicted in ritual and myth as 'obstructing' or 'obstructed.' In order to understand, following Clastres, Gledhill, Kapferer, and Bourdieu, the 'mythic logic' of this body and of the violence directed against it, I have employed the techniques of symbolic analysis. What has been uncovered is an implicit logic that suffused the thoughts and actions of social actors, gave form to their passions, and defined which violence in the context of 1994 Rwanda was the most gravid with meaning.

Finally, we need to understand that the violence against bodies in 1994 Rwanda was gendered. Both before and during the genocide, sexual and gender preoccupations were clearly on the minds of Hutu extremists. Ethnicity appears to have been the immediate cause of the Rwandan violence, but it was certainly not the only cause. Focusing solely on ethnicity has tended to obscure sex and gender. In examining Rwandan attitudes and representations of gender, it becomes clear that gender psychology, gender politics, and gender symbolism played a more important role in preparing the terrain and in shaping the violence than what has heretofore been suspected. Complex, ambivalent, and powerful sexual passions were unleashed during the genocide motivating the actions of the 'genocidaires'. These can only be partly understood as ideological, and are only partly amenable to conventional symbolic interpretation. A method integrating aspects of both along with social psychological analysis has been necessary.

In place of intellectual consistency, therefore, I have had to adopt a more dialectical method in this work, one that tacks between the poles of structure and agency, one that attempts to explain events and to explain forms, although not in terms to which both can be reduced. This method poses, yet does not resolve, the ultimate conundrum posed by the proposition that human beings, through their choices, create culture, including cultures of terror, but culture determines the framework of choice even under apparently anomic conditions. It is thus on a paradoxical note that I end, but one that is appropriate given the extraordinary nature of the Rwandan genocide, which, I believe, will always defy all but partial and contradictory understanding.

Bibliography

Anderson, B., *Imagined Communities: Reflections on the Origin and Spread of Nationalism*, London, Verso, 1991 (revised edition).

Assad, T., 'Market Model, Class Structure and Consent. A Reconsideration of Swat Political Organisation', *Man*, vol. 7, 1972: pp. 74-94.

Barth, F., 'Ecological Relations of Swat Ethnic Groups in Swat, North Pakistan', *American Anthropologist*, vol. 58, no. 6, 1956: pp. 1079-89.

Barth, F., *Political Leadership among the Swat Pathans*, London, Athlone, 1959.

Barth, F., 'Introduction', in F. Barth, ed., *Ethnic Groups and Boundaries, the Social Organization of Culture Difference*, Oslo, Universitets-forlaget (Scandinavian University Press), 1969: pp. 9-38.

Basch, L., 'Introduction: Rethinking Nationalism and Militarism from a Feminist Perspective', in C.Sutton (ed.), *Feminism. Nationalism, and Militarism*, Washington (DC), Association for Feminist Anthropology, American Anthropological Association, 1995: pp. 3-12.

Beattie, J, *Bunyoro, an African Kingdom*, New York, Holt, Rinehart, & Winston, 1960.

Beidelman, T., *Moral Imagination in Kaguru Modes of Thought*, Bloomington, Indiana University Press, 1986.

Birch, A., *Nationalism and National Integration*, London, Unwin Hyman, 1989.

Bourdieu, P., *Outline of a Theory of Practice*, Cambridge, Cambridge University Press, 1977.

Bourdieu, P., *The Logic of Practice*, Stanford, Stanford University Press, 1990.

Bourgeois, R., *Banyarwanda et Barundi, réligion et magie*, Brussels, Académie Royale des Sciences Colomales, 1956.

Boutros-Ghali, B., 'Introduction', *The United Nations and Rwanda 1993-1996*, New York, Department of Public Information, United Nations, 1996: pp. 3-1, 11.

Braeckman, C., *Rwanda. Histoire d'un genocide*, Paris, Fayard, 1994.

Chretien, J.-P., 'Burundi: le métier d'historien: Querelle d'école?' *Canadian Journal of African Studies*, vol. 25, no. 3, 1991: pp. 450-70.

Chretien, J.-P., *Rwanda: les médias du genocide*, Paris, Editions Karthala, 1995.

Chretien, J.-P., *Le Defi de l'Ethnisme: Rwanda et Burundi 1990–1996*, Paris, Editions Karthala, 1997.

Clastres, P., *La société contre l'etat: recherches d'anthropologie politigue*, Paris, Editions de Minuit, 1974.

Clifford, J., Marcus, G., *Writing Culture: the Poetics and Politics of Ethnography*, Berkeley, University of California Press, 1986.

Codere, H., *The Biography of an African Society, Rwanda 1900–1960: based on forty-eight Rwandan autobiographies*, Tervuren (Belgium), Musée Royal de l'Afrique Centrale, 1973.

Comaroff, J., and Coniaroff, J.L., 'Ethnography and the Historical Imagination', in Comaroff, J. and Comaroff, J.L. (eds) *Ethnography and the Historical Imagination*, Boulder (CO), Westview Press, 1992: pp. 3-48.

Comaroff, J. and Comaroff, J.L., 'Of Totemism and Ethnicity', in Comaroff, J. and Comaroff, J.L. (eds) *Ethnography and the Historical Imagination*, Boulder (CO), Westview Press, 1992: pp. 49–67.

Cornet, A., Histoire d'une Famine: Rwanda 1927–1930 crise alimentaire entre tradition et modernité', *Enquêtes et documents d'histoire africaine*, no. 13, Louvain (Belgium), Universite Catholique de Louvain, 1996.

Desmarais, J.C., 'Idéologies et races dans l'Ancien Rwanda', *These de philosophie*, Université de Montréal, 1977: p. 277.

Dumont, L., *Homo Hierarchicus*, Chicago, University of Chicago Press, 1970.

Ehret, C., *Ethiopians and East Africans*, Nairobi (Kenya): East African Publishing House, 1974.

Enloe, C., 'Feminism, Nationalism, and Militarism: Wariness Without Paralysis', in C. Sutton (ed.), *Feminism, Nationalism, and Militarism*, Washington (DC), Association for Feminist Anthropology, American Anthropological Association, 1995: pp. 13–32.

Eriksen, T., *Ethnicity and Nationalism: Anthropological Perspectives*, London, Pluto Press, 1993.

Evans, W., 'From the Land of Canaan to the Land of Guinea', *American Historical Review*, vol. 85, no. 1, 1980: 15–43.

Excoffier, L., Pellegrini, P., Sanchez-Moras, A., Simon C, and Langaney, A., 'Genetics and History of Sub-Saharan Africa', *Yearbook of Physical Anthropology*, vol. 30. 1987: pp. 151–94.

Fanon, F., *Les Damnés de la Terre*, Paris, Francois Maspero, 1968 [1961].

Farquhar, J., *Knowing Practice: the Clinical Encounter of Chinese Medicine*, Boulder (CO), Westview Press, 1994.

Fenton, J., 'A Short History of Anti-Hamitism', *New York Review of Books*, February 15, 1996: pp. 7–9.

Foucault, M., *Discipline and Punish: the Birth of the Prison*, New York, Pantheon Books, 1977.

Franche, D., 'Généalogie du genocide Rwandasi, Hutu et Tutsi: Gaulois et Francs?' *Les Temps Modernes*, no. 582, mai–juin, 1995: pp. 1–58.

Geertz. C., *After the Fact: two countries. four decades, one anthropologist,* Cambridge (MA), Harvard University Press, 1995.

Gledhill, J., *Power and Its Disguises: Anthropological Perspectives on Politics,* London, Pluto Press, 1994.

Goldhagen, D., *Hitler's Willing Executioners: Ordinary Germans and the Holocaust,* New York, Knopf, 1996.

Gould, S.J., *The Mismeasure of Man,* New York, Norton & Co., 1981.

Handler, R., *Nationalism and the Politics of Culture in Quebec,* Madison (WI), University of Wisconsin Press, 1988.

Harroy, J.-P., *Rwanda du féodalism à la démocratie (1955-1962),* Brussels, Hayez, 1984.

d'Hertefelt, M., *Les clans du Rwanda ancien,* Tervuren (Belgium), Musée Royal de l'Afrique Centrale, Serie in 80, Sciences Humaines, 1971.

d'Hertefelt, M., and Coupez, A., *La royautée sacrée de l'ancien Rwanda,* Tervuren (Belgium), Musée Royal de l'Afrique Centrale, Annales, Serie in 80, Sciences Humaines, no. 52, 1964.

Heusch, L. de, *Le Rwanda et la civilisation interlacustre,* Brussels: Université Libre de Bruxelles, Institut de Sociologie, 1966.

Heusch, L. de, *Sacrifice in Africa,* Cambridge, Cambridge University Press, 1985.

Heusch, L. de, 'Anthropologie d'un genocide: le Rwanda', *Les Temps Modernes,* no. 579, dec. 1994: pp. 1–19.

Hinton, A., 'Agents of Death: Explaining the Cambodian Genocide in terms of Psychosocial Dissonance', *American Anthropologist,* vol. 98, no. 4, 1996: pp. 818–31.

Hinton, A., 'Why Did You Kill? The Cambodian Genocide and the Dark Side of Face and Honor', *The Journal of Asian Studies,* vol. 57, no. 1, February, 1998: pp. 93–122.

Hobsbawm, E., *Nations and Nationalism since the 1780s: Programme. Myth, Reality,* Cambridge (UK), Cambridge University Press, 1990.

Hobsbawm, E., and Ranger, T., *The Invention of Tradition,* Cambridge (UK), Cambridge University Press, 1983.

Hubert, H., and Mauss, M., Sacrifice: Its Nature and Functions, Chicago, University of Chicago Press, 1981 [1964].

Jacob, I., *Dictionnaire Rwandais-Français: Extrait du dictionnaire de l'Institut National de Recherche Scientifique,* 3 volumes, Kigali (Rwanda), L'Imprimerie Scolaire, 1984, 1985, 1987.

Johnson, M., *The Body in the Mind: The Bodily Basis of Meaning. Imagination, and Reason,* Chicago, University of Chicago Press, 1987.

Kagame, A., *La philosophie bantu-rwandaise de l'être,* Brussels, Academie royale des sciences coloniales, Classe des sciences morales et politiques, Mem. In 8⁰, nouvelle serie, tome XII, fasc. 1, 1956.

Kagame, A., *Inganji Karnga,* 2 vols., Kabgayi (Rwanda): 1959.

Kakar, S., *Shamans, Mystics and Doctors: a Psychological Inquiry into India and its Healing Traditions,* Chicago, University of Chicago Press, 1982.

Kapferer, B., *Legends of People. Myths of State*, Washington DC, Smithsonian Institution Press, 1988.

Kapferer, B., 'Nationalist Ideologies and a Comparative Anthropology', *Ethnos*, vol. 54, nos 3–4, 1989: pp. 161–99.

Lacger, L. de, *Ruanda I. Le Ruanda ancien*, Kabgayi (Rwanda), 1930.

Lemarchand, R., *Rwanda and Burundi*, New York, Praeger, 1970.

Lemarchand, R., 'L'école historique burundo-française: Une école pas comme les autres', *Canadian Journal of African Studies*, vol. 24, no. 2, 1990:pp. 235–48.

Linden, I., *Church and Revolution in Rwanda*, Manchester (England): Manchester University Press, 1977.

Louis, R., *Ruanda-Urundi 1884–1919*, Clarendon Press, Oxford (UK), 1963.

Malkki, L., *Purity and Exile*, Chicago: University of Chicago Press, Chicago, 1995.

Maquet, J., *Le système des relations sociales dans le Ruanda ancien*, Tervuren (Belgium), Musée Royal de l'Afrique Centrale, 1954.

Moran, M., 'Warriors or Soldiers? Masculinity and Ritual Transvestism in the Liberian Civil War', in C. Sutton (ed.) *Feminism, Nationalism, and Militarism*, Washington (DC), Association for Feminist Anthropology, American Anthropological Association, 1995: pp. 73–88.

Nahimana, F., *Le Rwanda, émergence d'un état*, Paris, L'Harmattan, 1993.

Newbury, C., *The Cohesion of Oppression*, New York, Columbia University Press, 1988.

Nkundabagenzi, F., *Rwanda Politique 1958–60*, Dossiers du CRISP, 1962.

Nordstrom, C., and Martin, J-A., *The Paths to Domination, Terror, and Resistance*, Berkeley, University of California Press, 1992.

Oniaar, R., and De Waal, A., (eds) *Rwanda: Killing the Evidence*, London, African Rights, April, 1996.

Ortner, S., 'Resistance and the Problem of Ethnographic Refusal', *Comparative Studies in Society and History*, vol. 37, no. 1, Jan. 1995: pp. 173–93.

Pages, R., *Un royaume hamite au centre de l'Afrique*, Brussels, Institut Royal du Congo Belge, 1933.

Peters, E., *Torture*, Philadelphia, University of Pennsylvania Press, 1996.

Pitt-Rivers, J., *The Fate of Schechem: or, the politics of sex: essays in the anthropology of the Mediterranean*, Cambridge, Cambridge University Press, 1977.

Prunier, G., *The Rwanda Crisis*, New York, Columbia University Press, 1995.

Sanders, E., 'The Hamitic Hypothesis: Its Origins and Functions in Time Perspective', *Journal of African History*, vol. X, no. 4, 1969: pp. 521–32.

Schoenbrun, D., 'Early History in Eastern Africa's Great Lakes Region: Linguistic, Ecological, and Archaeological Approaches. ca. 500 B.C. to ca. 1000 A.D.', Ph.D. Dissertation, University of California at Los Angeles, 1990.

Schoenbrun, D., 'We are what we eat: Ancient Agriculture Between the Great Lakes', *Journal of African History*, vol. 34, 1993: pp. 1–31.

Schoenbrun, D., 'A Past Whose Time Has Come: Historical Context and History in Eastern Africa's Great Lakes', *History and Theory*, Beheft 32, Wesleyan University, 1993: pp. 32–56.

Seligman, C.G., *Races of Africa*, London, Oxford University Press, 1957 (1930).

Smith, P., *Le récit populaire au Rwanda*, Paris, Armand Colin, 1975.

Smith, S., 'Rwanda: Les fautes de la France', in *Libération*, 16 December 1998.

Speke, J.H., *Journal of the Discovery of the Source of the Nile*, London, J.M. Dent, 1969 [1863].

Sperber, D., *Le symbolisme en general*, Paris, Hermann, 1975.

Sutton, C., 'From City-States to Post-Colonial Nation-State: Yoruba Women's Changing Military Roles', in C. Sutton (ed.), *Feminism. Nationalism, and Militarism*, Washington (DC), Association for Feminist Anthropology, American Anthropological Association, 1995: pp. 89–103.

Taussig, M., 'Culture of Terror, Space of Death', *Comparative Studies in Society and History*, vol. 26, no. 3, 1984: pp. 467–97.

Taussig, M., *Shamanism, Colonialism and the Wild Man*, Chicago, University of Chicago Press, 1987.

Taylor, C., 'Milk, Honey and Money: Changing Concepts of Pathology in Rwandan Popular Medicine', PhD. dissertation, Univeristy of Virginia, 1988.

Taylor, C., 'The Concept of Flow in Rwandan popular Medicine,' *Social Science and Medicine*, vol. 27, no. 12, 1988: pp. 1343–8.

Taylor, C., *Milk, Honey and Money*, Washington (DC), Smithsonian Institution Press, 1992.

Turner, V., *The Ritual Process*, Ithaca (NY), Cornell University Press, 1977.

Vansina, J., *L'évolution du royaume du Rwanda des origines à 1900*, Brussels, Academie Royale des Sciences d'Outre Mer, 1967.

Verschave, F.-X., *Complicité de genocide?* Paris, La Decouverte, 1994.

Vidal, C., 'Le Rwanda des anthropologues et le fétichisme de la vache, *Cahiers d'Etudes Africanies*, vol. 9, no. 3, 1969: pp. 384–400.

Vidal, C., *Sociologie des passions*, Paris, Editions Karthala, 1991.

Warren, K., *The Violence Within*, Boulder, Westview Press, 1993.

Willame, J.-C., 'La Panne Rwandaise', *La Revue Nouvelle*, decembre, 1990: pp. 59–66.

Yelvington, K., 'Ethnicity as practice? A comment on Bentley', *Comparative Studies in Society History*, vol. 33, no. 1, 1991: pp. 158–68.

Index